interior design details
1,000 NEW IDEAS FOR THE HOME

Nonie Niesewand

COLLINS | DESIGN

An Imprint of HarperCollinsPublishers

interior design details

1,000 NEW IDEAS FOR THE HOME
by Nonie Niesewand

Interior Design Details has its own website: www.contemporarydetails.com

First Edition

First published in the United States and Canada in 2006 by:
Collins Design, *An Imprint of* HarperCollins*Publishers,*
10 East 53rd Street, New York, NY 10022
Tel: (212) 207-7000; Fax: (212) 207-7654
collinsdesign@harpercollins.com; www.harpercollins.com

Distributed throughout the United States and Canada by:
HarperCollins*Publishers,* 10 East 53rd Street, New York, NY 10022;
Fax: (212) 207-7654

Senior Executive Editor Anna Sanderson
Art Director Tim Foster
Art Editor Victoria Burley
Senior Editors Suzanne Arnold, Catherine Emslie
Editors Colette Campbell, Anne McDowall
Designer Sarah Rock
Picture Research Manager Giulia Hetherington
Picture Researchers Jenny Faithfull, Claire Gouldstone, Rebecca Douglas Home, Sarah Smithies, Sophie Spencer-Wood, Nick Wheldon
Production Controller Gary Hayes

Set in Frutiger
Library of Congress Control Number: 2006929857
ISBN-10: 0-06-113765-0
ISBN-13: 978-0-06-113765-5

Color reproduction by Sang Choy, Singapore
Printed and bound Toppan, China
First printing, 2006

contents

introduction

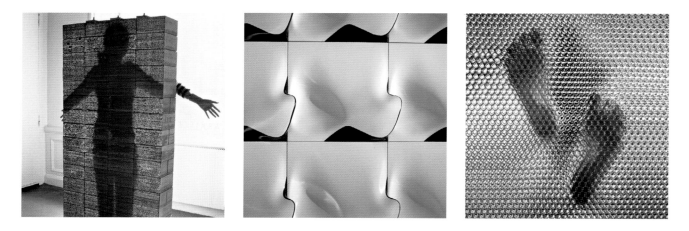

ABOVE LEFT See-through cement is the invention of the century by Áron Losonczi. Glass fiber optics ground into Litracon™ cement make a blurred black-and-white movie of activities behind the wall.

ABOVE CENTER Interlocking "Glacier White" Corian® tiles, thermo-formed like heat shields in Zaha Hadid's "Z" kitchen, conceal speakers and lights behind them, allowing both to escape from the furled corners.

ABOVE RIGHT Aircraft cabin floors are made of lightweight, immensely strong aluminum honeycomb. A glass membrane covers honeycomb aluminum floor tiles by Mykon.

Asked for the basic requirements of a house in 1929, Le Corbusier listed them as follows: "1. A shelter against heat, cold, rain, thieves, and the inquisitive. 2. A receptacle for light and sun. 3. A certain number of cells appropriated to cooking, work, and personal life." The wish list of the architect who spearheaded the modern movement holds as true today as it did then. *Interior Design Details* addresses those three requisites with advice, and the products to match it, in chapters on Walls and Ceilings, Flooring, and Heating and Cooling, which concern shelter; Windows, Doors, and Lighting, for light and sun; and Kitchens, Bathrooms, and Staircases, for carving up space for cooking, work, and personal life.

The requirements are the same, but the materials to build and shape them are very different. Le Corbusier would be astonished by the materials of the 21st century. Concrete becomes diaphanous with light-emitting LiTraCon™, which is as strong as concrete but has a shadowy translucence. Solid cement walls mixed with optical glass fibers silhouette the people moving around behind them, like extras in a French, grainy, black-and-white movie. Cement, wood, stone, and glass all morph into something new. Palladio wrote the recipe

in his fourth book on architecture for composites, mixing marble chips into a paste for hard flooring. Now resin is used to make quarried stone go further. Recycling pulped children's rubber boots into bright plastic sheets for soft flooring was something neither Palladio or Le Corbusier could have anticipated, but it exists, alongside recycled milk bottles, redundant circuitry boards, and gas-pipe off-cuts, as the flooring of the future. Wood that is cool to the touch yet feels just like grainy wood is cunningly reproduced in ceramics which are also convincing as slate, granite, limestone, and marble. As ceramics are good conductors of electricity, they are hybrids in the making, even able to bend and flex when mixed with silicone.

Mechanical is becoming electronic, and electronic is merging into the chemistry of materials, as Ed van Hinte observed in *Material World*. Glass gets smart with an IQ that makes it capable of tracking the sun to turn opaque at noon, which cuts the glare to cool down the interior and, as the light drops, to become transparent. It even cleans itself: Pilkington's Activ™ coating of titanium oxide gobbles dirt to wash it away in clean sheets when the next shower bursts.

ABOVE LEFT Crimson liquid gel sandwiched between the baseboard and thin laminated glass leaves an impression when walking across Rogier Sterk's floor. Footprints slowly fade.

ABOVE CENTER Ceramic convincingly replicates quarried stone and wood. Rex Ceramiche's slate floor from the "Pillarguri" collection is matched by its ceramic-clad pivoting door.

ABOVE RIGHT Celebrated architects take time off designing landmark buildings to turn their hand to door handles. Frank Gehry's "Arrowhead" stainless-steel handle for Fusital.

ABOVE LEFT A world first, Pilkington's self-cleaning "Activ™" glass makes window cleaners redundant. Titanium oxide coating reacts with ultraviolet light to break down dirt and when it rains a hydrophilic coating sweeps it away.

ABOVE CENTER Colored film sandwiched into laminated glass by Vanceva Solutia gives over a thousand colors in shatterproof window walls, the ideal solution on both counts for this nursery school in Spain.

ABOVE RIGHT Glass tough enough to make transparent stair treads and landings specified by architect Rick Mather filters natural light throughout a London house.

What used to be called the House of the Future is happening now, somewhere near you in a main street shop, out-of-town mall, or on the net. None of it is the stuff of science fiction. Everything featured in this book is in production, worldwide; a directory at the back of this book sources the products and gives websites.

Nonie Niesewand's *Contemporary Details,* which was published in 1992, featured real-life contemporary interiors from young architects chucking out the chintz. Fifteen years later, *Interior Design Details* features products that are mass-produced, marketed worldwide, and can be bought on-line. Many of the things from door handles to bathtubs and kitchen sinks are designed by celebrated international architects: Norman Foster, Zaha Hadid, Frank Gehry, (all three of whom have won the Pritzker Prize for architecture, the equivalent of an Oscar for actors), John Pawson, David Chipperfield, Ricardo Bofill, Jean Nouvel, Michael Graves, and Philip Johnson. The first book opened our eyes to modern interiors at a time when English country-house style piled on the patterns. In this book, real-life interiors are used for innovative ideas to outwit outmoded planning restrictions made in the pre-digital age.

Three stacked sash windows running up the back of a red-brick Edwardian house like a spine, made by architects Sanei and Hopkins, opens up their family house to light and sun. How to turn inelegant bay windows on a semi-detached that houses both a young family and a serious art collection into a light box fronting a white cube within is the secret shared by architect Niall McLaughlin. How Simon Conder beat Foster and Partners new Sage center in Britain and the much hyped Scottish Parliament to win the coveted Wood Trades award with something as simple as a staircase is another revelation. A floor painted gold then over-painted with coats of white gloss by Front designers means that, over time, a golden path emerges through a Swedish art gallery. Felt cut into baguettes and pasted over the walls and ceilings of Fluff, a New York bakery by Lewis Tsurumaki Lewis, shows us how young architects work, doing the cut-and-paste job themselves.

An archive of images representing buildings and interiors of the 20th century in *Contemporary Details* shows the extent to which color had slipped out of the language of architecture. In the new edition color resurfaces as a powerful force, on the façades of buildings with Schott glass, or Vanceva Solutia

ABOVE LEFT Cantilevered oak stairs with a twist by architect Simon Conder beat some of Britain's best buildings to win the coveted Wood Trade awards in a barn conversion in the countryside. Timber technology improves with computer-generated tests for stresses and strains on this freestanding staircase cut from a single oak tree.

ABOVE CENTER Energy-efficient BedZed housing beats British winters with solar roof panels to heat water stored in tanks below while white wind-driven cowls pump warm air into main rooms.

ABOVE RIGHT Architect Henry Harrison fuels gas-burning fires for the Platonic Fireplace Company with a "Woodscape" forest floor made of lava stone to retain heat more efficiently.

laminates, and inside with floors filled with shocking pink gel, sandwiched in shock-absorbing foam so that every footstep taken leaves an imprint that fades as slowly as footprints in wet sand. Often it is light that fills space with intense color, demarcating stair treads with an ethereal blue, suffusing a shower with mood-changing colors.

Pattern makes a tentative comeback with wallpaper backed with magnetic strips so that frogs can hop across lily ponds. Rugs that mix paper with linen are clipped to give the *Edward Scissorhands* special effect of straggly fringing in a close crop. Digital imaging, on everything from canvas to ceramic tiles and laminates, downloads photographs onto flooring, wall, and window treatments.

Products chosen for their heightened sensibility to the depletion of resources and sustainability, are highlighted in every chapter. Timber branded from the Forest Stewardship Council traces its roots back to the rainforest to ensure sustainable development. Exotic woods are used sparingly as a thin veneer covering pine base blocks. The argument goes that since most parquet flooring is anchored in concrete scree anyway, why bury good woods? Laminates made without

ABOVE LEFT Changing light at every angle, Foscarini's "Teorema" by Ferruccio Laviani refracts and reflects light from opaque and transparent baffles made in polymer mesh.

ABOVE CENTER Celebrated architects of the Tate Modern in Britain and the Walker Museum in the USA, Herzog and de Meuron designed the "Jingzi" light for Belux.

ABOVE RIGHT Revealing glass sides to a silky smooth Corian® curved recliner in the "Le Cob" bathtub, designed by Joseph Licciardi to drain into a pebbled mat at West One Bathrooms in London.

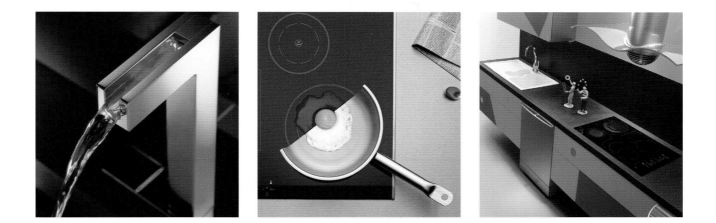

CFCs or corrosive glues are highlighted. Solar panels and wind machines that top up the national grid, together with geo-thermal systems capable of running underground heating feature. When the world turns into *Waterworld*, there is always the "Aqueon™" fireplace to top up with water – it turns water into hydrogen to burn a steady flame. Modern faucets can conserve water, and restrict power-shower flow, and wasteful flush systems can be replaced with dual-flush controls.

Electrolux asked industrial design students around the world for their designs to clean, cook, dishwash, and chill by the year 2015. Entry predictions were universal: the world will cluster in just 15 or so gigantic cities dotted about the planet; space will be at such a premium that not only appliances will downsize; water will be so precious that the "Rockpool" dishwasher can run without it.

Future generations may well look at some of these aids to contemporary living with the same amusement with which we view museum pieces of the last century such as log baskets, video recorders, and hostess carts. Let us hope they look kindly upon us, not angrily, as wasteful of the planet's resources.

ABOVE LEFT Hot water runs with a fine band of red LED light in the open spout of the "Hansacanyon" designed by Reinhard Zetsche and Bruno Sacco for HansaMurano. It turns blue when cold water runs.

ABOVE CENTER Frying an egg directly on ceramic glass induction hob by Siemens neatly demonstrates its versatility. The hob ignites when the ferrous bottom of a pan touches the magnetic field. The rest remains ice cool.

ABOVE RIGHT Suspended on a single-stainless steel unit and floating above the floor, the "Agreste" kitchen is designed by Alessandro Mendini for La Cucina Alessi collection of four kitchens.

walls and ceilings

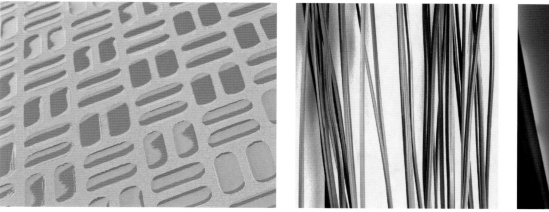

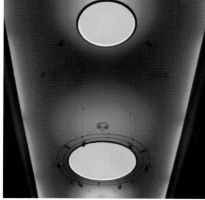

ABOVE LEFT TO RIGHT Color lifts walls and ceilings with graphic designs and LED glass panels:

ABOVE LEFT "Seed" ceramic tiles from Lea Ceramiche.

ABOVE CENTER Pravin Dewdhory's laminate design was influenced by nature and is available as part of Formica® Digital.

ABOVE RIGHT "SpectraGlass" from The Light Lab uses light-emitting diodes to evenly wash a dot matrix on glass panels and give over 15 million possible color combinations.

LEFT Narrow strips of felt, hand pasted over plywood-paneled walls and ceilings at the Fluff Bakery in New York draw passers-by into the coffee shop. Five kilometers (over three miles) of gray, black, and white felt were hand cut by the architects Lewis Tsurumaki Lewis (LTL), who did the cut-and-paste job themselves rather than get contractors to quote labor costs for the procedure. Laying the felt strips one by one like bricks, they graduated colors for a lighter ceiling with darker tones around the seating area. LTL also designed the chandelier.

Walls and ceilings are breaking out of the white box dictated by modernists and minimalists. In this digital age, walls are transformed by floor-to-ceiling screens, light installations, fiber optic grids, even the *Mona Lisa* painted in pixels of light smiles down from a high-resolution, gigantic plasma screen.

Walls of glass switch from transparent to opaque as the sun sets and rises. Smart glass cleans itself. Acoustic ceilings use technology developed for the aircraft industry, absorbing noise through a honeycomb core made of cardboard and coconut husks. Translucent concrete silhouettes the activities of people as intriguingly as traditional sliding Japanese shoji panels.

Freed from brick and stone by new materials, walls break into curves or slope vertiginously on the diagonal. At the Venice Biennale Architecture in 2004, the showcased buildings were curved in form and organic in construction. Biomorphic forms that had shapes drawn from living things, and surfaces more like membranes, were mostly public spaces, like Frank O Gehry's Walt Disney Concert Hall in Los Angeles, Daniel Libeskind's Grand Canal Theater in Dublin, and Zaha Hadid's Science Center in Wolfsburg, Germany.

At home, walls that stand four square can be given a wallcovering for the 21st century. New ways of looking afresh at familiar surface materials create interesting installations. Classic materials like paper and felt, metal, and glass, used imaginatively, can give a face-lift to walls and ceilings. Felt strips pasted onto plywood paneling sounds more like a children's game than an award-winning architectural finish to a bakery and coffee shop in New York. Architects Lewis Tsurumaki Lewis laid felt strips one by one, like bricks, graduating color from darker tones around the seating area to lighter tones at ceiling height where they created a chandelier from fluorescent tubes. Silk and plastic flowers, pasted onto walls in a Stockholm art gallery by art collective Front, make a striking 3D wallpaper, illuminated by a chandelier made from shredded strips of the gallery's exhibition posters. Artifice and nature, permanence and decay are the themes explored.

It's not only artists and architects who interpret classic materials in the 21st century, as industry adapts new technology to transform the familiar. Take cement. Mixing glass with cement makes it transparent. Hungarian architect Áron Losonczi's light-emitting concrete called LiTraCon™, in sheets 25mm (1in) or more thick, is as strong as regular concrete and can be used for walls, flooring, or sculpture, as in the European Gate in Komarom on the banks of the Danube where it celebrates Hungary's entrance into the EU.

An almost forgotten African craft of crushing the bark of *Ficus Natalensis* is revived to make fibrous bark cloth, now capable of being colored, fire-proofed, Teflon-covered, and laminated. Weaving can bring walls to life. Oxeon has developed traditional weaving to patent tape-woven carbon reinforcements with all kinds of fibers, including glass and ceramics: TeXtreme™, invented by Nandan Khokar with applications for aerospace and extreme sports, could have a future for shelters like aircraft cabins.

Paper impregnated with resin and bonded under high pressure at a high temperature is the basis of

ABOVE 3D wallpaper in the Tensta Konsthall in Stockholm striped with silk and plastic flowers by Front, a design team in Sweden. Like an art installation that explores permanence and decay, artificial flowers change with the seasons. A chandelier is made from shredded strips of the gallery's exhibition posters.

LEFT The cloakroom walls are festooned with plastic self-adhesive hooks, making a wallcovering out of a collection of mundane coat hooks, and inviting visitors to add to the display.

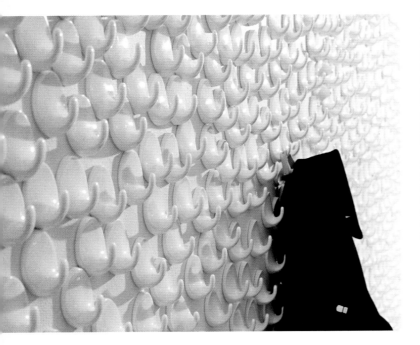

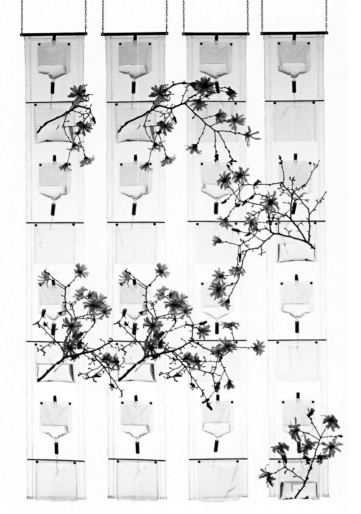

laminates. Invented in 1913 when two electrical engineers searching for a substitute insulation material to Mica formed the Formica® Insulation company, fake oak laminates were the first products. In the digital age, high-pressure laminates are light reflective, replicating metal foils and, with the advent of digital printing, computerized fractals.

Light is the magic ingredient that brings walls to life. Back-lit Lucite International Perspex® acrylic sheets in red, pink, and orange shimmered on stage around the catwalk at London Fashion Week. Ever more powerful and smaller, LEDs on computerized programs ensure walls are never static. Panels of iColor® tiles concealing 432 LEDs morph colored light waves over walls. Color-shifting thermo-plastic film from Sommers USA, sold in rolls like wallpaper, is made of two polyvinyl chloride

ABOVE LEFT "Erbale," designed by Becchelli, Bortolani, and Maffei for Driade, replicates blood transfusion bags as plant containers. Long, thin strips of transparent PVC to a height of 2.4m (8ft), and a width of 300mm (11⅞in) divide into eight bags: four for plants and four holding water.

ABOVE Despite the super-thin "Erbale" only having a depth of 100mm (3⅞in), Driade made a substantial wall of banked "Erbale" with a back-lit Perspex screen in the frescoed halls of the Palazzo Gallarati Scotti in Italy to showcase their "King Tubby" chair by Platt and Young and the "Thali" table by Miki Astori.

(PVC) sheets laminated on either side of a multilayered film. It refracts and transmits different colors with holographics that flex, bend, and stretch, just like rubber. Elumin8 demonstrated really cool lighting by bathing the tallest refrigerated wine tower with electro-luminescent (EL) light, the technology that lights computer monitors, in the Radisson SAS Hotel at Stansted airport.

The computer, which measures images in pixels of light, has allowed artists and designers to computer-generate mosaics and turn an age-old craft into an industrial wall application. Guest bedrooms in the Villa Oliverra at Portofino, belonging to fashion duo Dolce & Gabbana, have walls made of gold mosaic. The Midas behind this magical effect is minimalist architect, David Chipperfield who told American *Vogue* that "not everything has to be minimal and white and po-faced. I don't see why you can't do gold mosaics and broken tiles in a very disciplined and slightly rigorous way."

In the digital age walls turn into giant screens, changing at the flick of a keypad. Waiting for a change of scene is not like watching paint dry, as screens change constantly for entertainment and info-tainment.

Bill Gates heralded the revolution in the late 20th century. In his book *The Road Ahead* he explains how the emerging technologies of the digital age will transform lives. It was a design trend he observed when he described his own house on the shores of Lake Seattle in Washington. Beneath a sloping glass ceiling the eastern wall in his living room appears as wood paneling, most of the time. Twenty-four 1m (40in) video monitors stacked four high by six across display wood-grain veneers on the screen saver until, by remote control, they turn into great works of art.

The intelligent home is no longer the backdrop for science-fiction writers, but is a reality with affordable technology providing great potential to create changeable living environments.

OPPOSITE Mosaic pinpoints light in glass like no other material. The "Luxe" collection by Bisazza sandwiches 24-carat gold between two layers of glass. Used with white, the mosaic highlights the "Tulip" chair and table designed mid 20th century by Eero Saarinen. A new manufacturing process yields perfect squares in a consistent thickness of tesserae with bevelled edges.

BELOW Smooth and perfect, the stucco-like white wall of DuPont™ Corian® becomes animated with moving images, not projected upon it but emanating from the wall itself. Installed by Ron Arad with Ernest Mourman in the Gallery Gio Marconi in Milan, the "Lo-res-dolores-tabula-rasa" shows off the light-emitting qualities of DuPont™ Corian®.

RIGHT Bonded bronze lightweight panels in the "Mazatlan" pattern in the CabForms® series from Forms + Surfaces line the elevator. Bonded Metal® uses advanced mold-making techniques to cast metal granules in a matrix for fine details on a patterned and patinated surface.

BELOW "Neutra" from Casa Dolce Casa is a decorators' kit offering a collection of wall and floor tiles, both glass and porcelain, and mosaics with co-ordinated colors in matt and eggshell paints and grouting. Distressed walls in scumbled terracotta and ocher paint are anchored with big square charcoal "Carbone" floor tiles 600 x 600mm (23⅛ x 23⅛ in) grouted in anthracite.

walls and ceilings/light-emitting

Light is the single magical component that makes walls and ceilings come alive. Even solid structural walls are lightening up with light-emitting concrete LiTraCon™. Concrete infused with optical glass fibers makes the fibers a component of the cement, like small pieces of aggregate. The same light diffusing effect, but without the substance, comes from sliding paper screens called shoji in Japan. In his book *In Praise of Shadows*, now enjoying something of a cult following, Jun'ichiro Tanizaki explains its appeal: "Western paper turns away the light, while our paper seems to take it in, to envelop it gently like the soft surface of a first snowfall. It gives off no sound when it is crumpled or folded, it is quiet and pliant to the touch as the leaf of a tree."

Structural constraints can be overcome by light-diffusing wall treatments. In a London house conversion designed around a modern art collection, Irish architect Niall McLaughlin had to make the most of wall space for paintings, including one by Turner prize-winner Chris

Ofili. So he gutted the Edwardian semi-detached house of all its period features like cornices and baseboards, even removing sockets and light switches on the walls to create a white box, like a gallery. Unable to change the façade, and the big bay windows that he deemed inelegant, McLaughlin's solution was to block them with steel mesh screens, 300 panels 2-storys high, which filter the light and give the rooms an interesting dimension. Shadow gaps, small slits in between the ceiling and walls that take the place of cornicing, give the ceiling the illusion of weightlessness.

Light-emitting ceilings used to be plasterboard punctured with halogen downlighters. Now back-lit ceilings evenly diffuse light, rather than spot-light it, through opalescent Schott glass or intensely colored LED light. "System X" by Ross Lovegrove for Yamagiwa steps out of the background to create a modular, clip-together light system that fills the space required as easily as clipping together the modules.

1

2

Formica® High Pressure
1 Laminate from the "Authentix" collection wired together for a display at the Surface Design Show 2005. A range of textures includes Powdered and Brushed metallic finishes, and relief textures that are Quilted and Punched, in one of the most versatile and durable surfacing materials.

A two-story-high
2 permanent portcullis, made of 300 pieces of letter-sized punched metal on wires, conceals the original bay windows on a red-brick semi-detached house in north London. Architect Niall McLaughlin could not remove the bays so he turned them into a light box.

"The beauty of a Japanese room depends on a variation of shadows, heavy shadows against light shadows – it has nothing else. Westerners are amazed at the simplicity of Japanese rooms, perceiving in them no more than ashen walls bereft of ornament. Their reaction is understandable but it betrays a failure to comprehend the mystery of shadows. Out beyond the sitting room which the rays of the sun can at best but barely reach, we extend the eaves or build on a verandah, putting the sunlight at still greater a remove. The light from the garden steals in but dimly through paper paneled doors and it is precisely this indirect light that makes for us the charm of a room."

Jun'ichiro Tanizaki, *In Praise of Shadows*

⬆ DESIGN INFLUENCE

3

4

5

⬇ ALSO SEE

windows pp.86, 90, 91
lighting pp.134, 135

3 Soft light diffused through paper screens is a traditional Japanese shoji practice, but the modern chair is a clue to Shoji Designs Inc, which makes shoji screens for modern Western interiors, covering sliding glass doors with back-lit transom panels. Translucent sliding, bi-folding or shutter-style screens used as room dividers replace partition walls.

4 Mixing glass with cement creates a transparent concrete, Litracon™. Glass in the form of fiber optics allows light to filter through the material. Available in sheets 25mm (1in) or more thick, LiTraCon™ is as strong as regular concrete and can be used for walls, flooring, or sculpture.

5 "System X" architectural lighting solution is designed by Ross Lovegrove and made by Yamagiwa. A single X module in plastic and aluminum to a height of 680mm (2ft 2in), width of 5m (16ft 5in), and depth of 8.3m (27ft) weighs 2kg (4lb 4oz) and can be configured in ordered geometry to create zones of light, collectively or in single modules.

6 Planolux bonds an ultra-slim 40mm (1½in) metal board of Light Emitting Diodes to natural stone surfaces to create large panels of uniformly back-lit stone. Without any boundary frame it is suitable for many applications from walls and floorcoverings, inside and out, including swimming-pool linings.

7 Honeycomb polymer panels from Panelite are strong yet lightweight, which is why they can be lined up in a grid of transparent glass panes. The composite material reacts to light intensity as well as the angle of penetration, so that the panels constantly change opacity and depth of color to control the outlook and bathe the room in golden light. Below: detail of the honeycomb composite from Panelite.

8 After touching the interactive Lightfader walls by Rogier Sterk and TAL, handprints remain visible for about a minute. Then they vanish. Layers of materials in framed panels feature a scratch-resistant plastic on top, a 30mm (1in) thick glass base and in between, leveling with the wall surface, a thin film of colored liquid. Pressure displaces some of the fluid, leaving light prints.

9 Partition walls can change color with "SpectraGlass" from The Light Lab. Powered by LEDs giving more than 15 million color combinations, light emitted from one or both edges of the glass evenly washes the surface. Manual or computer-controlled sequencing and time-scheduling change the light to suit the mood or time of day.

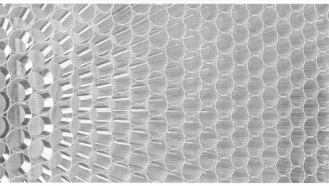

11

10

Light plays on the walls through electro-luminiscent technology, known as EL, the same source used to light computer screens. Designer Ginco dressed a real-life size room with light from the Elumin8 lighting system and called it Spacereactiv to illustrate that light can be a medium in its own right, just like color, to define space.

11

Light transmitting panels of Vanceva® glass interlaid with polyvinyl butyral film by Solutia light a stairwell without back-up lighting. Because laminated glass is bonded together by its plastic interlayer, the glass does not shatter and fall into pieces on impact, which makes it a safe option for overhead glazing.

12

Barkcloth revives an ancient African tradition of weaving to create a light-emitting fabric for interior decoration that is environmentally and socially responsible, from its cultivation in West Africa to finishing and distribution through a German-based company. A close detail of the cloth with a back-lit earth-colored room divider in an installation.

13

"SpectraGlass" by The Light Lab is used in a warehouse loft. A dotted pattern printed across the glass varies the size of the dots as the distance from the light source increases to give an even light distribution. The screen print is thermally enameled onto the glass in an abrasion- and solvent-proof material.

10

12

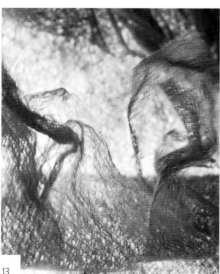

13

walls and ceilings/glass

There is no architectural material more versatile and beautiful than glass. It has far-reaching potential. Smart glass has revolutionized the way buildings look, inside and out, by making curtains and blinds irrelevant. High-tech glass can cut the glare by tracking the sun to darken at noon and brighten at dusk. It can filter out the heat, and dull sound. Noise is unwanted sound, a problem worldwide, and specialist glasses have acoustic insulating properties to meet demands for noise level control.

The world's first self-cleaning glass from Pilkington, "Activ™" has a titanium oxide coating which reacts to UV light to break down dirt. When it rains, a hydrophilic process means water flows across the glass in even sheets, leaving no spots or streaks.

In the Ming Dynasty, tea bowls had rice grains set in the porcelain bottom so that upon draining the last sip, the world beyond could be glimpsed in a grain of rice. Now Omnidecor has simple, small, frosted rice-grain shapes made of translucent glass etched onto opaque glass in its Decoridea Contemporary Cross collection.

1 Artista® by Schott, Europe's specialist glass manufacturer, pioneers thin glass only 1.5mm (1/20 in) thick, fused with the thicker, laminated glass to produce a safety glass that meets British Building Regulations. It allows endless designs to manipulate the view, blocking out unsightly buildings behind colorful panes, as it casts patterns of light that change with the sun.

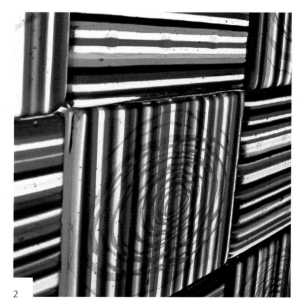

2 Fluorescent light tubes shimmer behind colorful double-glazed panels. Amanda J. Simmons calls her walls "New Directions," changing directions with horizontal and vertical stripes. For 3D-effects she slumps molten glass through steel to emerge like a wall of translucent marbles.

3 A kaleidoscopic wall of clear and colored Vanceva Design® glass specified by architect Angel Luis Lorenzo at a children's primary school, La Casa de Mama in Guadalajara in Spain. Heat and pressure bond the colorful PVB-based interlayers between two or more panes to produce a shatter-resistant glazing with a built-in Vanceva Solar® sun screen.

4 Kiln-cast glass walls by Fusion Glass Designs can be curved, made up in big panels, sandblasted, silvered and colored or frosted, as shown in the foyer of the Cumberland Hotel in London.

5 "Activ®" from Pilkington, is active all the time, breaking down bird droppings and tree sap on its surface to drain off in sheets during the next rain shower. After absorbing UV light, a catalytic process within its titanium oxide coating turns organic dirt into carbon dioxide and water vapour, and a hydrophilic process makes water run off in sheets rather than streams.

6 "Pegasus" glass bricks by VetroArredo have innovative outer edges that limit the gap between each block to only 2mm (¹⁄₁₆in) rather than the conventional 10mm (³⁄₈in). Large continuous surfaces, known as CGS (Continuous Glass Surface)™, are without perceptible interruptions and have the same strength as conventional glass block walls.

7 Nathan Allan Glass Studios designed these 12.7mm (½in) thick cast tempered-glass panels with a box-like container design indented in it for its client, Box Packaging. On one side of the design the box detail is indented in the glass, while on the other, it protrudes. The panels were specially designed to conceal the channels that hold them in place to appear frameless and self-supporting.

8 A rain-textured waterfall of 12.7mm (½in) thick tempered glass slides between a river rock wall by Nathan Allan Glass Studios, pin-mounted with stainless mounting rods that were set deep in the rocks and beyond to a concrete wall.

↓ ALSO SEE
staircases p.104

walls and ceilings/surfaces: metallic

Metallic finishes play tricks with the light. They can suggest changes of level and perspective, presence and absence. Some do not photograph as well as they perform, like "Solaris," the smart wallcovering from Muraspec which uses color-switch ink (previously only used in banknotes) which changes color as you pass, from gold to bronze to copper to silver. Designer Matthew Hayes describes the effect as being like "an expensive roll of shot silk or taffeta."

Metallics can be solid like silvered foil, or shot through ceramics like quarried copper or silver. Any product can be coated with a metallic finish, even glass and laminates. Real metal in metallic weaves has been made so lightweight by Forms + Surfaces that it can even be used to line elevator walls (*see* page 17).

Wire mesh first made an appearance in 1993 when Dominique Perrault designed the French National Library, using 30,000sq m (35,879sq yd) of mesh from GKD. Lit from behind, wire mesh is a translucent membrane; lit from the front, a solid shiny surface. With fiber optics woven into it, the mesh itself becomes a light source.

1

On the walls, "Metallic
1   Grass" from the Formica® Metallics collection of High Pressure Laminate. Created using real metal foils to combine the texture, color, and cool touch of real metal with the hardwearing, lightweight, flexible properties of High Pressure Laminate. Coppers, silvers, golds, and bronzes are replicated in this collection.

Small glass tesserae in
4   silver and bronze are set in a steely gray grouting in the "Casamood" collection from Casa Dolce Casa. Ceramics, glass, mosaics, paints, and grouting are the basis of an interior design collection for walls.

4

Frosted fronds deep carved
6   by Fusion Glass Designs, which makes structural architectural glass more decorative by etching, sandblasting, laminating, and back-painting, and acid-paste screen printing, all within a large kiln-cast capacity.

3

A watered moiré silk effect
2   from filigreed bronze wire mesh. "Mandarin" from GKD was chosen by architects Rainer Jensen and Ulrike Gorgi for the Asian Taku restaurant in Cologne to filter light from behind it. Woven mesh panels, up to 8m (26ft 3in) in width and practically endless lengths, create an apparently seamless veil that can be removed easily to change the light bulbs.

"Silver®" from Abet
3   Laminati is a collection that highlights a technological breakthrough with high-luster, pin-pricked, embossed and etched patterns like decorative Mexican tinware, yet made in laminates. The superficial metal vein, protected by a special anti-oxidization, was developed at the Center for Research Abet Laminati in Italy.

Metallic pewter coating
5   sprayed onto medium density fiberboard (MDF) wall panels by Metall-FX can be polished just like real metal three hours after application. These specialist coatings are made with real metal in a polymer base which can be painted or sprayed onto any shape or surface, including brickwork and wood.

5

6

Chain mail dating back
7   to medieval knights
in armor is still made for
protective clothing. Meters of
stainless-steel "Lamex," made
by Foin, line the walls, ceilings
and floors of the French
National Library (BNF) in Paris.
Graffiti-proof, strong, flexible,
and steely, it brings luster to
this windowless space.

A futon on a tiled platform
8   has a dramatic backdrop of
"Titanium" slabs, banded with
"Copper" strips from Hyperion
Tile's "Metal" collection.
Ceramic tiles look like Corten
steel yet have all the durable
qualities of ceramics. The
adjoining bathroom walls are
covered in small metallic
porcelain tiles.

8

7

▼ ALSO SEE
windows p.86

walls and ceilings/surfaces: pattern and color

Out of fashion in the 1990s, pattern returns in the 21st century. Possibilities for walls include writing all over them, then wiping them clean. You can paint your own paper, scratch and smell it, take a photo and set it in ceramics (if not stone, just yet). Digital printing has revitalized wallcoverings. A special transfer technique makes it possible to permanently imprint a photographic image on a glazed ceramic tile while virtually any image can be reproduced in laminate using digital printing. The most photographed paneled walls are in the Paris Eurostar lounge where Philippe Starck created large-scale images of tubas, teddy bears, and lobsters X-rayed inside suitcases, digitally printed on Abet laminates. And in the museum dedicated to its author, Roald Dahl, screen images from *Charlie and the Chocolate Factory* are digitally printed on walls of laminated Formica®.

"Gerbera Daisy"
2   wallpaper, designed by Jenny Willkinson and imported into the USA in rolls 521mm x 10m (20½in x 33ft) by 2Jane. Its Wallpaper-by-Numbers™ series delivers paints with wallpaper printed in black and white to color in. Strong graphic designs include "Hammerhead Sharks," "Pineapple," and "Tilly, the Flying Dog."

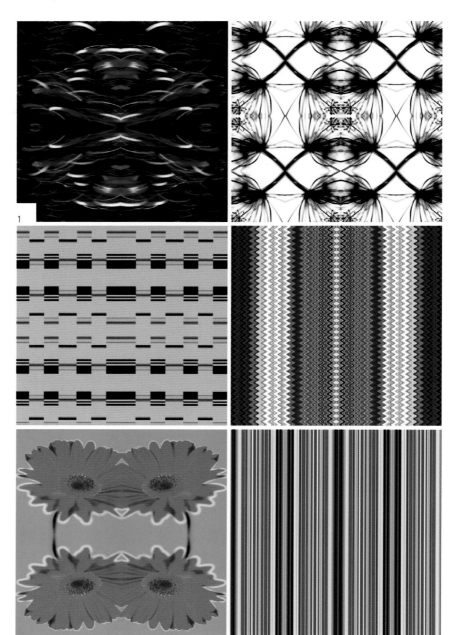

1

Formica Ltd commissioned
1   a collection of designs from photographer and graphic designer Michael Banks for Formica® Digital. Also available is a bespoke service which uses digital print technology to produce any images submitted as High Pressure Laminate. From the Michael Banks collection: top row, "Vegas" and "Lace"; middle, "Casa" and "Wave"; bottom, "Party" and "Rainbow Stripe".

Frogs spring from one
3   lily-pad to another on the world's first magnetic wallpaper. MagScapes™, developed by Pepper-mint with traditional British wallpaper manufacturers, Cole & Sons, hangs just like normal paper, but is receptive to the magnetic motifs like fridge magnets placed upon them.

2

3

Full-blown apple blossom
4   tapping at an illusory window pane is a graphic illustration of a mural digitally printed across 110 rectangular ceramic tiles. The "Artile" by H & R Johnson, the largest tile manufacturer in the UK, applies digital photographs or drawings to ceramic tiles, fired at such high temperatures that the UV-resistant glazed tiles can line a swimming pool and not fade.

4

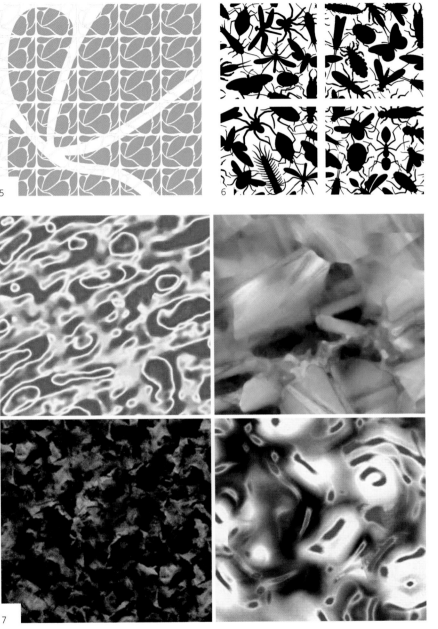

5

6

7

Digital printing on new
5   decorative laminate tiles made by Arpa in four collections: "Signs," "Motifs," "Geometric Shapes" and "Natural Elements." These stylized leaves in "Natural Elements" are united by the white brushstroke across some of them, enough to make patterns versatile.

"Insect" by Studio Job,
6   in a design reminiscent of Christopher Dresser, has bugs and butterflies swarming over tiles from Royal Tichelaar.

Using digital printing
7   technology, Abet Laminati morphs abstract images in its "Oceans" and "Sciences" collection. Its high-pressure laminates are made of Kraft paper impregnated with phenolic resin with a surface soaked in pure melamine resin.

8

9

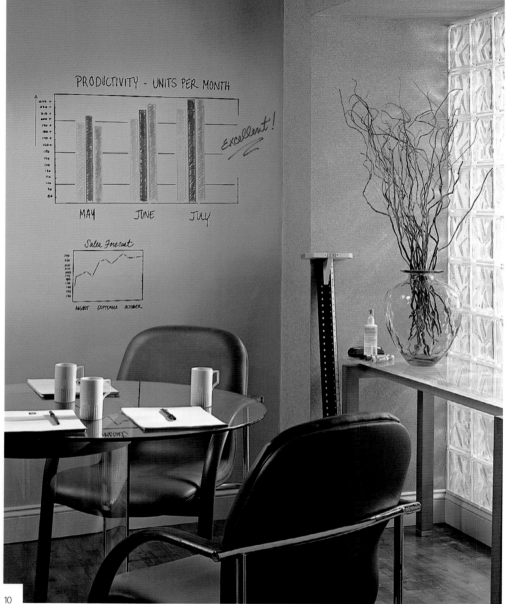

10

Leathers tanned by slow
8   washing, colored with
natural aniline dyes, are used
to make floor and wall panels.
Italian company Cuoioarredo
developed a woven leather
paneling suitable only for walls,
shown here with the patented
"Alterego" leather tiles on the
floor, that are easily installed on
a new flooring joint system.

Magiflex panels from Café
9   Interiors in fiery orange
give the illusion of flames
flickering across its surface.
Minute parabolic lenses molded
on both sides of
the vinyl or polycarbonate
plastic sheets, sold in rolls like
wallpaper, come alive under
light to create 3D shimmering
surfaces and stardust sparkles.

**"For me, color – with form – is representational.
For example, a building along a river or the
interior of a spa might use blue and white or
even golden tiles to represent the flicker of light
on water. A trellis supporting climbing vines
above a window or a porch made of wood might
be colored differently from the masonry body of
the building to correspond with its different use,
materials and scale."**

Michael Graves, *The Art of the Everyday Object*

"MemErase" is a
10   heavy-duty wallcovering
by Muraspec that encourages
graffiti with a standard dry-erase
marker which can then be
rubbed off with a gentle
detergent and warm water.
Its durable coating contains a
patented release agent applied
to a fabric-backed vinyl.

⬆ **DESIGN INFLUENCE**

An aerial view of
11   New York's Manhattan district digitally printed onto fine mesh panels by Louverlite. The room divider effectively filters daylight while allowing it to penetrate the core of a loft apartment. Digital technology makes it possible to print bespoke designs.

Winner of the best new
12   product of 2005 from the British Interior Design Association, Digetex images can be blown up to any size on durable matt, self-adhesive paper. This dramatic image of the New York skyline is printed in UV-stable and water-resistant inks.

11

12

A teenager's attic
14   bedroom under the watchful eye of a Dalmatian blown up along one wall to reach the eaves. Myfotowall.com® with Getty Images is a wallpaper service provided for interior design consultants who register online to browse through more than 700 images to select one, and input the required wall size. Using zoom and move tools, it is possible to see the image *in situ*. Printed on absorbent paper that can be wiped clean, the image is divided into 500mm (1ft 7½in) wallpaper widths.

14

This wall art with an
13   abstract geometric is from CanvasRUs which reproduces images on canvases as large as 2.5m (8ft) by 1.2m (4ft) or smaller. In this room, four panels are grouped to make

the painted wall become part of the graphic design, in much the same way as collaging four framed prints can complete one picture.

13

walls and ceilings/panels and tiles

After languishing beneath coats of white paint, walls are getting busy again. Quarried stone and composites, resins and rubbers, paneling, and tiles in ceramics add new depth to vertical surfaces with theatrical effect.

Droog Design from the Netherlands has become a household name for putting the fun back into functional. Looking afresh at the basic ceramic tile, Paul Hessels began with one that doubles as a power point. Peter van der Jagt, Erik Jan Kwakkel, and Arnout Visser took up the challenge with "Function Tiles" – a tile for hanging up towels, one that doubles as a memo pad, one integrated with a ventilation grid, a tile with a magnifying mirror, a built-in temperature indicator, an LCD screen, a pull-out tile-fronted drawer or, colored red, a medicine chest, and a tile that incorporates the plug to the kitchen sink.

Tiles made by Royal Tichelaar in the Netherlands illustrate two very different artistic approaches. Colorful, flat rectangular tiles by Ettore Sottsass depend upon color combinations to pattern the walls, whereas colorless tiles by Baukje Trenning are sculpted to create a rhythmic interplay of light and shadow. The relief on Trenning's tiles can be as deep as 12mm (½in), as she presses her thumb or fist into the soft clay. They invite touching, hence their name "TacTile."

1

2

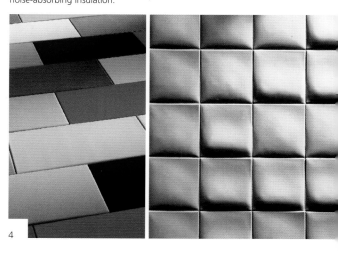

3

Droog's "Dry Bathing"
1   project began in 1995 with the "Power Tile" (top left) which has a receptacle, and was added to in 1997 with an ingeniously simple split in a tile that peels back to become a towel hook (top right), a tile that doubles as a ventilation grille (middle row, left), a tile with a built-in LCD screen and controls (right), and a tile that fronts a drawer in a niche which inspired the red cross medicine chest (bottom row).

Rubber is more commonly
2   used to run across the floor rather than up the wall. Architect Arthur Collin has used Dalsouple rubber, available in a variety of colors and textures, to striking effect on tabletops, and the floors and walls of the washrooms of a busy London restaurant, where it had to be of special wall fire-resistant (WFR) quality. Colorful, flexible and water-resistant, rubber has good acoustic noise-absorbing insulation.

Royal Tichelaar tiles on sale
4   in their shop with: (left) narrow rectangular strips of ceramic tiles in different colors in the Sottsass collection by Ettore Sottsass rely upon color for pattern making; (right) square white glazed ceramic "TacTiles" sculpted by Dutch designer Baukje Trenning create pattern in the raised surface.

Forever preserved
3   in transparent resin, bamboo, grasses, thatch (shown), and saplings, from 3-Form are planted by Futimis in light, strong resin panels which are eye-catching, durable, and scratch-resistant, as well as recyclable.

An irregular application of three shades of anthracite in the slender "Briques" ceramic collection by Rex Ceramiche intensified by candlelight.

"Marshmallow" is a 3D limestone mosaic available in sheets measuring 300 x 300mm (12 x 12in) from the Stone and Ceramic Warehouse, with a narrow red border.

5 Ceramic tiles that breathe are inspired by a flow of water. Wavy "Stream," created by the INAX corporation in Japan, are in a collection for Arma Architectural Materials. Called "Ecorat," hydrogen and oxygen are mixed into silicon, aluminum, and clay to produce 5.5mm (¼in) thin, light, durable tiles. The tile eliminates condensation and absorbs moisture to maintain humidity levels of between 40 and 70 per cent, even in the tropics.

8 The Project L14 by architect Gian Luca Soddu for Lea Ceramiche combines form and color to create a 3D wallcovering in four modular sizes. Shown here in red, "Matrix" is 200 x 200mm (8 x 8in) with an indented pattern and a white border tile measuring 100 x 400mm (4 x16in). The border replicates the grid on the red tile, but is upraised in relief like a waffle iron.

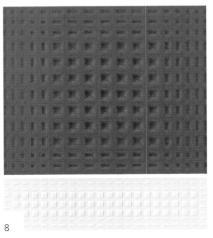

9 Cratered moonscape wall panels made by Total Stone reproduce the texture and color of stone but are thin and weigh between 5 and 6kg per sq m (11–13lb per sq yd). Panels are fixed with screws and mastic covers the holes.

walls and ceilings/screen, sound, controls

As walls turn into giant flat plasma screens, the word plasma has gone into the language as an object of desire. For picture quality the large plasma still has the edge but if size does not matter, LCDs are paving the way with high-resolution pictures. For now, truly big screens are the domain of plasma.

Watching a movie at home used to involve drawing the curtains, dimming the lights, switching on the audio and video equipment, and finding the remote controls, all before hitting the Play button. Now one button on a personally customized keypad can power up the configured electronics for home cinema. Walls do more

than screen plasma or LCD pictures. They can be programed to activate the home-alarm system, switch on a closed circuit TV in the baby's room, and track the musical requirements of different people moving around the house, emerging from virtually invisible loudspeakers mounted in the ceiling or walls. Lighting changes at the push of a button, a discreet wall-mounted keypad, or remote-control handset.

All it takes is for the walls to be fitted with a structured wiring system, not unlike the electrics in a car. Such a system needs to be meticulously planned to accommodate current and future requirements,

and is best installed during refurbishment or rewiring before the plasterers leave.

Bill Gates put a design team into his guest cottage at Lake Washington, Seattle, to test his ideas on a house that tracks its occupants, before creating his own smart house in 1996. Software in the cottage reacts to the tastes of the person inside and the time of day. It knows to make the temperature toasty on a cold morning before the guest is out of bed, and in the evening to dim the light if a television is on. When someone is in the cottage during the day, the cottage matches its inside brightness to that of the outdoors.

1 Decorflouscreen® by Omnidecor in a showroom at Como, Italy, is a glass panel that is perfect for professional projections. A special process used to manufacture them in large high impact formats makes the screen over 20 per cent brighter than conventional screens. When not in use, its surface looks better than the normal LCD blank screen.

2 Time was when TVs hid their cumbersome backs against the wall but this Sim 2 system by Giorgio Revoldini looks as good from the back as the front, with cabling reduced to a single optical fiber.

3 Dropping down off the walls to be set on a long low table and furnish the room against a window wall, the freestanding plasma surround sound system "Cabasse," with its two-drawer unit, frees up walls. The installation is worked out by professionals at Home Cinema.

Panasonic 1.5m (58in)
4   plasma TV and its digital
light processing™ technology
provides high contrast and
HDTV resolution. The company
won the 2005 Green TV of the
Year prize from the European
Imaging and Sound Association
for its 711mm (28in) TV, which
was designed to minimize
power consumption (just 1W
per hour on standby) while also
reducing environmental waste
by cutting down the amount of
wiring and other materials used
in its manufacture.

Sharp's "Aquos" designer
5   edition by Toshiyuki Kita
fuses art,technology and craft
with the most advanced
LCD technology, to make TV an
art form. Ultra-slim, lightweight,
with greater picture detail and
enhanced sound, this model
from the "Titanium Series"
pioneers high definition images
on a 1.1m (45in) screen.

Mission's "Elegante"
6   sound system is just that:
elegant. A pair of bookshelf e80
loudspeakers, an e8c center
channel and a compact 350W
subwoofer come with rigid wall
brackets for wall mounting.
They can also be used to lock
the speakers onto a specially
designed floor stand to match
the rest of the system, either
finished in anthracite or color-
matched to the interior design.

7

Outstanding speakers that
8   do not stand out from
Bowers & Wilkins. Clunky
speaker cabinets are made
redundant by these discreet
flat panel monitors providing
great sound in streamlined
contemporary cabinets designed
to hold 1m (42in), 1.2m (50 in),
and 1.5m (60in) speakers.

8

An installation of a home
7   cinema in London's
Cadogan Square relies on
Lutron's Homeworks to control
the projection screen and
lighting so that when the screen
comes down, the lights dim.
This ingenious system, which
won a consumer Electronics
Innovation award, also controls
the surround sound and the
security of the building so that
external lights go on and off
when required.

The Media Wall from
9   Danish loudspeaker
company Artcoustic hides TV
and speaker cables behind
white wall panels. The speakers
that hang on the wall on either
side of the plasma screen are
covered here in fabric printed
with tulips from Getty Images.
At a depth of 67mm (2⅜in),
they have interchangeable
screens so they can be
integrated into any interior
design scheme without
sacrificing the quality of sound.

9

10

A minimalist product with
10   maximum sound, the glass
sound® speaker by Glas Platz
sandwiches in thin transparent
glass a ring of glass, screen
printed to carry wireless signal
transmissions. Weighing only
2.2kg (4lb 8oz), it comes with
a wall-mounting set.

↓ ALSO SEE

lighting p.133

SmartComm's lounge has
12 a 1m (42in) Fujitsu plasma TV and three speakers set into the wall with surround sound via flush-mounted ceiling speakers. Specialists in the design of intelligent home systems, SmartComm integrates screen and sound systems with lighting and security. Then it is personalized, so that on a penthouse roof garden, touch controls operate light and heaters, and speakers are disguised as rocks.

A traditional barn in
13 southern England features an iLight system to control lights of differing intensity and color. Downlights focused on the stair treads and the halogen glow of the room in the eaves contrast with the color-changing feature of the living room below. LCD color-touch screens provide control of all internal and external lighting elements, as well as the heating and security systems.

The 50mm (20in) thick
11 "visiPad® SL18" by Visiomatic is a touch-screen wall-mounted pad with a built-in camera and microphone to control in-house technology, entertainment, telecommunications, and info-tainment. It filters, at your request, stock exchange info, weather and climate forecasts worldwide, traffic bulletins, and cinema and TV guides. It also regulates and monitors air-conditioning and heating systems, lighting, alarm system, and video monitoring.

12

13

Many sources of
14 entertainment and information are available in our homes. The Knekt system from Linn uses and integrates them seamlessly in one simple to control system. CD player, radio tuner, home theater satellite TV – up to 16 different sources – can be accessed from any point in the house via a wall-mounted room-control unit or hand-held remote control.

14

"My house is made of wood, glass, concrete and stone. It's built into a hillside and most of the glass faces west over Lake Washington. My house is also made of silicon and software. The installation of silicon microprocessors and memory chips and the software that makes them useful will let the house approximate some of the features the information highway will, in a few years, bring to millions of houses."

Bill Gates, *The Road Ahead*

↑ DESIGN INFLUENCE

walls and ceilings/storage

On the face of it storage space seems to have shrunk in size and importance in domestic situations. Yet paradoxically, in this age of consumerism we all seem to possess more things that need to be displayed or stored.

Its diminished role in interiors reflects a general esthetic movement introduced by minimalism to conceal most possessions behind closed doors. So doors have grown in importance as architects design pulls and handles and designers patent door mechanisms that slide, glide, and pivot across clutter, as well as collections. Open shelving with artful displays is largely a thing of the past for contemporary homes, unless it is combined with back paneling to take over the entire wall and provide cable management, formerly only a feature of office design. Storage systems, either stacked in a modular grid like a library to line a wall or sinuously designed as a monumental freestanding piece to frame objects, turn into working walls.

2

1

3

Bang & Olufsen designer
1   David Lewis has given its range of screen and sound systems a distinctive character, whether wall-mounted as shown here, or freestanding so that they look as good from the back as the front.

A modular stacking system
2   that climbs the walls. The "Frame" design by Pinuccio Borgonovo for Citterio has a distinctive little hinge like a clothes peg to hold the sliding drawer face on slender struts. Some drawer fronts are solid, others opaque, to allow many combinations to conceal clutter or, without doors, to frame displays of objects on shelves.

For a heavy-duty
3   modular storage system, "Cargo" by Feg offers cable management and open display. Substantial widths of paneling, double-banked back to back, hide all the cables behind the plasma screen in the center. The "Cargo" shelving system on either side of the plasma screen adjusts to offer a lot of storage for books and objects.

doors p.76
bathrooms p.174
kitchens p.192

4

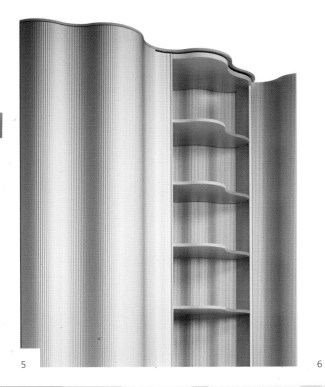

5

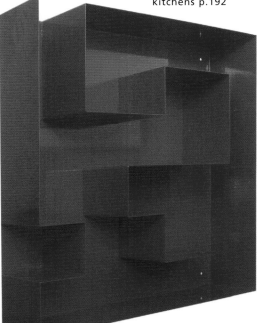

6

Just as an origami box
4 reveals hidden depths,
"Horizontal" by Shigeru Uchida
for the Dutch manufacturer
Pastoe has drawers which
slide open at just the lightest
fingertip touch. To work,
the unit needs generous
wall space on either side.

Flexible "Layout" by
5 Michele de Lucchi for Alias
comes in different heights,
760mm to 2m (2ft 4in to 6ft
7in), to adapt to the home or
the workplace. Just as cloud
forms change, so the footprint
of this unit adjusts to stretch
out horizontally, bunch into a
freestanding form in the room
center, or swivel to become a
linear piece set against the wall.

"Labyrinthe" shelving is
6 a modular system made
of steel painted in white, red,
eggplant, green, or orange
by Dool Design to hold books,
CDs, and other possessions.
Dimensions are 900mm (L)
x 900mm (W) x 230mm (D)
(3ft x 3ft x 9in).

"Home Project" by
7 Giuseppe Bavuso for
Alivar combines modular shelves
and consoles in wood and
aluminum with cabinets and
benches with glass or wooden
tops and drawers, as well as
mirrors and the centerpiece, the
TV unit. A flat-screen TV, DVD
player, or video recorder is
housed in an aluminum panel
on adjustable feet that hides
all cabling. Built into the TV
unit are fluorescent lights,
cable management, shelves
for records and decoder, and
a CD rack.

7

walls and ceilings/ceilings

What happens overhead is visually interesting as ceilings take on form (and volume) as well as function. Intelligent "Vektron" ceiling tiles by Kreon combine lighting with an integrated heating and cooling system in compact ceiling tiles that clip into the prefabricated metal frame which powers them. Easy to maintain, they are easily replaced. Downlighter tiles, for example, can be exchanged for ventilation grid tiles or a smoke detector tile. Different light sources include LED, halogen, metal halide, and fluorescents. With so many different functions, this gives the architect and homemaker a design strategy.

Glass ceilings reach new heights with back-lighting that changes color to make once transparent ceilings appear solid. Solid ceilings hide sound systems and speakers, light up at night, and balloon voluminously into weird shapes. They also muffle sound. Armstrong "Soundsoak®" acoustic panels absorb 50 to 90 per cent of sound striking its surface, three times more than traditional gypsum materials. Sound-proofed paneling made from cardboard honeycomb molded with coconut husks by Heideveld Polyester has a fluid wavy surface that resembles snakeskin. Alusion aluminum foam is packaged in a metallic shiny silver skin while Lambi Soundtube® panels channel sound in tubes behind a grooved varnished wood surface.

1

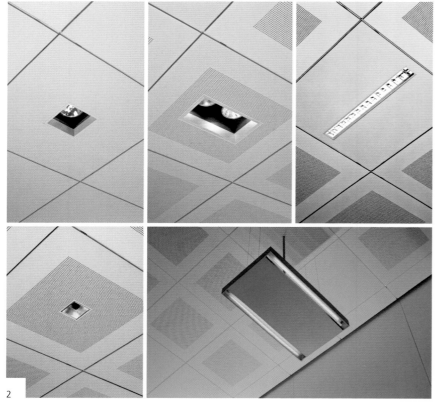

2

3

A ceiling suspended in waves high above the National Library in Paris. Architect Dominique Perrault chose metallic wire mesh ceilings by GKD in bronze and copper tones to reflect the colors of the walls. Semi-transparent wire mesh reduces the massiveness of structure which, lit from the side, appears opaque to conceal technical equipment like sprinklers and ventilation pipes.

"Vektron" ceiling tiles by Kreon, each always a regular square (600mm sq / 24in sq) contain different light sources: LED, fluorescent, halogen, and metal halide as well as heating and cooling systems, smoke detectors, ventilation grilles, and illuminated signage. Once specified, each tile can be clipped into the metal ceiling panel with a neuro connector that powers them. Top row from left: "Down 153," "Double Down 153," and "Down Long Mini." Below: "Down 76" and "Onn Air."

Invisibly installed in a home cinema ceiling, California-based Sonance's flat-panel speakers can be covered with the same surface finish as the ceiling without losing sound transmission quality. A motor attached to the back of a special diaphragm made of expanded polystyrene works as efficiently as conventional cone speakers, radiating vibrations from the entire surface without a drop in performance. Plaster, paint or wallpaper applied over the speaker will not affect its performance.

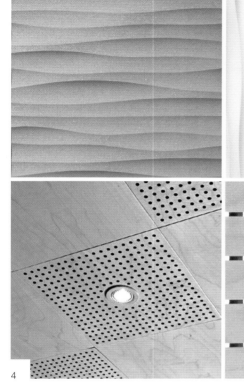

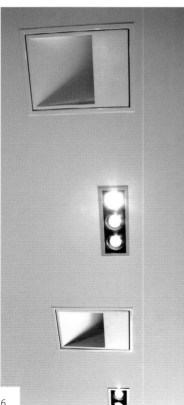

4

Four decorative
4 wood-paneled ceilings
from Marotte by designer
Georges Muquet. Minute
digital tools carve contoured
"Thalweg" ceilings made of
MDF, solid wood or fire-resistant
mineral fibers. Gouged rippled
effects and "Guilloche" carvings
like lino-cuts bring 3D waves,
dunes, and fold effects
enhanced by different layers
of colored wood veneers.
Perforated ceiling tiles with
built-in halogen downlights
are laser-cut.

5

A ceiling that breaks out
5 of the box with swooping
back-lit polymer resin panels by
3form® echoes the sinuous
swirls on the floor and furniture
in the Nordstrom restaurant,
San Jose, California.

A pair of "Bounce-One"
6 ceiling-mounted speakers
from Artcoustic whose ultra-slim
67mm (2⅝in) speakers conceal
high-performance quality sound
with a dynamic range higher
than conventional hi-fi.

Architects and designers
7 have an interest in
perforated materials because
the piercing provides solutions
to a number of design problems
from cabling, light transmission
and diffusion, and airflow. This
Gooding Aluminum slotted
ceiling panel shows the
perforations at actual size.

6

7

walls and ceilings/ceilings

This starburst ceiling by Swarovski above the indoor spa at the Hotel Residenz am Schwarzsee in Kitsbuhel, Austria is studded with small crystals lit by fiber optics with "Crystal 4 Reflex" reflected in the blue tiled pool. Once used mainly in night clubs and discos, fiber optic ceilings are moving into the home on long strands of cool light.

8

"Nebula" is an interactive projection system designed to make going to bed, sleeping, and waking a virtual experience. The Philips projector on the ceiling is linked via the internet to a database. Once users have selected the content for projection, they can manipulate it and personalize it. One algorithm in the system translates body positions and movements into moving imagery and text on video.

9

8

9

10

A skylight made of translucent silica "Nanogel®," the world's lightest and best insulating solid material by Cabot with Kalwall®, was chosen instead of glazing on this roof-top kitchen. When the sun shines, the panels transmit evenly distributed museum-quality light without the solar gain and shadows associated with glass. In winter, the panels transmit lots of light without cold air drafts.

10

An Opalika™ ceiling breathes life into a room, claims Schott, because it diffuses light evenly without shadows and guarantees a perfect rendering of color. Its application in museums and galleries has drawn the attention of interior designers. A colorless base glass, given a thin white flashed opal glass layer, means that even when not back-lit, it retains a pure white, even light distribution.

11

11

12

13

"SpectraGlass" is a new
12 material from The Light
Lab that uses light as a building
material. Above, the swimming
pool in a private residence in
London, with LED light evenly
bathing each individual
glass ceiling panel in intense
color is computer-controled
to change color under
scheduled sequencing.

Ideal for retro-fitting into
13 tiled surfaces, the "iColor®
Tile FX" from Color Kinetics is
a 600mm sq (2ft sq) panel
that conceals 144 individually
directed tri-color nodes
with 432 LEDs. Powered by
Chromasic®, waves of colored
light ripple across its surface or it
can be programed to light up a
logo, emblem or any pattern.

"Microabsorber" stretch
14 ceilings from Barrisol in
the Royal Academy of Arts
restaurant in London are
specially perforated for sound
absorption, and contain cold
cathode color-change lights.
Translucent polyester and
titanium stretch ceilings can
be back-lit, dimmed and
colorwashed via a remote
control, and shaped in many
ways, printed or painted. The
manufacturers boast that in the
event of a water leak it contains
water like a membrane.

14

flooring

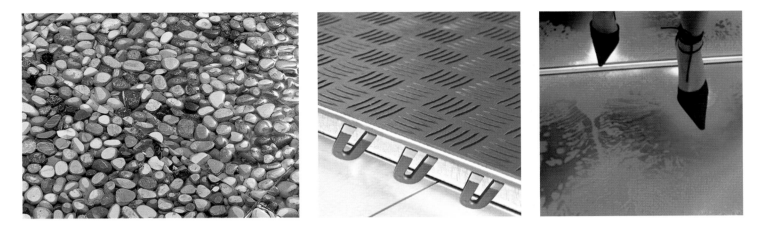

ABOVE LEFT A river bed replicated in floor tiles by Effepimarmi. Different sized marble pebbles and natural stone pieces bedded in transparent resin are raised above the floor level, yet the water-repellent waxy surface feels smooth underfoot.

ABOVE CENTRE The Dalsouple rubber tile has a magnetic backing to stick onto steel floors for cable management. Easy to lift, yet secure when laid, the magnetic force creates a stable walking surface.

ABOVE RIGHT Gel sealed in tough transparent floor tiles swirls under pressure. Café Interiors has installed these "Liquifloor" tiles in nightclubs, restaurants, museums and even yachts for a truly unsettling experience.

LEFT "Kilt" mosaic floor by Bisazza is formed of small pieces or tesserae of glass, stone, or marble, set in a mastic. Sold made up on 320 x 320mm (12½ x 12½in) mesh-backed panels and numbered with a template for quick installation by a specialist, panels are glued to the floor and grouting applied to fill in the grout lines.

Flooring is the biggest expanse – and consequently expense – in any furnishing scheme. All over the world real estate is measured in terms of the floorprint, or footprint as architects call it. In Japan, apartments are marketed according to the number of tatami mats (the traditional floorcovering of Japan) that the room will hold. That information immediately conveys the size of the room. Now GKD make "Tatami" floors out of sheets of woven stainless steel.

New materials, and new ways of looking at the familiar, make floors come alive. As if they were crossing wet sand, footprints blaze a trail through a liquid-filled foam floor, then gradually fade. Shock-absorbing foam (SAF) from Swisstex contours itself around a shape imprinted upon it and retains the memory of it. Artist Thom Faulders used SAF in his installation at the California College of Arts and Crafts (CCAC) to create the foam-padded "Mute Room," where people can walk or lounge, while listening to experimental electronic music. The shocking-pink memory foam floor means that every footprint is recorded momentarily.

To evaluate the impact that flooring makes in any room, try blocking out the floor in a photograph with

BELOW LEFT Rugs made of wool and flax from the Scandinavian Linie Design collection are hand woven in India. Danish designer Bodil Jerichau's "Cavi" in crimson is woven on a visible warp to give the bold geometric design an innovative surface.

BELOW RIGHT Laser-cut leather in a design called "Zhippo" by Riccardo Fattori from the "Intagli" collection by Parentesi Quadra. This collection of rugs designed by famous artists combines industrial technology with craftsmanship. Panels, which measure 900 x 800mm (36 x 31in), can be laid in strips or squared into decorative rugs.

RIGHT Anyone who steps onto Rogier Sterk's interactive light floor will be sure to make an impression. Footprints on the Lightfader, made by TAL, displace a layer of colored fluid sandwiched between scratch-resistant plastic and 3mm (⅒in) floor-grade glass, leaving an illuminated impression of each footprint. As a person walks across the floor, the fluid returns, making their footprints disappear slowly behind them. Sterk's illuminated tiles can be supported over a transparent ceiling below, making every step visible to everyone in the room below.

another color. Photoshop® makes it easier in the digital age to do this, but you can do it without a computer. A Post-it® note, cut to cover the existing floor in a photograph, will change it into citric yellow wall-to-wall carpeting. Block the wood-veneer maple floors with plain white paper. Imagine it to have rubber studs or just the glossy sheen of white ceramic tiles. Observe the room change, becoming more metropolitan, a canvas in which to introduce modern furniture.

The choice of floor can make a room shrink or widen, as it visually reorganizes space. This is why traditional interior designers such as Colefax & Fowler always include lozenge-patterned Brussels weave carpets in schemes to break up large expanses of a single color. Use pattern sparingly, however. Too much and your rooms look like a plasma screen test pattern.

The modernists laid patterned floor to rest in the late 20th century. The fashion to have floors under plain board, cement, or white tiles, still prevails. As minimalist John Pawson observes in his book *Minimum*: "The floorboards in my house are not really floorboards at all in one sense. They are actually laid on top of the original floorboards. They are as wide as the tree trunk from which they were cut and run the whole length of the house. Used like that you are able to enjoy the seamlessness of the material; there are no cuts in the boards. Seamlessness, to me, brings a sense of wholeness, it means not having your visual concentration broken. There is nothing jarring, you can sit anywhere in the room and always feel entirely comfortable visually."

If it is real wood, it must come from a sustainable source. The Forest Stewardship Council (FSC), a non-profit making concern, tracks wood from the forest floor to the consumer, demanding documentation and monitoring it for each piece of timber under strict accreditation. The government of the Netherlands only buys FSC-branded hardwoods for public buildings to ensure that woods are replaced by an ecologically sound forestry programe. California-based

ABOVE Crossing the foam surface of this cushioned floor is like walking on wet sand. Footprints gradually fade. Shock-absorbing foam (SAF) contours itself around a shape imprinted on it and retains the memory of it, which is why SAF by Swisstexis used for hospital mattresses and hearing aids.

This artistic installation by Thom Faulders of Beige Design, called "Mute Room" in CCAC, Berkeley, California, uses 25mm (1in) thick pink memory foam laminated onto flexible low-grade polyurethane foam. Visitors can walk around or lie down and listen to electronic music.

RIGHT Colorful, patterned ceramic tiles went out with the last century. Now the smart way to bring interest underfoot is to have the pattern in-built in the floor tiles, either in a textured, sculpted relief or by combining different surfaces. This floor contrasts matt and glossy finishes. Light falling from the window emphasizes the sheen on the gloss and contrasts it with the duller "Smoky Gray" matt finish in this "Globe" floor by Floor Gres, laid by Hyperion Tiles.

ABOVE First the floors in this Stockholm art gallery were painted gold. Then interior design team Front covered the gold with thick layers of white gloss paint. Visitors to the popular Tensta Konsthall wore a steady track through the layers of white paint to reveal the burnished gold beneath. Like a palimpsest, layers shine through.

ABOVE RIGHT Pale Jura limestone by Hyperion Tiles lines the shower tray sloping to the middle for drainage, and continues up the wall to create a wet zone. The bathtub appears to be paneled in the same stone, but this is really a paint finish. Because natural stone retains the heat well, underfloor heating is installed.

non-profit making society, ForestEthics, exists to make corporations aware of the impact of buying timber from any other source.

John Pawson is clear about the enduring appeal of real wood. He generally chooses natural materials for their sense of depth because they are living materials, "which I suppose is what distinguishes a natural material for me from an artificial one. When I used black vinyl on a floor, I was immediately unhappy with it. The eye stopped instantly, never giving a feeling that the material continued beneath the surface. On the whole, too, I prefer a rough or a matt finish," he writes in *Minimum*.

From the earth comes terracotta, ceramic tiles, marble and stone, bricks, and, at the other end of the scale, tamped earth. This age-old flooring inside nomadic mud and straw huts in the southern hemisphere is making a fashionable debut in the West as architects think organically – and laterally. In the Catskill mountains above New York the gigantic Z-dome by Jonathan Zimmerman is designed as a "residence for horses and their owners under one roof," a 650m sq (7,000 ft sq) concrete shell with sculpted earth excavated from the site, packed hard for a truly original earth floor. Hay is strewn over the floors in the stables and sawdust in the event ring.

Stone is a natural material that is quarried and

BELOW Limestone-clad floors slide beneath glass walls to line the pool deck of this Texan condominium. Continental Cut Stone prides itself on the laser cut technology it uses to shape fossilized limestone, a sedimentary rock composed of sea bottom fossils. Downlighting at the entrance, and uplighting in the pool, play upon the smooth pale plane of natural quarried stone.

ABOVE Nothing interrupts this view of Copenhagen's skyline as the solid oak floor appears to seamlessly slip beneath the glass curtain walls. Solid hardwood floors from Junckers can be planked thickly or narrowly. Solid beech floors, or ash, maple, merbau, European oak, American red and white oak floors, can be clipped together in a system which makes it easy – and quick – to install.

RIGHT Hard flooring flows in the fluid lines of the "Wave" by Effepimarmi. Small, natural stones graded in colors and assembled on a mesh support in this pattern can be laid on a prepared screed or smooth plaster floor. Loose stones are supplied to fill in any gaps.

shipped all over the world. As the selection of stone from North Africa, Portugal or Italy becomes harder to come by and importers only get a few blocks a year, marbles are used sparingly and local stones are sought for flooring. Indigenous stone creates vernacular architecture. Current favorite for floors in the USA is lichen-covered sandstone from Wyoming with a marble quartz appearance.

Reconstituted stone mixes made from limestone or marble chips mixed in a resin paste are both less expensive and more sustainable. Honing hardstone flooring in thinner slabs makes it go further, as does the recycling of sidewalk stones. In cities all around the world they are ripped them up for foundations, beneath which run fiber optic cabling. ASN Natural Stone's take on-line is that nothing is set in stone. "Stone keeps you guessing as new stones become available," they say. Tell that to a geologist.

Far from slipping unobtrusively into the background, flooring immediately draws attention to everything within the space. Whether naturals like seagrass, bamboo, and knotty pine reclaimed from river beds, are hard flooring choices, ceramics that double as wood or stone, are hard flooring choices, or carpets unevenly trimmed to resemble moss more than shag pile, are soft. Your choice of floorcovering invariably dictates the direction of the furnishing. Newer looms computerized to take complicated patterns and cut yarns combine different materials like silk and wool woven together in the same carpet. Great plains of savannah grass, moss, and lichen result from these unusual weaves and trims. For too long looked down upon and trampled underfoot, flooring moves into the foreground.

RIGHT Carpets have taken a bit of a knock as hard flooring – wood, tiles or stone – gained acreage in popularity. But carpets are back in the foreground to help with noise abatement. Carpets muffle sound more attractively than any other insulating material. Stepevi carpet is hand woven in Turkey and hand trimmed to vary the length of the pile. This raises tufts in wool with a shine flowing through the fluid matt wavy lines like ribbed sand.

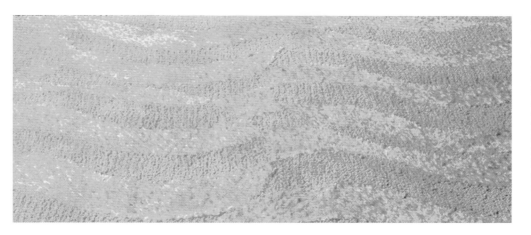

BELOW The "Original" laminate floor from Pergo replicates the warmth and pronounced grain of walnut with beveled edge planks. Its patina of real wood conceals the patented TitanX Surface™ protection coat which means that Pergo can withstand a catwalk of Manolo Blahnik stilettos. The SoundBloc™ sound-reducing underlay that is attached to the back of the plank reduces sound better than conventional loose underlay.

flooring/ceramics, stone, composites

Quarried stone, the favorite choice for French farmhouses and Versace shops, moves into the ground-floor apartments of modernists whose requirements are modest, and therefore affordable. The expense of freighting large slabs of stone across the world – and the environmental cost in terms of the depletion of quarries – has encouraged the use of regional stone. This approach is good for vernacular architecture: Coloradan yellow stone inside an Aspen ski chalet is more appropriate than imported Italian marble.

Reconstituting stone makes it go further, mixed with stone chips and pigments. Palladio published the recipe in 1570, but it looks just as good in a contemporary interior. Now that the laser is the stone mason's splitter, honing hard flooring in thinner slabs makes the real thing go further.

Do not be fooled by appearances. Some ceramic floor tiles replicate natural stone so well they feel like stone. Technological advances copy the naturally cleft texture of slate, marbled veins, and dappled colors that make stone floors beautiful.

1 Pattern on the floor, even apparently random like this one, works spatially to link furniture groupings and demarcate traffic routes. Resin colored like mother-of-pearl, by Gobbetto, spread over a flat, clean primed floor was decorated when dry by Dega Art with an irregular metallic finish sponged on to wind through tables and chairs like a snail trail.

2 Tiles that look like limestone are really ceramics from Iris Ceramica Marmi e Granti who call them "technological stones." Uniform ivory slabs flecked with tiny speckles that seemingly float throughout the material look as though they have lain on the sea-bed for millennia, just like real limestone.

1

2

Spanish Porcelanosa
3   pioneered ceramics
that replicate oxidized metal
in large clay slabs measuring
440 x 660mm (17¼in x 26in).
"Ferroker" black slabs
combined with "Osidi" in
gray, black, red ocher, or copper,
bounce light off its shiny
porcelain surface just
like burnished steel.

Tumbled cream-colored
4   travertine tiles from Malibu
Stone and Masonry Supply in
California are used in a modern
bathroom with a bluestone
border wrapped in curves
around the plunge pool. Greeks
and Romans built in travertine,
and their monuments stand
testament to the durability of
natural stone.

4

5

6

Real sandstone floors in the "Silk Collection," hand finished in an evenly adzed texture by Rhodes Architectural Stone, can be smoothly honed or lightly stippled in the finish it calls "Lychee" after the Chinese fruit. Rhodes has 16 factories around the world, using laser technology and hand craftsmanship to quarry stone according to its grain.

Ceramic tiles look and feel like coconut matting in "Cocos Café" from Iris Ceramica. Their MA.DE Collection, which stands for Materials and Design, explores 12 ways for tiles to be made in ceramic. Big squares are 600 x 600mm (24 x 24in), small ones 300 x 300mm (12 x 12in), and rectangular ones 600 x 300mm (24 x 12in).

This floor could be marble but is really high-tech "Cremo Delicato" by Ariostea, with a honed surface finish. Ariostea's ceramic tiles, 95mm thick (3⅝in), replicate quarry stone. Two examples (below): "Ardesia Amarilla," a light yellow base tile with ocher and greenish gray overtones that imitate the texture of naturally cleft stone and (bottom), "Ardesia Multicolor" which shows a realistic variation in marbled veining.

7

"Passato Prossimo," made in Italy by Aganippe Pavimenti, revives the tradition of mixing marble chips in white cement for contemporary interiors. The Ancient Greeks' paste of marble pieces set in marble grit was used in the 15th century by the Venetians.

8

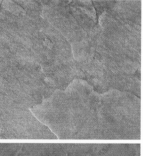

9

ALSO SEE

kitchens p.179

10

"Stone is real somehow. Concrete can never be real. The way to handle concrete, I suppose, since I've not handled it too much, is the way Corbusier does it with great deep shadows, extraordinarily rough, enormous overhangs, and deep cuts in black and white in a brutal fashion.

"As much as I admire Corbusier, my visit to the Marseilles building was quite a shock because of the ugliness of the materials. The extraordinarily bad lighting also affected me. I had to struggle to enjoy the forms."

Philip Johnson, *The Oral History of Modern Architecture*

↑ DESIGN INFLUENCE

Quarried in Italy, the
9 "Pietra Piasentina" limestone with a thermal finish can be cut as thinly as 10mm (⅜in) strips and slabs in the USA by ASN Natural Stone using modern technology. A flamed finish using special heat treatment gives the rough hewn stone an adzed texture.

Cement is as popular again
10 as DuPont™ Corian®, now 35 years old. So DuPont™ launched the "Concrete" colors collection, designed to fit in with Zodiaq® quartz surfaces. Unsuitable for flooring inside or out, it can be used to furnish rooftop terraces and weathers well out of doors, which is why the range of cement colors is included here.

Dense, hard limestone
11 quarried in Udine, Italy, and shipped to the USA by ASN Natural Stone, is hard enough to cut thinly to deck a rooftop terrace in San Francisco. Not many roofs could support the weight of natural stone flooring, unless finely honed.

11

flooring/tiles, mosaics

Contemporary floor tiles have fluid 3D sculpted surfaces that are comfortable to walk upon. Raised swirls and coils like earthworks or transparent raindrops made of glass fused to ceramic in the kiln are giving floors a higher profile. Ceramic tiles can even bend, mixed with silicone by Denis Santachiara in a project with Daniel Weidler he calls "Flex Stone."

Floor tiles are lightening up, quite literally, with holograms built into soft rubbery silicone tiles. They change color and image depending on the vantage point. Ceramics are a good conductor of electricity so LEDs (light-emitting diodes) built into ceramic tiles make floors pulsate with light.

Digital printing on ceramics can make your cat's paw prints crossing the floor a permanent fixture but surface decoration is more subtle than imagery. The secret lies in mixing and combining the various modules: matt surfaced anthracite tiles laid with glossy ones; small studs inset in big slabs; changes of tone within the same color, accent grouting. Tiled floors give the designer scope to create focal points and spatial awareness.

1

Mosaics adapt to any floor pattern imaginable. Shown here is an aerial view of a ceramic mosaic designed by Antonella Frezza – the Appiani collection in the "Nordico" color variation. Modular ceramic tiles, sized in 25 x 25mm (1 x 1in) pieces, are grouped tonally in four colorways, from birch and slate (shown here) to golden pine, dark green spruce, and Baltic blue.

2

3

2   The "Titanio" series of mosaics by Onix in Spain combines glass and ceramic tesserae made up into panels 250sq mm (9⅞sq in). Walls and floors paneled in the colorway called "Teide" shimmer when light falls upon them, like the sun playing upon a restless sea.

3   Borders and trims in the "Stonetech" porcelain tile collection by Apavisa Porcelanico inset among larger tiles make big expanses of tiled floors more interesting. Heavy-duty ceramic floor tiles are weather-proof and resistant to chemicals – excellent for use in public places.

4

5

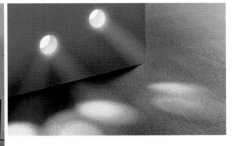

6

8

7

4 Wood and stone on a big scale in a dramatic contrast. The slate floor slabs are really ceramic "Gres" tiles from the "Pillarguri" collection made by Rex Ceramiche. Trolling through time to find inspiration, the collection celebrates the slate of the Norwegian fjords and a legendary woman warrior called Pillarguri who warned of a Scottish invasion in 1615. Wood effect ceramics are featured in their "Abisko" collection.

5 Stoneware is a term in the ceramics industry to describe a coarse kind of pottery baked hard and glazed. Deep-veined stoneware Almatec slabs 1.2 x 1.2m (48in x 48in) from Impronta Italgraniti are an alternative to marble, granite, and limestone.

6 Rather than transfer a printed pattern to a tile surface, smart ceramics have 3D patterns molded into each tile. "Fresh" by Ceracasa Ceramica shown in red and white, has an overall swirling pattern in relief, that is low in profile.

7 Uplighters in floors have been around long enough to inspire floor tile manufacturers to design a tile with an integral light embedded in the ceramic. Royal Mosa "Ultragres" ceramic tiles have integrated LED lights in the middle of each square 450 x 450mm (18 x 18in) or 600 x 600mm (24 x 24in) tile. Light-emitting diodes, like car brake lights, last a lifetime, and remain cool.

8 Glass globules like raindrops on the surface of ceramic "Drop" tiles stop slipping in the shower. Designed by Erik Jan Kwakkel and Arnout Visser for the Royal Tichelaar Museum in Holland, the non-slip tiles also give a foot massage. Drops of glass applied by hand melt in the kiln to bond with the ceramic tiles.

flooring/tiles, mosaics

Changes of scale across
9   large areas make flat
surfaces more interesting.
Mosaics in the same tonal
shades of natural stone as
the big porcelain tiles in the
"Brescia" collection by Ibero
Alcorense define the sleeping
zone in a studio. Edges
between the two floorcoverings
line up and the same grouting
unites them.

Big square "Dommo"
11   ceramic floor tiles, the
G31 from Azteca Ceramica in
a stone finish, are accompanied
by small matching trim pieces,
the R40. The reference numbers
relate to their sizes: great floor
tiles are 310mm sq (12¼ sq in)
and narrow rectangular wall
tiles are 400mm (16in) in length
with different widths.

9

Few floors are looked
10   down upon so frequently
as the floor in a shoe shop.
A Spanish shoe retailer
highlighted the central
showcase with a border of tiny
tiles in the "Chelsea" range by
Ceracasa Ceramica, designed
to mix with big slabs in the
same color called tobacco.
Grouting, pinpricked along
the seams before it dries,
looks like saddle stitching.

Just two shades of the
13   same color and two sizes of
ceramic tiles create a dramatic
tiled floor. Tiled by Reed Harris,
the "Habitat" collection by
Ceramicas Diago makes a
feature of an unusual tiled
bedhead, the same as the tiled
area on the floor around a
platform bed, studded with tiny
porcelain pieces that delineate
the color change like a rug.

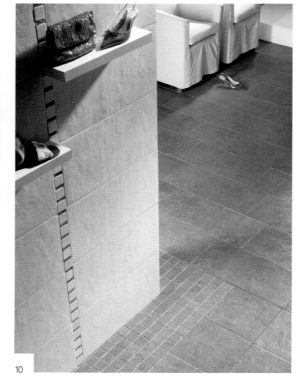

10

12

Ceramics arranged like
12   marquetry in the "Premier"
collection from Peronda. A
checkerboard of white and
brown porcelain pieces can be
scaled up to rug size in a room
or down as a detail to draw
attention to a column or
piece of furniture.

11

13

flooring/wood effect: ceramics

↓ **ALSO SEE**
flooring p.55

Touch it, feel it and you would never know the ebony floor underfoot was made of ceramic. Wood has a patina and the warmth of a living material that stoneware cannot replicate, but ceramic tiles are getting closer to that goal than ever before. New technologies allow cleft surfaces like the bark of trees, wood grains, knots and marbling just like a sawn tree trunk. Underfloor heating – and ceramic stone floors are an excellent conductor – makes them feel warm underfoot too. Ceramic tiles have for centuries played a part in beautiful gardens, now take on a new role indoors. And it's a green one, as they save the exotic species from extinction.

1

Tiles named after wood species – beech, oak, maple, and (shown) merbau – celebrate the beauty of wood. Stoneware tiles in the "Natura" collection by Grespania are even planked like boards in strips of 1.4m x 600mm (57in x 24in). Ceramics are suitable for use in bathrooms and kitchens, as no warping or fading will occur with condensation.

3 The "Forest" range of ceramic tiles by Azuvi is anything but rustic. They replicate woods from the temperate zones with sycamore, oak, ash, cherry, and walnut, as well as the exotic wenge wood from the tropics. The sheen on ceramics looks like highly polished wooden flooring and it comes in lengths of 624mm (24½in) in three different widths: 434mm (17in), 215mm (8½in), 106mm (4in).

2 Colored in honey, "Miel," and gold, "Dorado," the "Roble" series of ceramic tiles from Ceracasa are dappled and textured to replicate wood grain. Like floorboards, each 632mm- (25in-) long tile comes in three different widths of 150mm (6in), 74mm (3in), and 36mm (1½in).

4 When the demolition yard or the builders' merchant fails to unearth enough wide boards for a wooden floor there is always the porcelain plank alternative. Large format floor tiles that measure 450mm by 900mm (1ft 4in x 3ft), in the "Koa" series by Navarti, imitate wood from a time when very old tree trunks were large enough to be boarded in such massive widths. The girth of trees felled for real wooden floors makes such broad planks an antiquity.

5 For its ceramic tile collection, Italian tile manufacturer Rex Ceramiche was inspired by Scandinavian landscapes. First it looked to Norway for the slate collection. Then the national park of Sweden gave its name to the "Abisko" range of ceramic tiles that look like wood.

3

6 Gray wood-grained ceramic tiles in the "Midtown" collection by Lea Ceramiche. In this collection, different shades of cream tiles replicate leather, and four different gray, wooden effect tiles have grain and knots.

4

5

6

flooring/wood effect: laminates

Laminates that can be laid wall to wall as swiftly as unrolling the vinyl are putting a nail into real wooden floorboards. Technology works to replicate the finish of an exotic hardwood from an endangered species. Sophisticated finishes actually scrape the surface like boards, etch it like bark, and plank it so that it replicates tongue-and-groove boards. People who like the real thing are always amazed that laminates cost as much as they do, nearly as much as an inferior wood-veneer floor.

The final finish on golf balls, DuPont's ionomer coating Surlyn®, can be printed to realistically mimic any wood or stone. Sandwiched into flexible "Stratica" floors made in the UK by Amtico, it is one of the products listed in the *Eco Design Handbook* for the home and office as it is chlorine free, and has no plasticizers or Volatile Organic Compounds (VOCs).

What goes underneath both real wooden and laminate floors can reduce the sound of footsteps. Laminates muffle noise, but teamed with an underlay, they are doubly effective. Silencio 6 from Hunton Fiber (UK) is a 6mm thick (¼in) fiberboard underlay for laminates made entirely of recycled softwood fiber waste.

These oak floorboards
1   have the patina of age, swept and scoured over time. Yet this "Oak Colonial" floor in its metropolitan setting is really a mass-produced laminate. Each 9.5mm thick (⅜in) plank in the Quick-Step® "Country" collection has recessed edges on all sides just as purists would expect on felled timber floors. The detail shows the scraped finish.

In bathrooms and kitchens,
2   or any heavily glazed area with high condensation, laminates perform better than real wood. Bruce, a brand of Armstrong Floors, contains both real wooden floors and laminates like this "Acacia Torres." Its "American Home" collection replicates fine American hardwoods and fruitwoods in as many as three shades of the same species, embossed to feel like wood.

3

4

5

High-tech Alloc laminate
3   flooring resembles an oiled
teak ship deck. The first
company to manufacture
glueless, mechanical
interlocking laminate floors,
Alloc's "Teak Shipdeck" floor
has a distinctive low-sheen matt
finish just like that of real wood
soaked in linseed. Plates used to
mold the planks are scraped to
wood grain finish by hand in
three finishes, "Oiled Maple,"
"Oiled Teak," and "Teak
Shipdeck" which is a two-strip
design, varying planks with a
black infill and no end joints.

Heavy-duty areas such as
4   this dressing room passage
leading to a bathroom get a
new lease of life with "Classic
Oak" laminate flooring from
Amtico. Unlike natural wood,
"Classic Oak" will not warp,
crack, chip, or splinter because
it is made with the Multi
Performance System which
combines performance with
longevity. A polyurethane
treatment prevents scratches,
slips, and dents.

Broad boards of "Silver
5   Pine" in the "Country"
collection™ by Pergo® reflect
the fashion for lime-washed
wood emphasizing silvered
boards with two-way beveled
edges. This Scandinavian-style
laminate floor is so authentic it
could be a location in an Ingmar
Bergman movie.

flooring/wood

The razing of the rainforest is a horror story straight out of the Old Testament – floods or drought because the earth is heating up as equatorial forests are felled to fuel our flooring fancies, or for ranching and soya bean cultivation.

Just 30 years ago that green girdle around the earth's equator, the tropical rainforest, occupied nearly 30 per cent of the earth's surface. Today it takes up only 7 per cent. Every tropical hardwood product that does not come from a managed and sustainable source contributes to the destruction of the tropical rainforest.

International marketing tools like the Forest Stewardship Council, with its FSC logo branded on wood, guarantee that not only does the material come from

well-managed forests but that each step of production is monitored and traceable. Working with them to protect forests, and the people and wildlife that depend upon them, is ForestEthics, a non-profit organization based in San Franscisco whose mission is to harness corporate power to use the FSC tool to save forests, not only tropical rainforests but wood generally.

Everyone in the timber business, from the supplier to the architect specifying hardwood flooring for public places, right down to the home owner buying a floor, needs to source it from sustainably managed forest resources. Timber is one of the world's only truly renewable natural resources.

1

2

3

Marketed worldwide by the American Hardwood Export Council, the American hardwood species used for flooring includes: top, left to right, popular exports, American oak decking and broader, paler oak; middle, indigenous species popular at home, limited for export; hickory and beech; bottom, rare red elm, limited export, and black walnut, popular at home and abroad.

Natural wood veneers in many colors from parquet floor leader, Tabu, are Forest Stewardship Council certified. The color is solid all the way through the multi-laminates. Its "Caleidosystem" means that floors can be swiftly laid over existing floors, even carpeting, regardless of whether the floor is designed to be glued or to float.

Natural maple edging highlights a maple floor darkened in "Sierra" finish with a strip of walnut delineating the border. Three hardwood species from Mirage used in this way spatially change the room. The pale borders make the room appear larger, with the darkened center bordered with a walnut strip like a rug.

Ikea's particleboard floors 2 with pale blond wood veneers from the northern hemisphere are robust enough to withstand two sandings. Easy to lay at home over any existing hard flooring, each plank of the "Balk" maple floor measures 1190mm x 145mm (47in x 5⅝in). Boards are joined with a plastic strip which is included in the kit.

Australian beech shoots up 4 to 70m (230ft) in height with a perfectly straight trunk which is good for flooring. Boral Timber, which supports the Australian reserve system to protect the forest, grades its wood flooring simply: "Classic" which is traditional, and "Australiana" which has more character like gum veins, spirals, or even insect marking.

4

5

6

8

Mountain Lumber
6   Company reclaims wooden beams, floors and paneling from redundant buildings to plank them for contemporary interiors. Antique pine boards made from the great pine beams in an abandoned tobacco barn in Kentucky feature different weathered colors in warm brown, burnt orange, and deep amber. The planks have original saw marks.

7

Rivers that run through the
8   southern states of the USA are a rich source for timber floors. For over 30 years, scuba divers for the Goodwin Heart Pine Company have retrieved hardwood timbers shed from boats and logging rafts when they hit rapids or rocks. Flooring and stair parts made from Reclaimed River-Recovered® Heart Pine are more expensive but the dunking underwater makes the wood stronger and healthier.

Coconut palms are prolific
7   producers of nuts over their 80-year lifespan. So Smith & Fong, known for Plyboo® bamboo floorcoverings, turned the darker husk and shells into this handsome floor made solely from coconuts called Durapalm®. The 20mm thick (¾in), multiple-layered palm flooring is durable and harder than rock maple.

Bamboo is a highly
9   renewable resource, harvestable only four years after planting. Strong enough to be scaffolding in Asia, its low moisture absorption makes it ideal for the humid tropics – and bathroom floors in colder climes. Eco Timber's bamboo planks, 1.8m (6ft) wide, tough enough to sand, are on a plantation pine backing which can be nailed to plywood or glued to concrete sub floors.

The Forest Stewardship Council enables you to buy forest products of all kinds with confidence that you are not contributing to global forest destruction. FSC is branded on wood from certified forests all over the world to ensure long term timber supplies while protecting the environment and the lives of forest dependent people. A system of Chain of Custody certification traces forest products through the supply chain to the end consumer. Whenever you buy timber or timber products always look for the FSC logo.
Forest Stewardship Council

⬆ **DESIGN INFLUENCE**

9

flooring/wood

10

A solid hardwood ash floor 10 from Junckers with double dovetail joints is the perfect background to a designer fireplace and Scandinavian blond wood dining table with Arne Jacobsen's classic chairs designed in 1958. Naturally silvered ash wood grain is highlighted by the translucent white "Nordic" finish that seals the wide boards. No two hardwood floors from Junckers are alike. Hardwood species include ash, merbau, sycamore, oak, and press-dried beech.

11

American Hard Maple from 11 the colder mid-Atlantic and Lake States is a very hard, heavy wood that can be steam bent to create shapely stair treads that hit the deck in narrow boards. Exported all over the world by the American Hardwood Export Council, its distinctive color is known as "sugar maple."

For heavy traffic areas in 12 the home with hardwood floors, such as entrances and hallways, the prevention of indelible stains from paint, grease, and shoe polish is critical. An oak floor, "St Alban" from Mohawk Hardwood Flooring, is protected by Scotchguard™ Protector Advanced Repel Technology.

One of the hardest North 13 American woods, hickory, is used for tool handles as well as flooring. Eastern hardwood forests in the United States produce hickory hardwoods, split between true hickories and fruit-bearing pecan hickories. This hickory pecan, "Greenwich Plank" is from the Bruce hardwood brand by Armstrong.

12

13

Beech hardwood floor with
14   knots in the "Antique
Legend" collection by Italian
Stile. Produced in planks 15mm
(⅝in) thick, of which the top
4mm is solid wood above layers
of European conifer, glued to
another layer of hardwood
for stability. Tongue-and-groove
joints on four sides, with slightly
beveled edges, highlight the
dimension of each plank.

Blond woods held the floor
15   for the last part of the 20th
century, but now there is a
resurgence of rich, dark floors.
This solid black oak floor from
Junckers is fumed to draw the
dark coloring right through the
wood so that it can be sanded
and re-sealed.

14

15

16

"ShipStyle" parquet floor
16   laid in a brick-bond pattern
from Boen Parkett in Norway.
Only the top layer is solid
hardwood from certified
sustainable sources. The rest
is pine. As Boen point out,
even with solid parquet, it is
impossible to sand further than
the tongue-and-groove joint,
so why bury precious, slow
growing hardwoods? Lining
each pine plank is naturally
dyed hardwood.

Retro in style with its wide
17   plank, this white oak
parquet floor by Listone
Giordano is technologically
advanced. Different hardwood
surfaces, 5mm thick (¼ in), are
bonded to a second layer below
the surface to make selected
wood species go further –
wenge, Asian teak, iroko,
African doussie, Cabreva,
Canadian maple, and white
oak. Its Naturplus® finish
contains aluminum oxide for
maximum protection.

17

▼ ALSO SEE
heating p.123

flooring/soft coverings: leather, rubber, resin

Not all soft flooring has to be woollen. Soft, transparent, rubbery materials like polyurethane and silicone are smooth to touch and dazzling to view. Glitter in "Soft" silicone tiles by designer Saar Oosterhof in the Netherlands gave the illusion of depth, and her "Lens" tiles have hologram structures in pearlized pigments injection molded into them which change with the light.

Soft coverings for floors brighten up in the age of recycling. Smile Plastics in the UK began by recycling water bottles. Soon its processing plant gobbled up vending machine coffee cups, yogurt containers, dollar bills, CDs,

cell phones, and children's rubber boots to turn into sheet flooring. Its new venture has a never-ending supply chain: gas is piped into over 20 million homes in Britain in distinctive yellow pipes. All the off-cuts and scraps, with underground cabling, are turned by Smile Plastics into recycled plastic "Dapple" sheets.

Staples like water-resistant rubber floors are an environmentally friendly choice. Dalsouple's rubber is free from PVC, CFCs, formaldehyde, and plasticizers. Production waste is recycled in the UK factory and even its adhesives are water-based and solvent free.

1

2

3

Wall-to-wall leather
1   seems an impractical floorcovering but leather luggage designer Bill Amberg has mastered the art of installing one-off made-to-measure leather floors. Jewelry designer Solange Azagury had one installed when her teenage children were toddlers, which still looks good today. Waxing is required every two months.

A contrast in black and
2   white to rival the flourishing green of the garden beyond. This leather floor rug with a pattern of huge squares laid on the diagonal was designed by Michela Curetti for

Le Qr. It anchors the hard flooring, fringed with oversized, voluminous modular seating.

Leather ages as well as its
3   tannery. A tanning company near Florence, Cuoioarredo has mastered the art. Its leather tiles are laid the same as normal hardwood floors over an existing floor or a concrete screed. For stability, section bars supplied with the tiles can be glued into special grooves to align each row of tiles with the adjacent row.

↓ **ALSO SEE**

walls and ceilings p.28

4 Linoleums are mostly made from natural materials – linseed oil, pine resin, wood flour, and chalk – bonded under heat and pressure onto a jute backing. Mix and match linoleum panels and tiles in the "Marmoleum® Click" collection by Forbo Nairn simply click together without glue. They are made with lower emissions and lower acid output than PVC flooring or carpeting.

5 One of the hardest wearing floor finishes, rubber bump floor tiles from the Rubber Flooring Company will not fade in sunlight. Its vulcanized surface rebuffs burns, does not shrink and because nobody slips on it, rubber stud flooring is often installed in school and hospitals.

7 Children's out-grown rubber boots are sorted, shredded, flaked, and compressed into sheets (near right) by Smile Plastics to retain the myriad colors in a floorcovering. Coffee cups, yogurt containers, and redundant circuitry boards (far right) end up in a floor by Smile Plastics, who began by recycling plastic bottles into sheets.

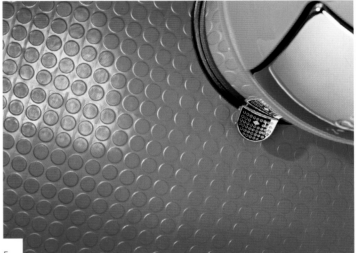

4

5

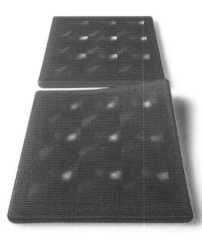

6 Images change according to the light and the viewing angle on these silicone and polyurethane "Soft" tiles with in-built holograms by Saar Oosterhof for Dutch design company, Droog. Sprinkled with glitter, the hand-cast floor tiles, 240mm sq x 14mm thick (9½in x ⅝in), give floors an illusion of depth.

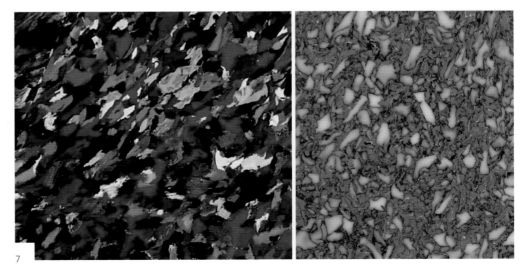

6

7

flooring/carpets and rugs

Carpets have taken a bit of a beating in the popularity stakes recently. Allergies, expense, and a general aversion to pattern and solid colors have made wall-to-wall carpets a rare sight in contemporary interiors. Architects have never liked them for breaking up their seamless floors that slip beneath walls into the shadow gap, that indentation in the plasterwork just above floorboards.

Yet, as any home owner knows, carpet and rugs can spatially alter a room as dramatically as any architect. A rug can make a room appear to be wider, or longer, than it is in reality. Pebble-shaped carpets made by Nani Marquina are like stepping stones across the room, taking the eye to new horizons. Or a rug can become the focal point of a room, drawing together furniture.

The Rug Company looks to the catwalk for dramatic effect, asking fashion designers to design a collection that is a talking point. Designers and manufacturers combine unusual materials with different tensions like paper and leather from Linie, silk and wool from Tufenkian, or linen with wool from Kasthall. As well as experimenting with materials and shapes, designers use different heights of pile within the same piece, trimming pile to create 3D patterns. Unevenly trimmed piles replicate moss, feathery grass, or sand ribbed by the sea, with raised textures.

1   "Stamp" from the "Figure Carpet" collection by Woodnotes is paper yarn woven with just 14 per cent cotton. Woodnotes produces a collection that ingeniously makes 64 designs out of combinations of just 10 patterns and 10 colors. Paper yarn does not gather dust or dirt, and due to the tight weave will not ignite easily. A soil-repellent treatment makes them impermeable.

2   At last, a flooring that can be laid over underfloor heating systems. Woven vinyl floorings with a fiberglass backing in the "Now" collection from Swedish manufacturer Bolon in intense colors – metallic pink or purple, bronze, and silver – will not fade in sunlight and are both noise and stain resistant.

1

2

3   Sisal from the agave family is a popular natural fiber that has shed its earnest homespun look. It emerges with a glamorous sheen, woven in a bobbly boucle finish in scarlet, by Alternative Flooring.

3

Strange bubbly weave on
4   the floor looks like rubber
bump or glossy relief tiles but
it's a carpet tile that is soft to
the touch. New wave
waterproof carpets in relief
from Heuga in the color
called "Marine" from the
"Waterworld" collection show
how carpets have come a long
way from boucle twists and
bobble tufts. A detail (far right)
reveals a surface that looks like
glistening water drops.

Tatami is a pressed rice
5   straw mat in Japan, used
as the real estate measurement
for floorspace in apartments.
"Tatami" by GKD is woven in
pure stainless-steel panels, 50
of them furnishing the futuristic
hotel lobby designed by French
architect Dominque Perrault.

4

5

Nylon carpet with a level
6   loop by Shaw in the
"Inspired Influence" collection is
both durable and natural, rather
than synthetic looking. Dirt is
hard to see on its 100 per cent
nylon surface which resists
permanent staining.

Antron® metallic yarns
7   called "Sparkle" from
Invista have graced palaces and
yachts. Hand knotted, hand
tufted and in both wool and
silk, custom-dyed yarns, metallic
color pigments are actually built
into the fiber, and will
not fade through prolonged
exposure to extreme sunlight.

6

Neutral shades in the
8   "A Touch of Silk" and
"Basics" collections designed
by handmade carpet specialist
Craigie Stockwell. These
contemporary mixes use
silk in two-tone patterns
with wool pile.

Get it wrong and animal
9   paw, claw or skin prints
on floorcoverings look
embarrassingly mawkish. Get
it right and you are on the side
of wildlife. "Mystical Zebra" is
what Karastan calls the stylish
black-and-white striped version
in its "Exotics" collection, but
there are leopard and giraffe
spots as carefully observed
as if on safari.

7

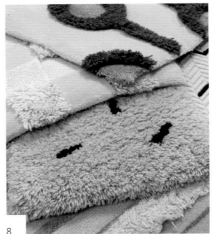

8

9

flooring/carpets and rugs

Attention-grabbing rugs in 10 The Rug Company "Designer Collection" by famous names in fashion and interior design. Flamboyant colors and bold designs illustrate individuality in the world of mass production. No two designs follow the same warp and weft pattern-making tradition to break out of formulaic manufacturing. Below left, "Canvas Rose" by Lulu Guinness; right, "Climbing Leopard" by Diane von Furstenberg; bottom left, "Swirl" by Paul Smith; bottom right, "Magnolia Black" by Vivienne Westwood.

Italian fashion house 11 Missoni, known the world over for myriad colored knits, clothing, fabrics, and objects for five decades, has a distinctive polychrome "Fleury" flower motif carpet hand knotted in China.

10

11

↓ **ALSO SEE**

walls and ceilings p.26

With raised silk stepping
12 stones winding through a background of New Zealand wool, Christine Van Der Hurd's "Follow the Drops" rug is cleverly made. She uses hand-knotted Tibetan weave for the 100 per cent woollen background and hand tufted petit point loop pile on the silken pebbles. From studios in London and New York, she works with architects, interior designers, hotels, stores, and residential clients worldwide to design flooring and area rugs.

"Igloo" in the
13 predominant shades of green and gold from James Tufenkian, designer and supplier of handmade Tibetan and Armenian carpets. A tireless traveler, his inspiration comes from things as varied as a painting in Assisi, a building in Kathmandu, the Chrysler building, and an Inuit shelter.

Stones made of wool
15 in Nani Marquina's collection are an amusing way to create stepping stones in a corridor, or leading towards a focal point in a room. Marquina sees her carpets as large canvases, albeit 3D ones – with which she can experiment with shape, like huge jigsaw pieces or these giant pebbles.

"Moss" hand tufted pile
16 rug by designer Gunilla Lagerhem Ullberg for Kasthall mixes long linen threads to a pile height of about 40mm (1½in) with short, coarse wool yarn, just like moss and lichen.

12

15

16

13

14

"The easiest way to make a pattern is to draw a row of motifs side by side and one below the other… Another way is to draw the motifs first looking one way and then the other, all along the line… A third arrangement is… where the motifs are drawn in columns and each column is dropped so that the top of the motif is level with the middle of the motif in the column before."

Lucienne Day in a 1950 BBC broadcast, *Looking At Things*

↑ **DESIGN INFLUENCE**

"Victor" by Riccardo
14 Fattori for Parentesi Quadra has its intricate design lasered onto a leather rug measuring 2.4 x 1.80m (8 x 6ft). This new Italian company looks to the 1960s and London's Carnaby Street fashion for patchwork in psychedelic colors on its rugs.

A careful combination of
17 natural materials, leather, and paper in the design Linie Design calls "Heavy." In reality, with its lightness of touch it brightens up any contemporary interior. There are three sizes: 1.4 x 2m (4ft 7in x 6ft 7in), 1.7 x 2.4m (5ft 7in x 8ft), and 2 x 3m (4ft 7in x 10ft).

17

doors

The classic Danish "d line" door handle, designed 30 years ago by Professor Knud Holscher and supplied by Allgood. Ergonomically shaped to fit the grasp, the handle is popular with architects.

ABOVE CENTER The sliding mechanism by Bisca in stainless steel, fitted to a toughened-glass door, runs on rollers along a track. Bisca stands for Brass, Iron, Steel, Copper, and Aluminum.

ABOVE RIGHT LED (light-emitting diodes) are fitted to the glass "Lina" door in the "Avantgarde Collection" at Inner Door.

LEFT A life drawing acid-etched onto the "Porte a bilico" door makes it highly visible. Patented by Portearredo to close flush against the wall without door posts or casings, the door operates on hidden oscillating vertical pivots. "Porte a bilico" can be integrated into any depth or type of wall, whether masonry or plasterboard.

In children's books, adventures always take place on the other side of a door. The lion and the witch in *The Chronicles of Narnia* by CS Lewis were found on the other side of the wardrobe and EE Nesbit's five children had to cross the threshold before they met the phoenix. Alice chanced upon Wonderland when she discovered in her pocket a golden key to one of the locked doors.

But it is not only in literature that we experience the thrill of stepping through a door to take charge of our destiny. In his endearing self-portrait, *The Curious Mr Sottsass*, Ettore Sottsass, who redefined the design of everyday objects in the Memphis Collection late last century, reveals, "I have always enjoyed taking photographs of doors, entrances and narrow passageways, particularly dark and dank ones. With a bit of experience you learn how it is that, by passing through such narrow gateways, you can step into brilliant sunshine, into open countryside, perhaps on to the beach and even into paradise itself."

There are curved doors and straight ones; doors that fit into regular frames or break out of them to hang suspended from invisible tracks like works of art on white walls. Doors can pivot and swing, slide and glide.

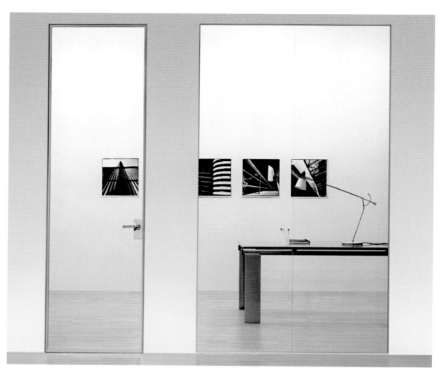

LEFT Milan-based architect Antonio Citterio designed a program for TRE-Più with the slender, full-height "Planus" hinged doors, shown as a pair. The doors fit into his mobile "Pavilion" walls, a door-furnishing system for full-height sliding or hinged doors, which can be made to measure.

ABOVE Two flush-mounted, clear-glass doors create a single and a double passageway through an apparently uninterrupted wall. The "Rasomuro" series from Lualdi Porte aligns perfectly with the wall, replacing the door frame with a thin, anodized-aluminum door jamb attached to the wall with clamps, and rubber gaskets for silent and smooth closing. An external hinge allows it to be opened outward, with a push, or inward, by pulling.

BELOW The same double door in the "Rasomuro" series by Lualdi Porte changes its appearance as easily as a new finish. "Grezzo" door, with its gray, lacquered surface and an extra-thin, smooth, anodized-aluminum frame, fits seamlessly into gray lacquered walls.

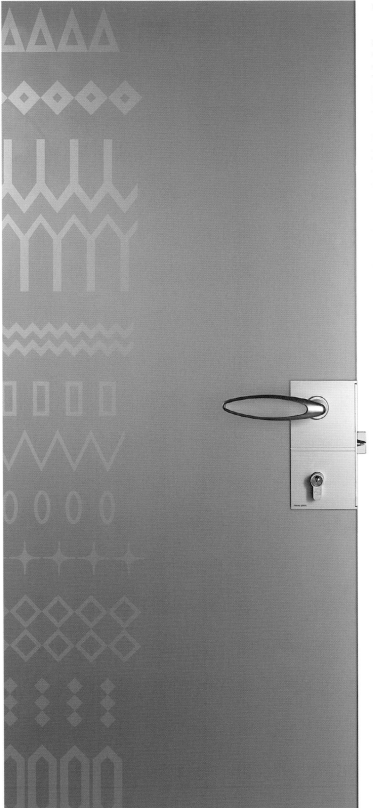

FAR LEFT Gracefully curved
"Lyra" sliding doors in the
"Orbitale" series by Scrigno
slide smoothly, held in curved
grooves fitted to the floor and
an architrave, both supplied
with the door. Curved door
panels, 40mm (1½in) thick, are
in white lacquer or dark or light
walnut, with matching posts.

LEFT Hieroglyphs and symbols
are sandblasted onto the
toughened-glass surface of
the "Ritmi" door in the "Segni
di Vetro" collection patented
by Henry Glass. Patterns from
birds and flowers to magic
carpet designs are revealed
through the glass lightly.
Sliding or hinged glass doors
can be made to measure
without any support frame
or traditional hinges.

Even the hinges are patented as designers devise new
ways of making doors move stealthily and then
disappear seamlessly when open.

Some of the world's most prestigious architects have
turned their hand to the design of door handles. Norman
Foster tells us why in his book *On Foster… Foster On*:
"A door handle can be likened to architecture in
miniature – it has to work well for those who use it
but it must also look good. In another sense it is an
important part of the furniture in a building – literally
one of the few points of physical contact. In the tactile
sense, the handle has to feel good. But then it is easy
to forget that architecture is all about the senses."

Recognizing that touch is one of the last senses
to fade, architects Renato Benedetti and Jonathan
McDowell used tactile grips on handrails at the Mulberry
House Nursing Home in London, putting different
sleeves over handrails. Red rubber bump rails lead to the
dining room, while blue, smooth rubber grips are used
on bathroom door handles. Doors facing the bed-ridden
are designed as display boards, allowing residents to keep
meaningful personal things while freeing bedside tables.

doors/doors and frames

Architect, furniture designer, and product designer, but best known as the leading figure of the Memphis design studio, Ettore Sottsass is a dominant force in the world of design. Memphis channeled all the vital energies of the 1980s into the decade's rebirth of design and taught us that design is figurative communication.

Cocif in Longiano, Italy, began making doors in 1945. Now, with an annual turnover of 63 million dollars, and a production line of 200,000 doors and 150,000 window frames a year, the company has introduced two contemporary design collections by Ettore Sottsass and Gae Aulenti. The door collection shown here, designed by Sottsass for worldwide

distribution from Cocif, illustrates the richness of a constant use of form. The door changes with every new application of color and material: most are of oak or beech, which may be lacquered and varnished, stained, or sanded and sealed. Frames visually change the door dimensions. Dark panels in a white frame lengthen them, pale ones in an extended architrave widen them. Sottsass named the collection after his travels in India – "Pakora," "Tikka," and "Goa."

Ettore Sottsass says, "I have photographed many doors, entrances and passageways… although we may imagine the consequences of crossing a threshold, when we actually do so, we are taking control of our destiny."

1

2   3

A wavy door that appears
4   to break out of its frame.
The curves on one side of the "Esse" by Eri Goshen for Lualdi Porte invite a gentle push to close it. Enameled in sea-green with inlaid metal ribbons, it comes in oak or cherry, with an anodized-aluminum door jamb.

Using a standard door by Cocif as an artist's canvas, Ettore Sottsass changes its dimensions visually simply by changing the decoration. They are shown in pairs from top right (1–3):

"Tikka" doors lengthen
1   with dark timber panels inset in white frames (left) and widen in blonde wood framed in oak to show off the extended architrave (right).

A sea-green "Goa" door
2   in a black frame with horizontal bars seems more substantial than its companion (right) in a white frame.

A red door in a red frame
3   abstracts the "Pakora" door from the broad-banded version (right), with honeyed horizontal stripes interset with pale wood.

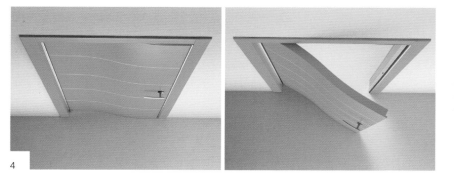

4

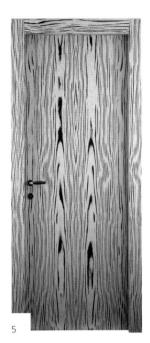

5

Porte Zanini launched its decorative "Paola" collection of exotic-veneered doors at the Abitare interior design fair in Verona in 2005. Behind "Zebrato" (shown) lies a double-thickness (44mm/1¾in) of MDF, framed in solid wood.

Red-lacquered "Outline," 2.9m (9ft 6in) tall in the XL version, 2.1m (7ft) in the standard, steps out of the wall like a work of art. Lualdi Porte attach the door to the wall with a simplified system that does not require the use of a counter frame, only an aluminum one. "The door is a panel of great visual and tactile impact," says the designer Erik Morvan, "that detaches itself from the wall with the same effect that a column creates inside a space, to emphasize its decorative value."

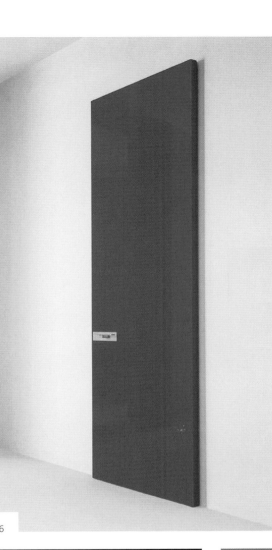

6

7

A bleached oak, single sliding door in the "Unique" series by Scrigno, the "Appeal" makes a feature of its sliding mechanism by extending the oak architrave it slides behind when open. Framed in slender aluminum posts, the "Unique" project seeks to reduce the volume of door parts while increasing the quality of the materials used.

ALSO SEE

walls and ceilings p.17
flooring p.63
bathrooms p.145

8

9

Hidden in the thin aluminum door frame of the "Plana Slim," designed by Giuseppe Bavuso for Rimadesio, is the technology that makes it possible to hang a heavy glass, wood, or aluminum door on a minimalist aluminum frame. It adjusts to walls that are out of plumb within a range of 105–125mm (4–5in). The door handle helps delineate the width of the door with an inlaid strip behind.

Known worldwide for designs of Nikon cameras, Swatch watches, and Apple computers, Giugiaro Design, who were responsible for the "Iki" collection for GD Dorigo, made a feature of the frame, combining aluminum posts with wood and lacquers. On this model, amber wood veneer meets zebrano in a jagged pattern, framed between aluminum door jambs with a wooden architrave.

10

11

A fashionable wenge wood finish to a sandwich-board door by Laura Meroni smoothly slides with a finger slot grip. Standard doors from 2.1–3m (7–10ft) tall, in widths of 0.7–1m (2ft 3in–3ft 3in), are available in rosewood, maple, cherry, pear, and ebony veneers with satin-brushed-steel handles and patented locks.

The solid wood "Dibla" door and frame is designed and made by Fernando Garofoli in response to "all those who once thought that solid wood doors looked old fashioned." Two etched grooves running almost the length of the door zig-zag at the handle, a visual reminder of handcrafted detailing, which can be mass produced in a factory today.

doors/folding and sliding

Folding and sliding mechanisms are so ingenious that designers patent them.

Jeld-wen®, named Energy Star in the USA in 2005 for its energy-efficient doors and windows, patented its "IWP® Aurora™" exterior patio folding doors. Operating like an accordion, they slide, pleated, on tracks to stack at the sides.

Austrian architect Norbert Wangen patented his grooved, plastic, three-pinned hinges on the "S201" floor-to-ceiling cupboard doors for Boffi. Even though the doors are 2.34m (7ft 6in) tall, just two tiny hinges, top and bottom, allow them to close seamlessly and, open, to slide out of sight into vents on either side of the door frame. They jut out of the 120mm (4¾in) frame like bookends on shelves. Laser precision in manufacturing makes this the joint most architects dream about, but Wangen says: "Technical details alone don't serve to realize an idea. Architects who plan houses by starting with the car in the garage will never capture the emotion of a building. I think about improving the occupant's life functionally but with esthetic consequences."

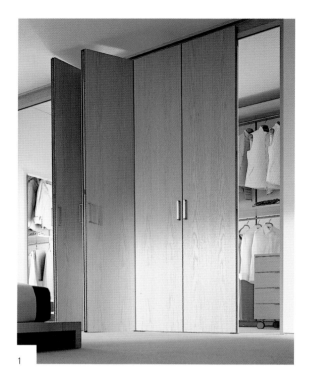

Moving doors is the goal
1 Italian company Movi set itself with "Flectoarm." Folding doors fitted to the "MyWall" storage system by architect Raul Barbieri concertina gracefully into pleats. They can be replaced by sliding "Andros" doors if floorspace is limited.

Lightly woven wood on
2 a sliding panel blind turns a window dressing into an architectonic room divider. "Tobago Teak" doors by LouverLite filter daylight when closed while stacked behind one another when open, they allow daylight into the room.

1

2

Jeld-wen® patented its
3 IWP® folding door, which was unveiled in 2006 at the International Builders' show in the USA. Energy-efficient, low-E glass is framed in either real wood or the award-winning "IWP® Aurora™" custom fibreglass, impossible to tell from real wood. A concertina folding section on an overhead track holds doors in heights up to 3m (10ft) in wood and 2.4m (8ft) in fibreglass.

The substantial "Andros"
4 door by Movi on smooth running tracks makes up in substance and width what it frees in floorspace. Sliding behind one another on overhead tracks, the door panels feature vertically grooved fingertip controls lined in anodized aluminum that run a quarter of the length of the panels.

3

4

Absolutely flat aluminum doorposts frame double sliding "Flyer" doors in dot-etched glass. One of five product lines in the Scrigno "Unique" collection developed with Studio Ugolini Design, the doors can be either single or double and are available in glass, or bleached oak, walnut, or cherry.

5

From LouverLite, the "Manhattan" sliding panel blind in suede effectively blocks the light when closed. Anchored with a bar at floor level in teak or aluminum, this versatile system impacts lightly upon the room while controlling light and offering privacy.

"Mira" folding double doors in light Tanganyika wood veneer glide on the "Applauso" system by Scrigno. Opaque glass panels shown are not supplied with the doors so they could be replaced with handmade paper like shoji screens in Japan, which let light glimmer through into innermost rooms.

Rimadesio "Graphis," designed by Giuseppe Bavuso, is a system of sliding panels characterized by a rigorous design that divides space into rooms. Structural aluminum tracks of minimal thickness hold double-glazed, sound-proofed glass panels, always made to measure in both height and width. Shown in glossy black lacquered glass, the panels are available in 12 lacquered colors and in gray or blue opaque glass. Handles feature a retractable grip.

6

↓ ALSO SEE

walls and ceilings p.19
windows p.91

7

8

doors/transparent doors

Not so long ago, the only all-glass doors at home were found on shower stalls. Now they step out of the bathroom to take center stage in contemporary interiors. Acid etched or sandblasted, pattern makes glass doors come alive, and sheets suffused in intense color make patterns of colored light within the room.

The Victorians decorated front doors with stained-glass panels to bring some individuality to terraced houses. The same technique to produce lead-bound panels of mouthblown colored glass is applied to contemporary designs on all-glass doors, which can be mass produced. Henry Glass has patented a system that combines craftwork with high-quality technology to manufacture sliding or swinging glass doors with artists' handmade panels positioned in them. The technique allows delicate tapestry handwoven in Renata Bonfanti's studio to be set into frosted or clear glass panels.

Almost as clever are the hidden mechanisms that allow toughened glass to open or close. "Agile 50," developed by Dorma, is a compact rail system for sliding doors, with a loadbearing capacity of up to 50kg (110lb), yet the clamp fittings and roller carrier are invisible, concealed behind a slender aluminum frame. A lightweight alternative to glass is a light-emitting mesh, used in the "Siparium" sliding panels from Rimadesio, which maintains privacy but allows light to pass through.

3

The "Concerto" door
1 in the "Tuttovetro" collection from Henry Glass.

Sandwiched between
2 glass in this door is the "Arianna" handwoven tapestry by Italian artist Renata Bonfanti, one of several designs she created for the "Vetro Veneto" collection by Henry Glass (detail shown).

1

2

4

5

Yves Klein blue on
3 "Imera®" anti-reflective glass from Schott. Coated on both sides using a special dipping method, it reduces light reflection from eight per cent to only one per cent. Ideal for doors, it invites a reflection-free view through to the other side, and can be laminated and insulated.

Small lead-bound glass
4 panels on sliding or hinged glass doors in the "Vetro Veneto" collection for Henry Glass are designed by Afra and Tobia Scarpa (left) and Alessandro Mendini (right).

A modern take in cast
5 glass on medieval studded doors. Action and events taking place behind these frosted-glass double doors in the offices of Vancouver-based interior design firm Robert M Ledingham Incorporated are a bit blurred but intriguing. Nathan Allan Glass Studios cast the glass with studs by pouring molten glass into a mould.

6

7

With a track rail depth
6   of just 50mm (2in), the
"Agile 50" from Dorma
sliding-door system is designed
to carry up to 50kg (110lb) on
clamps fitted to a roller-carrier
unit concealed within the
aluminum track profile. Easy
to install, with an almost silent
operation, the system permits
a precise latching of the door.

The "Onda" glass door in
7   the "Appeal" collection by
Scrigno includes changes of
light and depth with its novel
surfacing – a combination of
dot-etched glass with a small
stud impression and a
continuous wave pattern
sandblasted over it.

 ALSO SEE

flooring p.48

Gray etched glass
8   "Ghost' by Giuseppe
Bavuso for Rimadesio is a door
characterized by the thin
aluminum frame that appears
to effortlessly carry a solid span
of luminous toughened glass.
The exclusive telescopic jamb
hidden in the thin frame makes
up for any difference in the
thickness of the walls.

"Fly" by Fioravazzi is a
9   sliding glass door framed
in aluminum, which is
lacquered in the RAL color
9006. Large sheets of matt,
engraved glass are carried
effortlessly on tracks.

8

9

World leader in the production of handles, door furniture, and bathroom accessories, Valli & Valli collaborate with top architects and designers for their Fusital brand, shown on this spread. More examples of classic designs made by other worldwide manufacturers are shown on pages 82–3.

A review by Norman Foster of the "d line" handles designed 30 years ago by Knud Holscher (see page 71) reveals turns a door handle into a classic. In most of the buildings Foster and Partners designs, including its own, the "d" handle, with a semi-matt finish in aluminum or stainless steel, is specified. The design is "intellectually satisfying, sparse and abstract, even though it is acceptably comfortable to use. In that sense it is an excellent compromise with an agreeable economy of production – it is, after all, a simple bent bar."

Designs of door handles often hold the key to the thinking behind their designers. Frank Gehry's handle has the forceful twist of his buildings, while Norman Foster, inspired by high speed flight, has a lightness of touch. Two door handles with the biggest presence are Jean Nouvel's solid block handle which mirrors light and shade, and Ron Arad's, reduced in substance to a twist of paper. Simplicity is the secret of this collection of highly original pieces.

2

Two collections designed by Frank O Gehry, one of the most celebrated architects in the world since the opening of the Guggenheim Museum in Bilbao which he designed. Part of the "Duemilaquattro" series for Fusital, the "FOG" (his initials) handle in brass reflects a sculptural theme most characteristic of Gehry: the fish. Below, the stainless-steel "Arrowhead Series H5021" appears, like his buildings, to have a centrifugal force.

The concept of separate laminations or layers on the "H334" (top) and "H328" by Norman Foster in the "Novantotto" collection for Fusital began with a wing section for high-speed flight known as a laminar-flow aerofoil. An international jet-setter who flies his own plane to his buildings around the world, Norman Foster was awarded the Pritzker Prize and a life peerage in 1999.

3

4

The "H329" in the "Novantacinque" series by Ricardo Bofill's Taller de Arquitectura in Barcelona. His ability to endow commonplace building types with eloquence and dignity has given concrete an edgy new face in the suburbs of Europe where his housing complexes flourish.

The "H335" in the "Novantotto" series for Fusital from the American architect Richard Meier makes a feature of the clasp where the lever meets the door plate, a junction usually overlooked for detailing. His clean-cut geometries and rigorously ordered white spaces are found in museums around the world, most famously at the Getty Center near Santa Monica, California.

1

Handles designed by Antonio Citterio in the "Novantacinque" collection for Fusital. Top to bottom: "H317," "H321," "H327," and "H326." The Milan-based architect and product designer is working on the revamp of Line I of the Milan Metro, a chain of luxury hotels for Bulgari, and a new settlement called the Technogym Village in Cesena.

5

6

Jean Nouvel's "H344" in the "Duamilauno" series makes as much of the base plate as of the handle that mirrors it. The resulting play of light and shade is reflective of the building that made his name in 1987, the Institut du Monde Arabe in Paris, clad in camera lenses that track the sun.

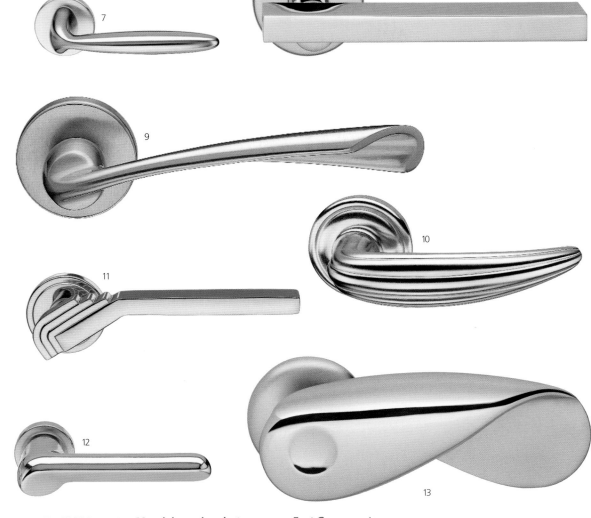

7 Matteo Thun's "H330" in the "Novantasette" series for Fusital. His handle combines both high touch and high-tech. He believes that "It's not enough to design a vase or a handle without the eye sending the signal 'I love this object' for its color, its texture, and the values that are prominent on the surface and not inside."

8 Esthetically pared down without being plain, the "H343" by John Pawson in the "Duemila" series for Fusital. Pawson maintains his rigorous stance on beauty and usefulness maintaining the minimum of material needed to perform its purpose safely than exaggerated styling tends to look better."

9 The "H333" in the "Novantotto" series for Fusital by Piano Design Workshop spearheaded by Renzo Piano, whose Pompidou Center with Richard Rogers set the anarchical 1960s right in the heart of Paris. Design, he believes, is not a linear process which begins with a single idea on paper and proceeds sequentially to a building – or a product. Rather, it is a circular process with sketches followed by models in ply of foam, then factory made prototypes.

11 Sottsass Associates designed the "H38" in the "Quattro" series for Fusital way back. "In order to appreciate how to draw a door and to understand the door itself," Sottsass observed, "I have photographed lots of them. Not all doors indiscriminately, just those through which I would like to have passed."

12 The "H37" in series "Tre B" for Fusital by architect Cini Boeri, who designed the first seats to be built exlusively in polyurethane foam with the support of an internal frame for Italian furniture maker Arflex. Her style uses clean cuts, straight lines, flat surfaces, nothing extraneous: the idea is not hidden but displayed with simplicity and clarity.

"In 1993 I went to Magdeburg, in what was once East Germany, to give a lecture. Although the Cathedral in the city had been closed to the public under the Communist regime, it had miraculously survived as one of the most outstanding medieval buildings in Germany.

"The interior is a magnificent space, which at the time of my visit was entered through a door on one of the long sides of the building. I was intrigued by the handle to this door, which was cast in metal in the form of a stylized bird. It was not only good to look at; in its own way it was also eye catching. But more importantly and equally memorable, was the way in which it sat in the hand – so comfortable and generous…

"When we accepted the challenge to design a range of door handles for Fusital I was reminded of my experience in Magdeburg and indirectly that was one of a number of influences on the project."

Norman Foster in *The Human Touch 1995,* published in *On Foster… Foster On*

10 The "H331" in the "Novantotto" series for Fusital by Michael Graves, whose houseware for Targett stores in America has made him a household name in the USA. "As an architect," he says, "I never understood why I had to stop at the door." Graves' shorthand to his team of product designers is "House of Cards," an indirect reference to the game designed by Charles and Ray Eames, and a reference to intersecting planes.

13 The "H342" in the "Duemila" series for Fusital is designed by prolific designer and architect, Ron Arad RA, Professor at the Royal College of Art in London. Arad's design treats a substantial brass steelplated door handle like a lightweight piece of paper, unfurling it with delicacy to fit the grip. The patented assembly system of the handle with the spring, screw on rose, and security ring guarantees a sound anchorage to the frame.

14 Alan Ritchie and Philip Johnson (then in his 80s), jointly designed the "H351" in the "Duemiladue" series for Fusital with grooves etched on the rectangular lever that fits to its round door plate with a bolt-like stud, at once both industrial and decorative. "One of the most obvious and consistent trends in modern architecture has been the tendency to simplify, through standardization and repetition, and through elimination of every element which might be left out," Johnson wrote in the *Architectural Forum* in 1943.

15 David Chipperfield's "H348" in the "Duemiladue" series. Elegantly reductive door handles, honed and pared down to the basics, have a strong presence. The celebrated British architect has made his name in Europe with the Neues States museum in Berlin, a commission he won in the final jump-off between him and Frank Gehry, and for hotels in the USA.

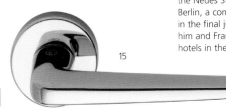

doors/door handles

16

The "1191" horn-like lever handle on a big round backplate made in aluminum was designed by Philippe Starck for FSB.

Another aluminum *tour de force*, the "1144" by Jasper Morrison for FSB, the manufacturers ,who describes it as "chaste" and "unassuming."

Made of square or rectangular chromium-plated bars by Olivari, "Time" by Alessandro Mendini draws inspiration from parallelepiped geometry, and results in a simple and Euclidean esthetic.

"Space," also from Olivari by Alessandro Mendini.

The fluid and dynamic "Selene" by Massimo Iosa Ghini made in brass finished with chrome for Olivari.

An antidote to all designer labels, the "Startec" handle was designed and made in-house by Hafele, who call it "a generic handle created for the commercial market."

The new patches for sliding and swing glass doors with interchangeable lever handles and a dead lock were made by Henry Glass to complement the "Tuttovetro" collection.

The "Viola" series by the young design team of Angeletti e Ruzza for Colombo Design is rationalist in its straight-lined profile, which hides a curve to help get a grip.

17

18

20

21

19

22

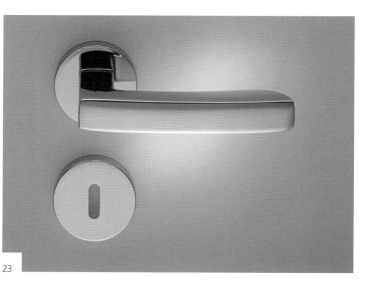

23

25

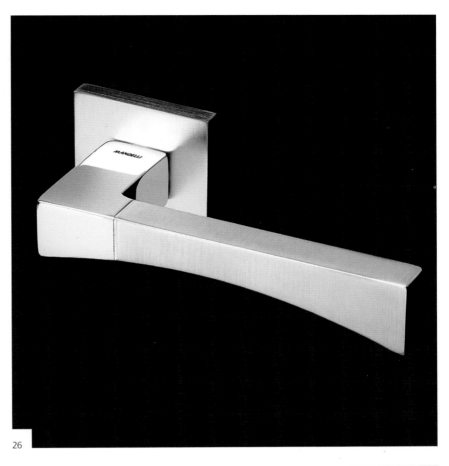

24

Brigitta Westmeier's
24 brushed stainless-steel
door lever for Technoline slides
through a rubber ball in black,
red, green, or blue.

Dieter Rams distinctive
25 nickel-plated lever with its
thumb grip for Technoline is
available for both a round rose
and rounded long plate .

"Life" Number 1171 door
26 handle in the "Life" series

by Studio Mandelli in die-cast
brass contrasts a satin-polished,
chrome-finish door plate with a
brushed chrome lever.

Plain, slender, mitred lever
27 handle, simply numbered
"1015," by architect CF Møller
in the "Randi Line®" collection
by Danish Ingersoll Rand.

Interior designers like
28 the plain tailoring and
colorful finishes of Ghidini

handles. This aquamarine
Murano glass door handle, the
"Athena" by Ghidini, is also
available in rose, opaque glass,
cobalt blue, and emerald.

Colorful lacquered lever
29 handle on the "Ginevra"
by Fabrizio Bianchetti for Ghidini.

"Leonardo" by Fabrizio
30 Bianchetti for Ghidini,
shown in satin chrome-plated
brass, is also available in a
matt-black finish.

Hewi's product design for
31 a standard door fitting
numbered "111R01.130"
is 25 years old. Tactile
and ergonomically sound, it
remains a favorite within
the construction industry.

26

27

28

29

30

31

windows

ABOVE LEFT Narrow strips of DecorFlou® glass by OmniDecor acid-etched in gray are banked above square panes on the NCC building in Aarhus, Denmark. Neither opaque nor transparent, the acid-etched filter diffuses light evenly.

ABOVE CENTRE Under the eaves of this timber shingle-clad house in the USA, energy efficient metal-clad wood windows in the "Caradco®" collection by Jeld-Wen® use Impact Gard™ glazing.

ABOVE RIGHT Forty rows of 6mm (¼in) laminated glass in a brise-soleil by Vanceva® Solutia color the façade of an office in Barcelona. Architect Fermin Vasquez based the palette on traditional colored awnings in the neighborhood. From within, the view outside is transparent.

LEFT Opening up the back elevation of their Edwardian brick semi-detached house, architects Abigail Hopkins and Amir Sanei stacked three sash windows 11m (36ft) high to illuminate the staircase running centrally up four stories.

Glass shapes façades dramatically. Look up at public buildings around you to see how technological developments in glass manufacture influence design. In the 1970s smoked glass brazenly cloaked corporate cathedrals raised to the sky, begging the question, when does a window become a wall? In the 1990s mountaineers abseiling over huge glass edifices answered the question. Now glass cleans itself. Float glass is smart enough to track the sun, repel its noon rays and muffle noise.

Three sash windows stacked four stories high by young British architects Amir Sanei and Abigail Hopkins up the spine of the back elevation of their Edwardian red-brick house in London illustrate the point that standard windows can be used architecturally to dramatic effect. The bottom sash rises to open out into the garden, the middle is fixed, and the top drops for ventilation, all three creating one tall window.

Bringing color back to our cities, Solutia works with Vanceva® to pioneer colored interlayers on laminated glass. By allowing a combination of up to four colors, it is possible to produce over a thousand different shades with a seamless transition from one shade to another.

A perforated Venetian
1   blind by Silent Gliss
doubles the energy efficiency
of double-glazed windows,
as well as making light
management easy.

"Shadoglass" by Colt
2   requires no electrics or
mechanics to track the sun, just
the Girasol solar-powered sun
tracking device which works the
louvers via two 3m (10ft) tubes.
As the sun moves across the
building, one heats up while the
other cools down, expanding or
contracting the fluid in each
tube to rotate the louvers and
reduce solar heat gain while
maintaining daylight levels.

The Bois de Boulogne in
3   Paris is swathed in a silvery
steel mesh curtain by Groupe
Foin "Chainex" metal to
attract attention to this resilient
window covering. More often
seen on the catwalk, or on
firemen's helmets for protective
visages, the steel mesh gives a
new use to ages-old chain mail.

Two views from the same
4   high-rise building.
Transparent at one glance, but
then opaque when seen from a
different angle, "Lumisty" is a
view-control film from Madico,
developed as a privacy
protection filter for computer
screens. The film bends the light
to increase the optical angle
while maintaining the quality of
the frontal image. Sold in rolls
1.25m (4ft) wide and 15m
(49ft) long to stick on windows,
it changes the view, depending
on the angle viewed.

Designing a big office block in a residential area in Barcelona, architect Fermin Vasquez took the awnings that shield the street from the noon sun to create a brise-soleil in red, yellow, and orange. Imperceptible gradations in color on just one face lower air-conditioning intake in the offices by controlling solar light reaching the interior.

When Philip Johnson curated an architectural exhibition on deconstruction at MOMA in 1988, it highlighted the fact that architects, like scientists and philosophers and writers, mirror the change riven when the atom was split to reflect the point of impact and refraction. Every city showcases buildings by famous architects that challenge our perception of shelter as four walls supporting flat or pointed roofs with a regular array of windows. Windows like shards of glass pierce the stone façade of Daniel Libeskind's Jewish Museum in Berlin. They zigzag precariously around the Scottish Parliament by Barcelona architect Miralles, each frame handmade at huge cost.

Smart glass has to find ways of cooling down. "Farb Effekt™" from Schott changes color depending on the intensity of the daylight, the angle of view, and the background. Metal oxide coatings on base glass allow light to be reflected from the junction of layers, intensifying as the layers grow further apart. Smartest of all, and crossing swiftly into the domestic market for conservatories and atriums, is Pilkington's self-cleaning glass. "Activ®" absorbs ultraviolet rays from the sun, and through a catalytic reaction, breaks down organic dirt like bird droppings and leaves. The glass coating is also hydrophilic to reduce the surface tension of water, so it runs off the glass in sheets rather than forming droplets.

Window coverings smarten up, too, not just in good looks but in performance. The "Shadoglass" system by Colt maximizes natural daylight while controlling solar heat gain and glare. Integrated in the louvers are photovoltaic cells controlled by the Girasol self-sun tracking device that closes or opens them without electricity or electronic controls. Two 3m (10 ft) long tubes fixed to the louver blade, filled with CFC-free thermo hydraulic fluid, track the sun as it moves across the building. One tube heats up while the other cools down, expanding and contracting the fluid in each tube to rotate the louvers.

Home owners with rooms that are overlooked could consider frosted window film which looks like etched glass at a smidgeon of the price. View-control film from Madico in Massachusetts changes the view depending on the angle viewed. Developed as a privacy protection filter for computer screens, viewed frontally, it is transparent, but from a more oblique angle, it is opaque.

Typhoons that swept the coastal regions of the USA in 2005 led to a change in building regulations for windows and doors required to withstand the strong impact of wind-borne debris, pounding seas, and

BELOW Marvin's "Case Master" window in pine purchased from reliable raw lumber suppliers with sound forest management practices subscribing to the Sustainable Forest Initiative, SFI. Tested in gale-force winds in tunnels before release in 2006, new laminated "StormPlus" glass meets building codes in Florida to sustain winds from 193–225km/h (120–140mph).

gale-force winds. Windows on seaside houses appear old-fashioned in mullioned wooden frames, but the glass has been tested in gale-force winds in wind tunnels to be impact resistant and its fasteners withstand corrosion. Impact Gard™ laminated glass from Jeld-Wen® can withstand a 9lb piece of lumber striking the glass head-on at approximately 56km/h (35mph). It reduces sound transmission and blocks up to 95 per cent of harmful UV rays, meeting the strictest building codes in hurricane-prone areas. Pella's "HurricaneShield®" impact-resistant glass gives laminated glass an advanced polymer technology, with a protective ionoplast layer sandwiched between two layers of glass offering 100 times the rigidity and 5 times the tear resistance of a commonly used impact-resistant laminated glass.

LEFT Made in vinyl by Weather Shield and modeled on historic wood single-hung windows, the "Lifeguard" could have been a prop on location at Tara in *Gone with the Wind*. Its historic look disguises high performance impact-resistance and energy efficiency requirements.

ABOVE Stormproof Scandinavian slow-grown redwood windows with natural oil-based finishes. The "Ecoplus" window range made by the Green Building Store was selected by Greenpeace for their showcase house. Sourced from properly managed forests, care is taken in the choice of preservatives, paints, and stains. Timber windows are "by far the best environmental choice", Greenpeace says.

The advent of float glass sheets, laminated, toughened, wired or treated with coatings and film, dramatically improved the performance of large expanses of glass.

Architects like window glass walls because they blur the distinction between outside and in. Sliding panels and walls of glass are common to most modern houses. The clerestory window, the peaked two-story window that accompanies a cathedral-like living room, or an A-frame, and the window that turns the corner are some of the more conspicuous divergences in design taking the place of old double-hung or casement windows. French windows are, as the French name *croisé* suggests, casement windows carried down to the floor so as to open like doors. First used at Versailles in the 1680s, they are popular today in a more security conscious world

Having achieved such openness, architectural window screening leads to panels, mesh screens, and louvered shutters that allow daylight to move across the interior with interesting patterns of light and shade. Vertical louvers, a sidewise adaptation of the Venetian blind, control light on the immense all glass façades of modern buildings. Now the driving force behind all these advances is to keep the simplicity and to be energy-efficient. Beyond good looks, window shades have to conserve energy because heat moves toward cold surfaces, such as glass windows in winter. Experts calculate that almost 40 per cent of all heat within a home escapes this way.

1

Roller blinds by Hunter
1   Douglas hung horizontally are ideal for windows that are taller than they are wide. Raised and lowered at a bank of windows, they allow light to fall in slabs of changing pattern and light intensity throughout the day.

2

Vertical blinds that slide
2   open and close from side to side are well suited for windows that are wider than they are tall. The "Somner™" custom vertical blinds in vinyl or fabric in the "Premium" collection by Hunter Douglas feature a wide range of vinyl and fabric styles which provide sound absorption and translucency.

"Sivoia QED", which
3   stands for Quiet Electronic Drive, by Lutron offers a near-silent electronic drive (44dBA at 1m, 3ft), to operate blinds and let in light, closing with minimal light gaps around each blind. Simple to install, they work anywhere.

3

4

5

↓ **ALSO SEE**

walls and ceilings p.18, 19

Israel's Balcony Ltd bends
5 aluminum and glass
on both sliding and hinged
systems into arc-shaped doors
and windows. "Panoramic"
thermal windows use a
specially patented system which
joins different elements of
curved thermal aluminum
extrusions. The shutter does
not rely on gravity to close but
moves left or right horizontally.

Four fabrics, from sheer
4 to the opaque linen-like
"Batiste", filter light through
crisp seamless pleats on the
"Duette® Honeycomb" energy-
efficient shades by Hunter
Douglas. Big expanses of glass
require electronic controls for
roller blinds on a pocket-sized,
wall-mounted pad.

7

6

8

Louverlite's panel blind
6 collection in natural fabrics,
mesh screens, and faux suedes
doubles as window shades for
big spans of glass like these
French windows and as room
dividers. The wide panels of
"Panama Pebble" reflect and
filter daylight. Panels stack
neatly and discreetly behind
one another when open, and
when closed, slide silently
on tracks to filter the light.

Glazing bars create a
7 changing pattern of light
on the floor. Shielded by trees
outside, the mullioned windows
by Pella® are left unadorned
to become a feature of the
interior decoration. The Pella®
"Designer" series of windows
allows on-line subscribers to
design their own window or
patio door within minutes,
selecting from a product range
for their own measurements.

For floor-to-ceiling glass,
8 the Panel Fold System up
to 5m (16ft 5in) long with a
maximum drop of 3m (10 ft) by
Silent Gliss answers an obvious
design dilemma. Why should
panels have to be flat? These
fabric panels hang from
discreet gliders, using a Velcro
carrier for quick changes.
Closed, panels stack against
each other. Open, they slide
vertically across the glass.

9

10

11

In Andersen's "400 Series", "Frenchwood" four-panel gliding patio door in oak, maple, pine, or white, (and colored outside in white, sandstone, terracotta, or forest green), has reach-out locks to pull tight against the frame. "High Performance™ Low-E" glass offers optimum temperature control.

Self cleaning glass from Pilkington, the "Activ™" solar control glass uses daylight and rainwater to break down and wash away any organic dirt from exterior surfaces coated with titanium oxide. Dirt runs off in rain in sheets, rather than droplets, with a hydrophilic coating.

A large conservatory needs shade to stop plants scorching and occupants over-heating. The Silent Gliss skylight system was developed especially for glazed areas like atriums and conservatories. Parallel fabric panels move to provide shade, either hand-operated or motorized.

Deep laminated mullions made of Douglas fir by Wood Trade in Germany are integrated into an unusual glass curtain façade designed by architect Stefan Eberding with Seufert-Niklaus who specializes in window designs combining wood and glass. The flat flush glazing system on a curtain wall opens to the outside like a casement window in this school in Alzenau, Bavaria.

12

Not everyone has smart glass to track the sun and control solar gain any more than they have acres of glass window walls with a view and the budget to invest in motorized controls. The kind of standard window, too small to stifle in sheers, too central to the room to muffle in curtains, poses a problem. It needs to be dressed for privacy and light control.

The small standard window is not overlooked by window manufacturers, who recognize that the smaller the glazed area, the more important the window

dressing. Roman blinds in wood or fabric can make a feature of it. Curtains can ripple tidily across the window without forming great bunches at either side of a small window.

Nowadays interior designers and curtain manufacturers are as concerned about the quality and control of light as an architect, though they approach it from different ways. Diffusion today is more important that it was ten years ago because homes built closer together block the light.

Fabric vanes in the
1   "Silhouette®" brand by Hunter Douglas suspended between two sheer panels let in precise amounts of light. Fully open, vanes appear to float with no visible cords. Fabrics range from semi-sheer to the light-dimming "Matisse collection™" which transforms the room with luminous light.

Curtains hang in a
2   smooth, simple and continuous wave effect. An alternative to traditional pinch, pencil pleat or goblet headings, "Wave™" is a new curtain heading system by Silent Gliss. The heading tracks back neatly to take up less space and the glider cord is not visible when the curtain is closed. Cordless 70mm (2¾in) tape sewn along the top of the curtain has pockets in exactly the right position for the track system.

Flush fin window frames
3   can fit on top of an old window frame, installed with a sealant between the old and new frames to form a watertight seal. Jeld-Wen® make the "Premium Vinyl"

collection to combine with Jeld-Wen® wood-clad casement windows for a unified look.

Simply sliding in and
4   out of the wall, these "Granbelvedere" shutters by Scrigno disappear from sight into a metal box. Designed to make the most of the large windows and minimize any framing obstructions, the casing system uses two parallel pull-down sliding and retractable shutters.

ALSO SEE

walls and ceilings p.20
doors p.79

1

2

3

4

windows/skylights

Skylights allow natural daylight into space that might be dark and lifeless: a stairwell, perhaps, or a rooftop living space. At night skylights can become oppressive black mirrors, reflecting every move. To prevent this, they can be lit. If accessibility for changing bulbs is awkward consider LED or fiber optics. Rectilinear light fittings to fit the pitch of a glass room can be accentuated with recessed wall lights. Domes flooded with natural light by day are set about with LEDs evenly spaced to provide a soft twinkle, echoing stars above.

Velux's prototype for airing an inner-city apartment is a unit on top of existing apartment blocks in Copenhagen. The design of the 8.4m sq (90.4ft sq) prefab is based on careful placement of vertical windows in combination with roof windows in a sloping roof. "Think vertically when establishing new housing in the city. Higher up we find fresh air and light – two qualities in high demand in the housing sector," was the conclusion.

1

Pella® skylights open wider on a hidden motorized system that provides an unobstructed view with a built-in rain sensor that automatically closes the skylight when it detects a shower. The natural wood on the interior can be painted to match walls or left plain while the "Hassle Free™" aluminum exterior blends in with most roofs, and the glass is either tempered or laminated with low E insulating glass. A rust-free fiberglass screen to stop insects is fitted on all venting units.

2 The "Skylux®" spherical dome by AG Plastics can be acrylic or polycarbonate. Either way, it is lightweight while being waterproof.

3 Daylight from roof windows penetrates deeper into the interior while Venetian blinds help regulate the sun's heat. Danish company

Velux's skylights let daylight and fresh air through the roof. They are available in many sizes, types and variants with sun-screening products.

4 Skylights are often in awkward spaces like stairwells. Velux installed three windows on a motorized system to show them closed, partially open and fully open, each on an individual setting. "Io-homecontrol" is their wireless communication that controls motorized and manual equipment in the home (roller blinds, shutter, garage doors, roof windows, heating, lighting, alarms, and locks).

2

3

↓ **ALSO SEE**

walls and ceilings p.38

5

4

An illumination design project by Targetti, "Aria" lights up the sky. More than just an indirect ceiling downlighter for fluorescent lamps, the blue silk-screened image of a clear sky is endlessly reproduced by mirrors on four sides of the fixture. Fluorescent lamps hidden inside the aluminum frame beam down a patch of blue sky.

5

Getting light down from a roof bubble through a winding warren into a room that needs it is a skillful business. SolaLighting specializes in low-cost, energy-efficient daylight solutions for houses and businesses. Invented in Australia in 1986, "Solatube®" tubular skylights are simple in concept yet effective.

6

6

"How wonderful, I feel, as a semi-historian, to live in a period where you have that calmness of an acceptance of a style of architecture. The first time since the eighteenth century when everybody knew when a window was well placed or not. In Wren's time they knew the difference between a thick muntin and a thin muntin. Now we know the difference between well spaced columns and oversized lumpy columns."

Philip Johnson, *The Oral History of Architecture*

↑ **DESIGN INFLUENCE**

staircases

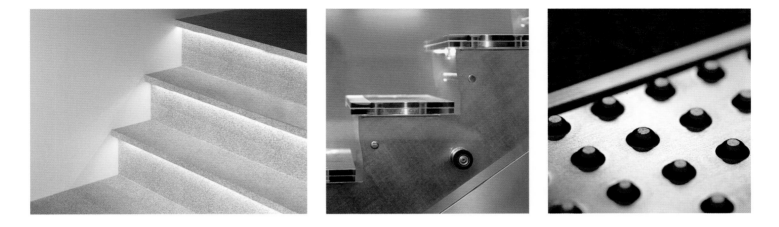

ABOVE LEFT A teflon-coated fiber optic tube with a 60-degree output angle from LightGraphix, installed along stair tread nosing, provides continuous linear illumination five times greater than that of conventional fiber optics.

ABOVE CENTER A glass staircase designed by Bisca maximizes light in an open-plan mews house modernized by architects Barrett Lloyd Davis. Glass on stainless-steel stringers that are just 10mm (⅜in) thick is illuminated by fiber optics embedded in the wall next to the treads.

ABOVE RIGHT Flat-surfaced, dot-matrix stair trims from the Gooding Aluminum "Step Up" collection.

LEFT Helical stairs designed by Eva Jiricna in a London house seem poised for flight from a 300mm (12in) diameter steel tube sprayed with silver metallic paint. Newels, banisters, and handrails made from thinner, 12mm (½in) steel, polished or satin brushed, lighten the structure visually. Sandblasted glass treads with a nonslip, diamond-patterned finish carry light throughout the house.

Stairs, with all their components – risers, treads, nosing, balustrades, handrails, and supports – which are loadbearing and act as safety barriers, have to be built on a gradient that makes ascent and descent painless. They are, therefore, tricky to design. The design of a staircase will depend on whether it is straight or flying, dogleg or spiral, suspended or cantilevered. And its position will be determined by scale and proportion as well as by more pedestrian issues such as traffic flow.

Designers seeking the perfect growth pattern for stairs look to nature for inspiration. Patterns emerge in the natural world, which demonstrate not chaos or chance but order, harmony, and proportion. The Golden Section, developed by the Ancient Greeks for their temples, is based on proportions found in nature. This section, in which the smaller is to the larger what the larger is to the whole (or roughly 3:5), divides a line in such a way as to create an ideal relationship between the parts.

Staircases, like spiny backbones or seashell spirals in stainless steel, use the Golden Section. The growth patterns of shells are logarithmic spirals of the Golden Section proportions. Le Corbusier pointed out that

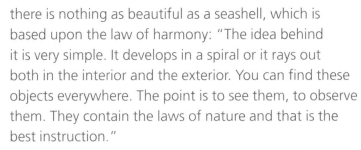

there is nothing as beautiful as a seashell, which is based upon the law of harmony: "The idea behind it is very simple. It develops in a spiral or it rays out both in the interior and the exterior. You can find these objects everywhere. The point is to see them, to observe them. They contain the laws of nature and that is the best instruction."

The discovery in the mid 20th century that a DNA molecule consists of two intertwined helices has been a further influence on the shape of stairs. Ross Lovegrove, winner of the 2005 World Technology award for design, called the staircase he designed for his London studio and made in fiberglass and carbon fiber the "DNA."

FAR LEFT The "DNA" staircase, designed and manufactured by Ross Lovegrove, was made with a new technology, bladder molding, which combines high-performance composite materials such as carbon fiber and fiberglass. Like bone structure, the design of the staircase achieves much through minimalism, with form, material, and technology working in unison. Lovegrove describes it as being "informed with evolutionary purpose."

OPPOSITE An aerial view of the Edilco spiral staircase unfolding as beautifully as a nautilus shell. The staircase is sold in kit form for self assembly. Edilco was founded in the 1960s after patenting a modular and self-supporting system of prefabricated treads in reinforced concrete to be installed and finished with cladding on site. The treads are joined together by metal brackets and reinforcements. The staircase has no central supporting column, moving upward like a spiralling well.

ABOVE Contemporary design meets traditional timber technology in a barn conversion by Simon Conder Associates. The timber spiral staircase, made of 50mm (2in) thick, finger-jointed European oak, has matching grains and is cut from one log controlled by the architects. It links an open-plan living area in the former cattle shed with bedrooms in what was once the hay loft. Conder load tested a 1:5 scale model, then built an on-site model because of the inherent 3D variation of timber properties. The 3.5m (11ft 6in) high, freestanding, curved-glass drum that surrounds the staircase in no way supports it.

Architect Eva Jiricna has designed dramatic one-off staircases in steel and glass in retail outlets and private apartments all over the world. All the components of her staircases are structural rather than merely decorative yet she fashions them like jewellery. They are beautifully detailed and have a lightness of touch that belies their substantial span and loadbearing capacity.

In 2005, a timber staircase that is anything but wooden won Simon Conder the coveted Wood Award for the best building in competition with a clutch of Britain's biggest-budget buildings, including the Scottish Parliament, the National Assembly for Wales, and Norman Foster's Sage Gateshead.

staircases/straight

The straight staircase is standard in most houses but the interpretation of it in the height and dimension of the stairs, and the materials used, make the difference between a dynamic first impression and indifference. Even the banisters and the stair rods that hold down a stair runner can smarten up stairs. Unlike spiral or helical staircases, flights running in straight lines allow virtually unlimited upward movement.

Straight stairs can go straight up like a ladder, make a quarter turn with a landing, like a set square, or a quarter turn with winders fanning out where the landing would be. The biggest space-grabber of all is a half-turn flight with two landings, which is like a picture frame missing one side. A dogleg staircase consists of two flights at right angles with a half landing. In older buildings where space was not a premium, the most commonly used type of staircase is one that runs up in three flights at right angles around an open well with intermediate landings.

Straight stairs, always the simplest solution, do not have to be chunky and set into the solid sides of the stairwell. Albini & Fontanot's "Chic" line from the "Scenik" collection is a freestanding version that has a steel backbone supporting open treads, the sides rigged with cables. Sometimes a straight flight of stairs begins to wind at the top, like the staircase by Bisca that balloons out to break the linear grid of the flight of steps at the Hotel du Vin in Harrogate, UK (*see* page 106, picture 8). American stair manufacturers Arcways argue that putting a camber on a curve to the straight staircase gives it more distinction than an L-shaped stair, without altering the floorplan.

1

2

3

4

"Limeira" staircase from
1   the LimeStone Gallery in cool white and consistent oolitic limestone contains microscopic shells and the occasional larger gray fossils. High density and low porosity make the material suitable for heavy traffic. The bold slab stairs, which are illuminated at different levels by built-in wall lights, look substantial but take up very little space.

"Spruzzo" tempered
3   and laminated glass from "Studio Line," specified by architect Pierre Archambault, in the headquarters of its manufacturer, Joel Berman Glass Studios on Granville Island off Vancouver, Canada. Organic and linear patterns molded in kiln-cast glass won the gold award at NeoCon® 2005 in the USA.

Perfect where space is at a
2   premium, "Karina" in black or white from the "Arke" collection by Albini & Fontanot climbs like a loft ladder up its modular spine, which supports broad paddle treads and a single-sided, steel-frame handrail. "Karina" is height adjustable on site between 2.3 and 2.8m (7ft 6in and 9ft 2in) with additional tread kits available to stretch the height to 3.3m (10ft 10in).

Straight staircases in a
4   small stairwell have to turn corners. This complication is resolved beautifully by architect Luigi Rosselli within a restricted space and on a shallow gradient in this house in Sydney, Australia. Broad treads and risers that extend visually beyond the entrance make the small step up in height more dramatic and emphasize the irregular stone-slab wall finish.

Factory-made by Edilco,
6   the "M1/44" is a simple framework system for straight-flight stairs. Two lateral, self-supporting trusses in 8mm (⅓in) thick, laser-cut iron are assembled at home by means of external, visible pins in hexagonal sockets. Special modules placed at the beginning and end of the flight allow the staircase to adapt to most designs.

6

5

A stainless-steel cable
5   balustrade with feature fins marks the climb up a seven-story staircase in the City of London by architects Pelta Associates with Boundary Metal. Rigged horizontally with yachting cables, the decorative fins create a safety barrier along open treads that lighten the appearance of this substantial staircase.

This flight of stairs by
7   Canal Engineering cantilevers from the stairwell without any support other than the bonding of the steps into the stairwell. Cornering on a tight turn, the fully folded, stainless-steel stairs are concertinaed into a small space. Slender banisters and the handrail emphasize the elegant solution, which makes a feature of the stairs in profile.

7

staircases/helix

The difference between spiral and helix staircases is that a helix uncoils to become a straight line when the surface unrolls as a plane, whereas a spiral is a plane curved. Think of a tightly wound ribbon uncoiling onto a tabletop as opposed to a corkscrew. Or think anatomically: the rim of an ear is a helix. Often referred to as a spiral stair without a central column, the helix staircase is supported on a stringer, its ribbonlike centrifugal force shaped like a cyclonic twister running the length of the stairs. The dramatic look and grace of a helix staircase is unparalleled.

Geometry becomes more complicated with the double helix. Since the mid 20th century, when scientists James Watson and Francis Crick discovered the structure of the DNA molecule as two intertwined helices, this form has been popular with designers. In staircases, the double helix reveals itself when the inner coil of the tread and the inner handrail banister uncoil separately side by side in opposite directions. Double-helix staircases have more generous treads and risers on a larger radius than spiral stairs. Arcways Inc. in the USA has uncomplicated the geometry to make a freestanding, open-riser, double-helix stairway that will fit into a standard stairwell opening of 1.93m sq (6ft 4in sq).

Nearly every flight of fancy that began as a custom-built staircase is marketed in kit form. Edilco's patented design for reinforced concrete stairs which can be assembled on-site as a straight – or spiral – staircase is undoubtedly a more modest discovery than the DNA chain, but heralds an evolution within the industry.

2

1 Inspired by Frank Lloyd Wright's Prairie houses, which exploit the horizontal rather than the vertical, architect John Corrigan for Corrigan Soundy Kilaiditi used open treads – known as beach treads – for this light-filled staircase in an industrial designer's Axis House in Windsor, UK. The staircase, which is supported by a single column rather than a stringer, ends in an opaque, sandblasted glass landing.

3

2 Edilco's concrete, modular freestanding staircase profiles the wooden stair treads and risers in relief at the back of the stairs, which are seen as the helix staircase gracefully uncoils.

3 Bisca's helical staircase with generously sized beechwood stair treads and risers permits a larger radius than spiral stairs on a central column could support. This custom-built staircase installed in a home in the north of England features a mild steel stringer support with rolled stainless-steel cladding and satin-polished finish. The stair balustrade in stainless steel is forged upright with a double curve at the end; the handrail is in rolled stainless steel.

1

The benefits of the double-
4   helix staircase, which
include handrails on both sides,
greater tread widths, and more
generously proportioned stairs,
are obvious in the new Tacchini
headquarters outside Milan,
designed by Roberto Grossi.
The "Girola" chairs are designed
by Lievore, Altherr, Molina.

⬇ **ALSO SEE**

walls and ceilings p.31
flooring p.61
doors p.71
lighting p.141

Edilco uses industrial
5   marble, granite, cement,
and stone for its modular
staircases but specializes in
handcrafted finishes. The green-
marbled, paint-finish effect
makes a focal point of this
freestanding concrete staircase.

4

An interplay of uprights
6   and curves in white plaster
emphasizes the ziggurat in the
profile of the stairs outlined
with Brazilian cherry treads.
The staircase is in a 330m sq
(3,550ft sq) Manhattan
apartment by architects Calvin
Tsao and Zach McKown, who
were inspired by Le Corbusier
and the Modern movement.

The discovery of the double-
helix structure of DNA was
first published by James
Watson and Francis Crick in
1953. The scientists
constructed a molecular
model of DNA in which there
were two complementary,
anti-parallel (side by side in
opposite directions) strands,
each one forming a helix. The
two helices are held together
by hydrogen bonds and ionic
forces to form a double helix.

⬆ **DESIGN INFLUENCE**

5

6

staircases/spirals

Spiral staircases feature circular or winding stairs with a solid central post that supports the narrow ends of the steps. Palladio invented the first flying spiral staircase – spiral stairs without any support other than the bonding of the steps into the outer wall – at the convent of the Carita in Venice, which was planned in 1561.

In the last century, spiral staircases were cast in iron and tacked onto the outside of big buildings as the ultimate fire escape. Steel spiral staircases, once used almost exclusively in industrial buildings, now appear in contemporary households. Some of the best kits for self assembly allow combinations of both steel and wood – silvered steel with light walnut or bronzed steel with dark cherry for a more dramatic effect. Modern spiral staircases also make use of new materials; for example, Mykon bonds honeycomb aluminum from the aeronautical industry in glass for resilient, lightweight treads.

1

2

3

4

1 With its combination of bronze newel and handrail with cherry treads, the "round" staircase from Albini & Fontanot has a dramatic ascent, rigged horizontally. Teamed with Albini & Fontanot's "Sport" balustrades, cabling laces form an open-mesh balustrade up the spiral.

2 This spiral staircase made by Bisca, whose company name stands for "Brass, Iron, Steel, Copper, and Aluminum," has green oak block treads, rolled stainless-steel profile and a stainless-steel newel post at the end of the flight of stairs.

3 The "Genius" series by Albini & Fontanot, whose multilingual catalog reveals its worldwide distribution of ready-made staircases. The staircases in the "Genius" range consist of a steel frame with different treads and sectional handrails. The silvered steel and light walnut "Round" staircase shown here has horizontal rigging.

4 Clear-glass treads from Nathan Allan's "Josiah J." collection on a spiral staircase for River Glass Designs. Two layers of 12mm (½in) thick, clear, tempered glass are dropped into the installation, which has black railing supports that turn upward to become banisters hinged onto the handrail – a decorative device that strengthens the structure.

staircases/details

Detailing on staircases has to be more than decorative: it must also make stairs safe to climb. Some detailing is clearly designed with safety in mind, such as corrugated or grooved aluminum tread edges, or acid-etched raised patterns on glass treads. Other details are less obvious and more suggestive. For Mulberry House Nursing Home in London, architects McDowell and Benedetti used different raised surfaces on handrails so that residents whose sight might be failing, or who might be finding routes confusing, could reach their destination by association through tactile signals (*see also* page 73).

Nowhere is lighting more important than on stairs. New materials, such as electro-luminescent film (EL) glued onto stairs or fiber optic tubes, delineate each tread without adding weight or bulk. LightGraphix "Light Tube" fiber optics system is featured on page 97. EL film is silkscreen printed with phosphor ink and plugged into an electrical socket with an inverter (it only works on AC) to become integral lighting strips on stairs. Austrian Light & Motion Lichttechnik used EL on stairs for a Dutch theater set and called them "Stairway to Heaven." The only disadvantage of these ultra-thin, lightweight, and flexible light strips, which are cut and pasted on site, is their cost.

Projects such as these, and products that are easy to install, such as the Muvis "Magritte," offer consumers possibilities and technologies that are typical of the lighting systems designed for theater and movie sets.

2

1

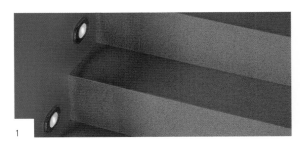

3

4

5

1 "Blue Step" lighting from LightGraphix uses cold, intense, light-emitting diodes (LEDs) in a range of fixtures manufactured from stainless steel and die-cast aluminum, which can be set flush, recessed, or inclined.

2 A floor lamp from the Muvis "Magritte" collection highlights these helical stairs. An in-built mechanism allows the light source to be guided along two axes, each having a range of motion of more than 180 degrees. Beams of light can be adjusted in size, their intensity regulated and color changed. A tiny but powerful chip enables each lamp to be operated from a remote control within a distance of 40m (130ft). The system can command up to 128 lighting fixtures in the same area and can be used with lamps already in the home. Each lamp comes equipped with energy-saving devices and there are no special installation requirements.

3 "Night & Day" from Albini & Fontanot's "Scenik" collection of straight and spiral stairs highlights the dramatic, slim profile of open treads.

4 Uplighters in the basement floor beam light up this dramatic stainless-steel and glass staircase with oak treads, which was designed by Bisca for a large London home. To maximize natural light, a toughened float-glass wall lines the stairwell between the basement and ground-floor level to a height of 4.5m (14ft 9in) and balustrades are of 12mm (½in) thick, clear, toughened glass.

5 A panel of six spotlights inset below the staircase where the stairs hit the landing are concealed by a tread in a refurbishment by Pelta Associates over seven floors of the SEB bank in the City of London. Boundary Metal upgraded a 1960s staircase, leaving the standard uprights to support the handrails and sliding sleeves of steel over them like fins to rig with steel cable and lighten up a dark staircase.

The swirl in the stainless-steel balustrades and handrail above stairs made from reclaimed oak railway sleepers, designed and installed by Bisca at the Hotel du Vin in Harrogate, UK, breaks the commonly held belief that banisters should rigorously line up with the edge of a flight of steps. The staircase rises upon a single tubular helix of mild steel from the ground-floor reception to a hallway on the first floor.

6

8

Heavy-duty stair carpet covers the treads and risers up a straight flight of steps. Toughened glass panels held in a groove at the base of the stairwell and capped by a circular grip handrail, designed by Balcony Ltd, act as a safety barrier.

6

The "Genius" collection from Albini & Fontanot allows mixing and matching different shapes, dimensions, and materials. Here, the "Steel Flight" spindles and steel-cable rigging are shown with light walnut open treads and landing.

7

7

"The future will bring constant increasing progress to the architectural possibilities both in height and depth. Life itself will shape the age-old horizontal line of the earth's surface with the infinite perpendicular in height and depth of the elevator, and with the spirals of the airplane and dirigible. The future is preparing us for a sky invaded by architectonic scaffoldings."

Umberto Boccioni, *Scenes of the World to Come*

⬆ **DESIGN INFLUENCE**

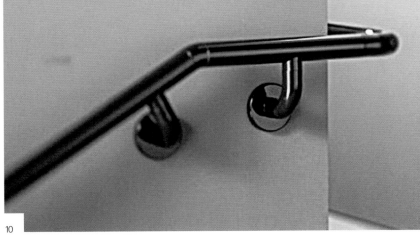

Stainless-steel balustrade
10   and handrail by hewi, the suppliers to architects of systems for handrails and balustrades, signage, electronic locking systems, and sanitaryware to include a range for the disabled. The stair rails in rounded shapes allow a good grip, which is why Hewi is used all over the world in public spaces.

10

9

11

        Raw stone and toughened
9   textural glass meet in a staircase by Andrew Moor Architectural Glass Associates. Structural balustrades in toughened, kiln-cast glass are set flush in a panel above the stone steps. This sophisticated combination of hard materials with purposefully roughened textures dramatizes a straight flight of stairs.

        This sea-green, clear-glass
12   flight of stairs, tempered and laminated to a dappled, luminous finish, is called "Spruzzo" by its maker, Joel Berman Glass Studios. The staircase, in a private residence in Vancouver, Canada, flows to a glassy pool of a landing and beyond, its fluid lines followed by a stainless-steel handrail.

        Stairs installed around a
11   fireman's pole in a fire station at Mansfield, UK. The stairs wrap around a central, perforated steel cage, which conceals the fireman's pole for emergency descent, engineered by Canal Engineering.

12

heating and cooling

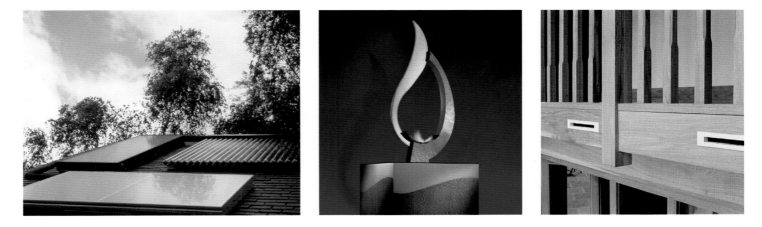

ABOVE LEFT A ridged solar water-heating panel shown beside two solar electric photovoltaic panels on a slate roof at CAT, the Center for Alternative Technology.

ABOVE CENTER "Aqueon™" creates fire from water. The world's first hydrogen-burning fireplace (1.5m x 0.7m/60 x 28in), invented by Heat & Glo™, ignites with a heat output of 31,000BTUs (the standard measuring unit in the industry).

ABOVE RIGHT Unobtrusive ventilation ducts on the Unico heating and cooling system can be sanded and stained to match the wooden floor in this stable conversion.

LEFT Architect Bill Dunster's own home keeps warm in British winters without consuming oil or gas. Sun tubes mounted on the conservatory roof heat household water, and 20 solar electric panels (photovoltaic cells) convert sunlight into electricity. The first-floor living room, heated by a wood-waste-burning stove, is reached up a gangway made from recycled steel.

Rising global energy prices reflect our diminishing resources of gas, oil, and water, putting energy consumption high on the agenda of every government. In Japan, a nationwide campaign led to heating in public buildings and businesses being set no higher than 20°C (68°F) all winter. In the summer Prime Minister Junichiro Koizumi asked companies to set office air conditioners no cooler than 28°C (82.4°F). In Tokyo alone, the campaign saved 70 million kilowatts of power between June and August – enough to power a city of a quarter of a million people for one month, according to Tokyo Electric Power company. The Reichstag in Berlin, capped with Norman Foster's dazzling elliptical dome, is partially powered by rape seed burning in huge generators below ground.

Energy-efficient houses that are increasingly reliant upon renewable resources are being built all over the world. Britain's first award-winning green housing development of 100 homes built on the site of an old sewage works is called BedZED, standing for Beddington Zero Energy Development. On site, a combined heat and power plant runs on willow coppice, and gray water is recycled. Colorful, passive heat-recovery wind cowls take stale warm air from each home to heat incoming cool air, which is trapped as each cowl rotates. Super insulation, triple-glazing, rainwater recyclers, and solar electric panels on every house are designed to save maximum energy.

The architect behind the scheme, Bill Dunster, prototyped his sustainable ideas with his wife, Sue, in their own London house (*see also* page 109), which tries to be carbon neutral and keep warm without drawing on oil or gas. The south-facing, full-height conservatory acts as the powerhouse: sunshine falling on photovoltaic cells generates enough electricity. Solar tubes on the roof, filled with water that heats in sunlight, warm household water via a heat exchanger and a special hot-water tank. In winter, it is topped up with heat from the living-room wood stove, which burns waste from the timber industry. To cut heating and electricity bills in a three-bedroom house, Bill Dunster recommends one wind turbine plugged into the electricity on the roof, twenty solar electric photovoltaic cells on a low-energy lighting circuit, eight solar tubes on the roof to warm household water, and a water tank compatible with a clean-burn wood stove.

One of tomorrow's main sources of solar energy is the photovoltaic cell, which converts sunlight directly into electricity. Once an eyesore glinting in the sun on rooftops, solar panels now get architects' attention for

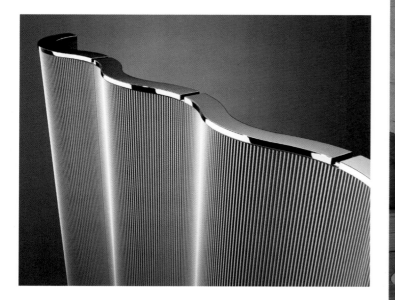

FAR LEFT Eileen Gray's classic chair in yellow leather is pulled up in front of an open gas fire from the Platonic Fireplace Company. Rather than burn fake logs, architect Henry Harrison ignites a collection of geometric shapes cast in fire cement he calls "Geologs" on a solid slab of stone below a cylindrical steel, fan-assisted extractor system.

LEFT Dominique Imbert first made this fireplace for British architect Norman Foster, who commissioned it for a commercial project. Adapting the model for residential use resulted in the "Filiofocus Telescopic." The hood and the entire flue can be drawn right down to the base, manually or by remote control, to form a closed fireplace.

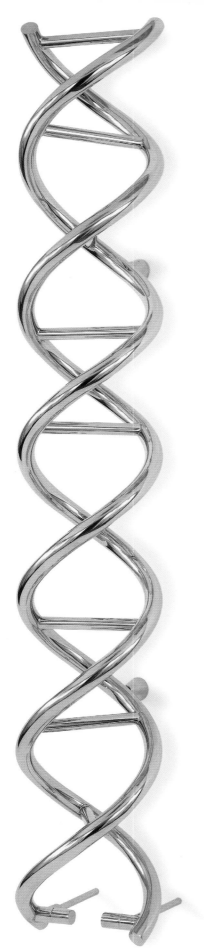

LEFT "Velum" is a new concept for heating designed by Perry King and Santiago Miranda for Runtal. Tubes to carry warmed water are concealed behind the corrugated aluminum surface. The purchaser buys lengths to fit any space, horizontally or vertically, in pairs or threesomes or single panels cut to any height. Once configured, "Velum" heating panels clip into different shaped fixings curved like a harp (shown) or flat on a modular system.

their good looks as much as their performance. Simon Conder's design for a country house in England makes a feature of copper-wired glass solar panels made by Viessmann. Sunovation in Germany have designed a modular system of photovoltaic cells elastically encapsulated between two sheets of polycarbonate that is flexible as well as significantly lighter than glass but just as strong and weatherproof. A thermo-forming process shapes them into any form imaginable.

CAT, the Center for Alternative Technology in Wales, says that for most people, solar water heating is the most economical way to use renewable energy at home. Solar water tubes on the roof that warm water in pipes can provide up to 50 or 60 per cent of a household's hot water. Solar electric (photovoltaic) panels are ideal for remote situations where there is no grid connection but they can be expensive compared to grid electricity. The British government has introduced a grant to offset some of the cost, while in the USA, house owners who install solar systems are given bonus points from the grid.

Underfloor heating was prototyped by the Romans drawing hot air from furnaces through hypocausts deep underground into flues in the walls. Today it can be an electrically heated mat beneath carpets for small areas, pipes circulating warm water heated by a boiler, or geothermal systems. The temperature underground is a constant 10°C (50°F). Geothermal pipes laid 90m (300ft)

FAR LEFT "DNA" is a radiator with an intertwined twist designed by Damian Evans for Bisque. The radiator is 1.8m (6ft) tall and manufactured from stainless steel polished to brightness. "I was reading an article about the discovery of DNA," says Evans. "I immediately saw how the linked double helix would translate into a tubular radiator."

ABOVE Faceted ceramic plates, clipped onto each other on a hooking plate with flexible connections, retain temperature and radiate heat longer. The radiating plate, which is covered with a titanium sheet, comes in different sizes and rotates to clean. Thin, flexible, and light, the "Add-on" by Satyendra Packhalè for Tubes Radiators literally climbs all over walls.

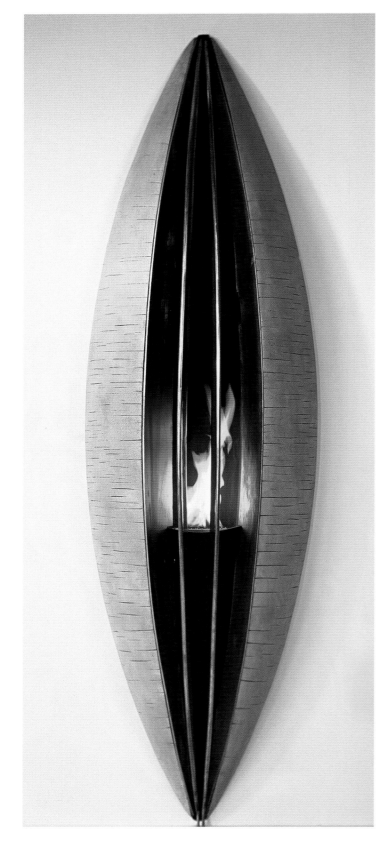

LEFT A flueless fire by CVO, housed in a wall-mounted pod called the "Seed," comes in bronze and limestone, stainless steel, bronze, or granite.

BELOW A flame picture is achieved with a flueless fire in a frame by CVO, which burns either natural gas or liquid propane gas so cleanly it does not require a catalytic converter. Carbon dioxide emission is about 90 per cent below the legal limit, while carbon monoxide emission is 94 per cent below the legal limit without any heat loss.

deep and a heat exchanger will heat water to 40°C (104°F). A ground source heat pump has pipes laid horizontally 1m (3ft) below the surface to harness solar energy. Pumping up the water uses energy.

When wood, natural gas, and liquid propane do run out, the sculptural "Aqueon™" fireplace (see page 109) will run on water. This invention by American-based company Heat & Glo™ is fueled purely by water fed into it. A process of electrolysis, an electrical current passing through water, separates the hydrogen from oxygen, channeling the two elements individually, and the hydrogen ignites in a stainless-steel and copper freestanding fireplace. It burns so cleanly it does not require venting or a sealed glass front.

Contemporary gas fires look more like sculptures than fake logs burning in a grate. Fires can be lit in a giant seed pod, or in pebbles cast in fire-clay filling a stone bowl.

Energy efficiency ensures that radiators are no longer hidden behind decorative grilles. Satyendra Packhale's design of radiant ceramic modules (see page 111), with either three or four facets that allow them to be linked

RIGHT The slender "Lily" by The Radiator Company is designed to be hung vertically with no horizontal applications. It visually extends the height of any room with its simple vertical lines. The height is unchanging but the width is variable. "Lily" can be colored to match the interior decoration.

FAR RIGHT "Missme," designed by Andrea Crosetta for Antrax Art, is a quirky outline of a figure on the wall, with the mist-free mirror as the head. The lithe tubes project from the wall.

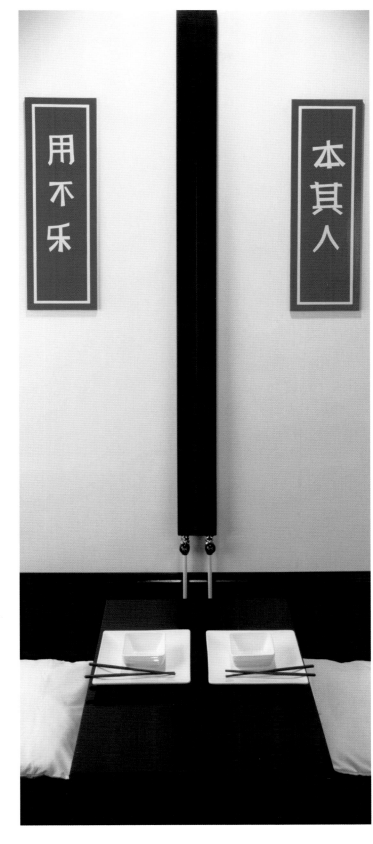

together to create an endless radiator, overcomes problems associated with buying radiators: an obligation to choose them at the first phase of building and the inability to amend radiator sizes. Flexibility after installation is a real innovation in the industry.

The fact that panel radiators are sectional in construction means that the length and output of the radiator can be adjusted by simply adding (or removing) sections, an idea ingeniously developed by designers Perry King and Santiago Miranda for Runtal. "Velum" (*see* page 111) is corrugated aluminum radiator sheeting sold in rolls like wallpaper. The undulating aluminum is a good heat diffusor, concealing tubes of tungsten or steel (depending on the weight of loadbearing walls), through which hot water passes. Panels cut to any length, fitted horizontally or vertically, can stretch from wall to ceiling or fit neatly below a window.

Modern underfloor heating (UFH) systems work on the Roman principle of pumping hot water through pipes below the floor surface, although electricity replaces the furnace. The Tall House in Wimbledon, south London, is just that, five stories tall, skillfully slotted into a narrow site by architect Terry Pawson. Built in timber and brick like its Edwardian neighbors, the vernacular is given a modern spin with sunlit spaces opening out from the principal stairs, central to the plan as both the conduit and the divider between open living spaces that face the backyard and the reclusive bedrooms in the tower.

Pawson chose underfloor central heating to free walls from "the clutter of radiators and pipework." The system pumps water warmed by a conventional energy-efficient condensing domestic boiler located on the first floor all around the house beneath the floors. Thermostats in every room control each room individually.

Floors throughout the house are an important architectural element. Natural dark green–gray slate flooring winds seamlessly from the garden patio through the kitchen and dining zones, and up the stairs, warming up underfoot once indoors. Slate covering solid concrete floors and walls in main living areas makes warm floors vanish seamlessly into shadow gaps where they meet the walls. Upstairs, the oak flooring conceals heating pipes laid in 25mm (1in) scree over a polythene membrane. The oak boards, 20mm thick and varnished, stop at the walls with a minimal 5mm oak lip.

1

2

3

1 Underfloor heating in The Tall House, Wimbledon, frees walls of the normal domestic clutter of radiators and pipework. Low heat emission over the entire floor works well within tall, double-height spaces. The living space facing the backyard has slate floors that slide seamlessly into shadow gaps in the walls.

2 The Tall House is five stories high, slotted onto a narrow site in leafy south London. Architect Terry Pawson maximizes space and light with a simplicity of plan combined with interlocking geometry that opens out views and lets sunlight stream in. The boundary between outside and inside is seamless.

3 Bedrooms in the timber-clad tower have underfloor heating covered with oak boards. Small oak baseboards, made from the same timber as the flooring to match grain and color, are detailed to give only a minimal 5mm (⅛in) lip over the edge of the plasterboard.

heating and cooling/radiators

When you are faced with winter and rising fuel bills, energy-efficient radiators will take the chill out of your rooms. Contemporary radiators can be freestanding columns or wall-mounted panels. They can double as towel rails, room dividers, or works of art. Industrial cast-iron radiators are making a comeback with a modern performance.

Radiator choice often has to be made before the room is finished. Before choosing a style, make sure that you calculate the required BTU (British Thermal Unit) output for the intended room. All radiators are given a temperature output rating, calculated and listed as BTUs per hour, a standard measurement that is used throughout the heating industry. To match the room heat requirement to the BTUs per hour from a radiator, multiply the width and length and height of the room in meters. (To convert cubic feet to cubic meters, divide the total figure by 35.31). Then multiply this figure by six to find the BTU requirement. (Alternatively, use the online BTU calculator at www.theradiatorcompany.co.uk). Once you have this figure, you can calculate how many radiators you need and which model equals the required output.

Quickest to heat, aluminum is the Porsche of radiator materials: it can be accurately controlled and used only when rooms are occupied. Cast iron takes the longest time to heat, but the material holds the heat well. Even against a support wall, a cast-iron radiator should stand alone. Steel radiators can be bent, cut, welded, and shaped into all manner of designs and have thermal properties that fall between the two.

1

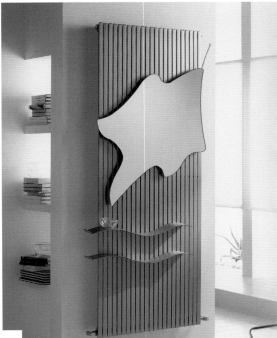

2

3

4

3   "La Scala" takes center stage in this conservatory dining room. Its 3D profile, which concertinas out in a zig-zag, is made by Bisque in Switzerland. Shown in white in this luminous space, it is available in more than 1,000 colors and looks dramatic against a painted wall in an anthracite finish.

1   "Lune," designed by architect Luigi Molinis for Officina Delle Idee, part of IRSAP, is a radiating panel painted in aluminum gray with black-stained tubular pipes. It also wittily rearranges geometry with its vertical lines penetrated by concentric spaces and, unusually for a panel radiator, has hidden depths.

2   "Line," designed by Mariano Moroni in the "Inox®" collection of seven designer radiators for Cordivari. Compatible with all water circuits, this radiator stands 2m (6ft 6in) tall and 805mm (2ft 8in) wide. Made of high-output, vertical, multi-column stainless steels with a satin finish, this wall-mounted radiator not so much glows as sparkles.

4   The flowing pipework of Bisque "X-Stream" creates a focal point in a room. Standing 1.9m (6ft 3in) high with an output of 2,009W, this dramatic piece needs space, though another model, the "Half X-Stream," cuts it down to size. It is available in more than 1,500 different colors and finishes, including chrome and aluminum.

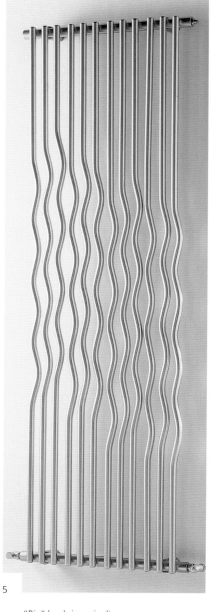

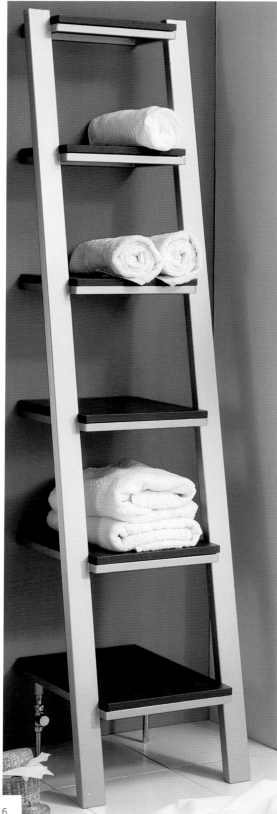

7

"Stax" is exactly how this
6   heated towel rail from
MHS performs: it has room for
stacks of towels on six metal
steps lined with black or white
oak, which store and warm
towels as well as heat the space
around them. At 1.9m high by
0.45m wide and deep (6ft 3in x
1ft 6in x 1ft 6in) and weighing
17kg (37½lb), this vertical
radiator combines form
and function with an output
of 780W.

From the JIS "Coastal"
7   range, the "Malin"
radiator, which is made in broad
planks of stainless steel like boat
decking, runs off the central
heating system or electricity on
a dual-fuel format so that towel
radiators remain warm when
the heating is turned off in
summer. The radiator is
produced from more than
90 per cent recycled metal,
manufactured environmentally,
and is recyclable.

5

"Rio" has brio, wriggling
5   the rigorous line-up of
radiating tubes in stainless steel.
Designed by Mariano Moroni
for Aestus, it is compatible with
all water circuits. Steel has good
thermal properties and bends,
cuts, and welds to shape up to
demanding designs.

The "Orb" towel rail
8   heater in the "Vanilla"
range by Vogue uses curved
radiating tubes that encircle
each other like a crossbow.
Fixed to the wall on four
mountings, its curvaceous
presence in bathrooms
means it is used where
space is not a problem.

6   8

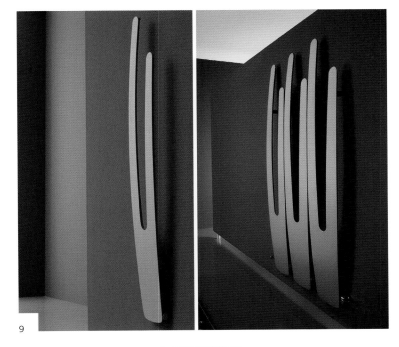

9

A stand-alone radiator that
9   can join a group resolves
the problem of matching heat
output to the requirements of a
room. Designs such as "Vu" by
Antrax, shown here, which can
be used alone or grouped,
when it triples the heat output,
perform well and look good in
either configuration.

An Ecolec® stainless-steel
10   electric heater operates
from a wireless-controlled
thermostat that can send a
signal within a range of 30m
(100ft) to maintain a surface
temperature of 70°C (158°F).
The "Eco" 1500W heater
weighs 14kg (31lb) and
measures 0.5m wide by 1.5m
high and 40mm deep (1ft 8in x
5ft x 1½in). The heating system
for the whole home has a
thermostat and timer, which
uses radio to relay control
signals to all Ecolec panel
heaters registered to it.

10

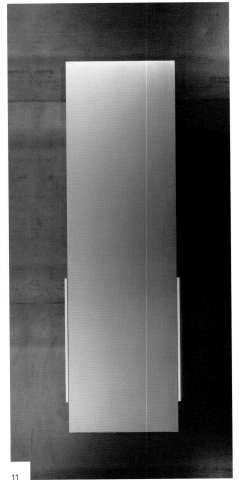

11

Designers Tiberio Cerato,
11   Giulio Gianturco, and
Mario Tessarollos' experience at
builders' merchants revealed
the problems of choosing
radiators: the need to decide
on their size at the first phase
and the difficulty of accessing
the back for cleaning and wall
painting. "T-OT" is their
solution. This deceptively simple
panel radiator from Tubes is
based upon one hooking
radiating plate with flexible
connections onto which an
ultra-slim and light titanium
heating panel of different sizes
can be placed either vertically
or horizontally. This heating
panel can also rotate so that at
right angles to the wall it
doubles as a room divider.

The French company
12   Fondis believes that the
living room is a place where
it is essential to feel well and
in harmony. The exclusive
technology of OHDS heating
glass by SOLARIS® develops a
radiant power to emit a heat
that feels more like sunbathing
because it maintains a uniform
temperature from the floor to
the ceiling.

12

**"The house of tomorrow will be
reduced to an empty envelope:
the temperature will be
controlled from the floor,
the light will be an electro
luminescence provided by
windows of liquid crystals,
sound and pictures will
come from the walls."**

Philippe Starck in conversation
with Sophie Tasma Anargyros
in *Starck*

↑   **DESIGN INFLUENCE**

heating and cooling/radiators

Zehnder radiators are
14 specifically designed for awkward spaces: "Zip" radiant ceiling panels are ideal for sports halls or warehouses where space is at a premium, for example. In this home, which has windows banked close to floor level, the long, low, Zehnder "Stratos" provides energy-saving heat with a good, uniform distribution along its surface.

"Zeb," made in mild steel,
15 only works off the central heating system and shuts down in summer. Aestus manufacture this industrial classic in four different lengths – 0.5, 1, 1.5, and 2m (1ft 8in, 3ft 3in, 5ft, and 6ft 7in) to a height of 200mm (8in) – with a satin nickel finish, or in various colors to special order. The maximum output is 2800BTUs.

14

15

16

The "Plinth" at the
16 Radiator Company is an excellent space-saving alternative to radiators. Available in electric or hydronic (water and electricity with a catalytic convertor) versions, it fits under kitchen cupboards that stand on plinths. It comes in brushed steel or with a white fascia that can be painted to match kitchen units.

A freestanding column
17 radiator turns into an occasional table and food warmer. "Tris" by IRSAP, in quartz-gray tubular steel on cherrywood feet, supports a glass tabletop pierced with holes to encourage the movement of hot air, and a Plexiglas dome. It could have been inspired by the work of Austrian designer Josef Hoffmann, who founded the Vienna Workshop in 1903.

17

The "Milwaukee" pierced
18 stainless-steel radiator on
a roll resembles the gigantic
exhausts on silver American
freight trucks. Made by
Brandoni, it comes in one size
only to deliver a great blast of
heat into the wide open spaces
of loft apartments.

An architectonic radiator,
19 the "Serpentine" by
Radiating Style in sleek stainless
steel is retro modern design by
Peter Rankin. He cites as his
inspiration Alberto Alessi, the
steel-with-style household
name, for his ability "to
humanize inanimate objects."

↓ **ALSO SEE**

flooring p.57
bathrooms p.152

18

19

A modern take on the
20 traditional concertina-
style of radiators found in
institutions and public spaces
in the mid 20th century, the
Bisque "Classic" is updated
visually with a pastel palette
and in performance with
improved heat output. There
is a wall-mounted, vertical
"Classic" to save floorspace,
and an electric version for
heating rooms independently
of central heating.

The no-frills industrial
21 styling of "Vienna" by
Brandoni incorporates the
classic disk design. This
freestanding radiator, which
suits almost any space, is
supplied with integral valves
concealed within its sturdy feet.

20

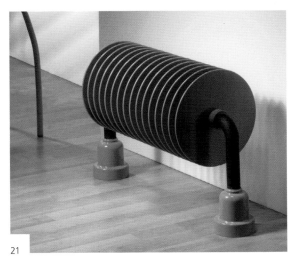

21

heating and cooling/fires

Fires can be cupped in a stone shell rising out of beach shingle, smolder in an open stone bowl, flicker in a cube, or become a room divider in a freestanding piece. Modern heating should have made fireplaces redundant, but the pleasure of pulling up a chair in front of a fire has ensured their rise in popularity.

Of course, no interior designer in the 21st century wants to replicate a mock Georgian fireplace or stick a piece of fake Grinling Gibbons molded in polystyrene around the hearth, and the hearth was the first thing to go in a modern interior. The next was solid fuel. Fueled by gas or electricity rather than by replicate fire logs or coal lumps on the hearth, flames lick around pebbles or autumn leaves with fire twigs. Architect Henry Harrison named the geometric cubes and cones that burn in his Platonic Company fireplaces "Geologs."

The new flueless gas fires will convert 100 per cent of the gas to heat, by comparison with open, coal-effect fires, which convert as little as ten per cent. To avoid losing up to eighty per cent of heat generated by whatever means, cavity wall and loft insulation are essential.

Now Heat & Glo™ – a brand of Hearth & Home Technologies™ Inc., the world's largest fireplace manufacturer – fuels a fire with water, feeding the "Aqueon™" to burn brightly on hydrogen generated. The manufacturer claims its product is the future in fireplaces, acknowledging that while fossil fuels generate the electric current necessary for operation, renewable energy sources such as solar, wind, hydro, geothermal, or bio-mass can realize the fire's full potential as an environmentally friendly product. (*See also* pages 109 and 112).

1 Award winner for energy efficiency, CVO's bronze "Firebowl" in a bronze porthole won the Prince of Wales Medal at the V&A Classic Design Awards in 2001. A smaller, more accessible version is available made in white or black concrete.

2 Contemporary rooms demand careful positioning of focal points. Fireplaces and TVs are obvious points around which furniture is arranged. The new "Firescheme" series by Henry Harrison, owner of the Platonic Fireplace Company, customizes fireplaces from the existing product range and creates one-off designs. The service is ideal for fireplaces in unusual situations such as this one, where the room has been opened out, leaving just the central section of the wall, for more light and space.

5 French designer-craftsman Dominique Imbert's "Focus" collection, imported into the UK by Diligence, and Celsius in Italy, contains 40 designs that breathe life into fires. The fireplaces are always fabricated to order. Whether gas or solid fuel, positioned centrally, wall or corner mounted, or built in, "Focus" fires are always architectural. In the model shown here, the diagonal tilt of the giant steel plate contrasts with the very slender chimney piece, an elaborate exercise in scale that delights the eye as much as the fire burning in the perfectly regular hearth.

2

3

4

3 This may look like an old-fashioned wood-burning stove, but Gruppo Piazzetta's stoves burn pellets made from compressed sawdust and can run for several hours without attention. The example shown is the "P960."

4 "Paloma™" freestanding gas fire by Heat & Glo™ is the winner of the top hearth industry award in the USA. Its compact footprint, clean lines, and parabolic shape are stylish yet provide a good view of the fire from virtually any angle. Available as a stand-alone unit or with a cast-stone surround, it also features a double glass-front design in four tints.

5

Another fire for small
8   spaces, the "Avola" from
Dimplex features electric flames
that flicker from either pebbles
or artificial coal in a rounded
grate. Colored insets,
emphasize the curves that
tuck neatly into 410 or 460mm
(16 or 18in) fireplaces with
minimal projection into the
room. The fire can also become
freestanding with the optional
spacer kit.

"Berlin" from the Elgin &
9   Hall "Essentials" collection
is such a handsome rectangular
fireplace that it is framed twice
and elevated off the floor to
make a feature of it. Its position
above ankle height is ideal for
rooms with high ceilings, such
as loft spaces or barns.

The "Bathyscafocus,"
6   designed and made in
France by Dominque Imbert,
looks like something Jules Verne
could have invented, or in
which Jacques Cousteau might
have immersed himself in an
undersea exploration. The oval
fireplace suspended from the
ceiling on a slender chimney
allows the fire to breathe.

The "Fire Cube" reinvents
7   the traditional grate – an
item that manufacturer CVO
had nearly made obsolete with
its fires in bowls – with gas
flames licking through slices cut
into a stainless-steel cube.
Designed for a small hearth, it is
nonetheless an attention seeker.

6

7

8

9

heating and cooling/fires

10

A mesmerizing, spinning gas flame spirals in "Cyclone™," which Heat & Glo™ describe as "Fire Art" rather than a conventional fireplace. Available as a system or customized, and generating 15,000BTUs (British Thermal Units), "Cyclone" offers a comfortable level of heat for small areas such as foyers and hallways. The system includes everything for installation, including a decorative front in nickel or brushed or black copper, the base, and the remote controls that operate the fire.

11

The "Bench Hearth" in Bianco Neve from the LimeStone Gallery elevates the hearth to become part of the furniture in a contemporary interior, and allows the stone to be fully appreciated. A made-to-measure service means that standard-size fire surrounds can be adjusted to cater for many non-standard fireplaces.

12

13

12 DuPont Surfaces invited fireplace manufacturer Brilliant Fires to design three fireplaces from its award-winning range made with DuPont™ Corian®. The "Ledge" fire is shown with a full surround made from Corian® in one of the new colors, Jasmine White. This minimalist fire sits in an elevated position on the wall, which replaces the space-consuming hearth, and is operated by remote control.

13 Another fire made in France by Dominique Imbert in his "Focus" collection (*see also* pages 110, 120, and 121). The "Metafocus" frames the square hole-in-the-wall fire with outsized plates of steel.

14

The "Mondrian" from the
14   Platonic Fireplace
Company is a four-sided
fireplace inspired by abstract
forms that juxtaposes the
monumentality of cast stone
and the precision of stainless
steel. The fireplace can be
tailored with either an elegant
wave-form shelf (shown) or the
simplified bow-fronted version.

15

At Rudloe Stoneworks,
16   fireplace surrounds are
designed for purity of line and
form. Classical proportions are
combined with the slim profile
of a picture-frame surround in
the "Rothko." Sized to permit
the use of a wide variety of fire
appliances, the fireplace can be
tailored precisely to feature in
any room.

16

17

The "Vision" fireplace by
15   Gruppo Piazzetta slides
easily into the flue with its
simple stainless-steel surrounds,
which frame the fire.

"Saxo Scenic" from
17   Drugasar is a glass-
fronted, balanced-flue gas fire
occupying the full width of the
chimney breast to give a three-
sided view of the flames. The
fire is available in two formats:
the inset version (shown),
which nestles discreetly in the
chimney, and an outset version,
which fits flush to the front of
the chimney breast. Colored in
alu-metallic, sand metallic,
or anthracite, it is powered by
remote control, with a room
temperature display. It includes
the patented feature of Vario
Burner® for an all around
glow and the Sandwich Door
system®, which enables the
glass front to be hinged open
for cleaning and routine
maintenance.

⬇ ALSO SEE

flooring pp.51, 62

heating and cooling/cooling

Friends of the Earth spells out a warning on its website: avoid using air conditioning wherever possible. Harmful CFCs (chlorinated fluorocarbons) in the units' slip streams contribute hugely to global warming.

Aware that today's cooling units may well be museum pieces in the future, manufacturers of heating and cooling systems are working on more energy-efficient, integrated systems. Clivet balances indoor temperatures with constantly changing weather in the "ELFOSystem," which cuts in to acclimatize only when absolutely necessary by prioritizing the use of existing thermal energy. But Friends of the Earth warns that efficiency of use is not enough on its own to cut the emission of CFCs. Fast forward to geothermal underground pipes in the backyard which feed warmed water to underfloor pipes indoors, controlled by a small pump and manifold connected to a thermostat. If groundwater is accessible, Clivet's "GeoComfort" unit fitted to the pump recovers thermal energy to cool water in summer and warm it in winter while reducing electricity consumption. At the Building Research Establishment's Environmental Building in the UK, architects Feilden Clegg with Buro Happold and Max Fordham pioneered a natural cooling system that uses the thermal mass of the building and automated monitoring systems to make the building regulate its own climate. Natural ventilation at night when temperatures drop, combined with groundwater pumped through the concrete floors and ceilings, has an efficiency of 1kWh output for pumping to an equivalent 12–16kWh cooling energy output. This could be the blueprint for high-density housing developments of the future.

2

1

1   LG "Art Cool" duct-free design for an air-conditioning unit was heralded as a "really cool" product when it was launched in the USA in 2005. The discreet, slimline, interior-wall-mounted evaporator unit linked to an outdoor condensing unit looks good enough to hang on the walls. The ultra-quiet machine has an air purifier and dehumidifier, a wireless remote control, and changeable panels.

2   Unobtrusive, 80mm (3in) diameter, slim ducts, which silently breathe out warm air in winter and cool air in summer in this timbered stable conversion in the UK, are the only visible signs of the Unico System. It conceals modular air handlers and coils in ceilings, crawlspaces, and floors. The small-duct central heating, air conditioning, and ventilation system creates even room temperatures without draughts.

Transparent plastic blades,
3   wrapped around the
motor and freed from a
cumbersome body, silently
drive the "Artemis" ceiling fan
designed by Mark Gajewski of
G Squared Art and made by
Californian company Minka
Aire. Translucent wings with
a 1.47m (5ft 10in) span are
available in mahogany, maple,
or pearl, and are operated by
a handheld or wall-mounted,
radio-frequency remote control.

The "Ball," designed by
4   Ron Rezek for Gregory
Lighting at the Modern Fan
Company, is a sphere in brushed
aluminum that moves air on
silvery, square-ended blades.
Optional direct or indirect
lighting can be installed in the
fan, which is made of die-cast
aluminum with a 1.07m
(3ft 6in) or 1.32m (4ft 4in)
blade span. Hanging heights
range from 280mm (11in) to
more than 2.1m (7ft), with
alternative switching packages,
including remote control.

3

5

"Windward" by Hampton
5   Bay from Home Depot
Stores throughout the USA has
five thick-set chopper blades
with a wing span of 1.38m
(4ft 6in) set on a short stem.
Its geometric shape without
ornamentation doubles as an
unobtrusive ceiling downlighter
with a 40W "Circline" lamp
behind a translucent diffuser.

Hunter Fans claim there is
6   no ceiling on innovation
with "Lugano" so they register
their trademarks and patents.
Five round-edged paddle blades
powered by the patented
Airmax® motor run both cooler
and quieter. Wobblefree™
canopy and Easy Lock™ blades
and glass shades to diffuse the
light are designed for quick
home assembly.

The scoops taken out of
7   the elliptical blades on
"Silverado", engineered by
Casa Vieja, are not purely
ornamental but are designed
for efficient air circulation. They
stir up warm air that rises
indoors to cool it in summer
and circulate heated air in
winter. This fan, from Lamps
Plus, has a contemporary finish
of brushed aluminium.

4

6

7

8

9

The owners of this seaside
8   home in England decided
on air conditioning only at a late
stage. They chose the Unico
System because it permits
insulated narrow tubes to slide
easily into existing wall and
ceiling voids without disruption.
Underfloor central heating
already had been installed
throughout, including in the
travertine-lined bathroom.

A view of the sweeping
9   stairs to the first-floor,
open-plan living area shows the
unobtrusive slender ducts in the
ceiling, which breathe out warm
air in winter, when the Unico
System backs up the slow-
response underfloor heating,
and cool air in summer. It works
so silently that the owners say
they hardly know it's there.

10

ALSO SEE

walls and ceilings p.34
flooring pp.51, 54
kitchens p.195

This self-build house (photos 8 to 11) on the coast of Devon, UK, was inspired by the Art Deco houses on Palm Beach in Miami, Florida. Key Art Deco elements in the house include glass blocks and terrazzo floors with underfloor heating for British winters, the travertine staircase, and uncluttered open space. Walls and ceilings rendered white have air conditioning unobtrusively installed in them. The house was featured in the British television Channel 4 *Grand Designs* program.

DESIGN INFLUENCE

Double-height,
11 window-to-ceiling glass walls that face south are a sun trap. Forty per cent of the surface area of the seaside house is glazed, which is why the owners decided to install air conditioning to cool it in summer and, in winter, to assist the underfloor heating and the focal fireplace, which is suspended and underlit so that it appears to float in space.

In the dining and
10 cooking area, which has spectacular views out to sea, a cylindrical, stainless-steel ventilation hood above the hob in the white Pedini kitchen is flanked by two Unico air-conditioning ducts in the ceiling. Their white plastic fasciae painted to match the ceiling make the ducting even less obtrusive than the low-voltage halogen downlighters dotted alongside them. Zoning in on the cylindrical extractor ventilation hood above the cooking area shows the ceiling-mounted halogen downlighters, the 22 x 220mm (1 x 8½in) slot for the Unico cooling and warming ducts, and, behind them, ceiling-mounted speakers for the sound system.

11

lighting

ABOVE LEFT Chandeliers make a comeback with Murano glass. "Odile" chandelier by Barovier & Toso in crimson.

ABOVE CENTER Unlike the garden crocus that flowers in a fortnight, a long-lasting "Crocus" bulb from Matsushita, maker of Panasonic. The energy-efficient compact fluorescent consumes less energy, which means lower power costs and a longer life.

ABOVE RIGHT Putting the fun back into function with the "Milk Bottle Lamp," which has 12 bottles hanging in a cluster just above the ground on long cables. Designed by Tejo Remy in 1991 for Droog Design, it burns 15W lamps in sandblasted milk bottles, made by DMD Voorburg.

LEFT At the Byblos Art Hotel in Venice, architect Alessandro Mendini has mixed baroque with rock 'n roll. The chandeliers by Barovier & Toso bridge the dazzling mix of classical 17th-century Veronese architecture with modern art and design classics in the salon. Vanessa Beecroft's photographs, set in the garlanded cornice, are lit in a way that spotlights could never have fulfilled.

For such a recent invention, electricity has had a dramatic effect upon society, revolutionizing the way the world receives information by enabling its delivery through pixels on a screen. Yet the science of light is still inexact. Music can be written on a score but light cannot be drawn. You can describe sound, but not the qualities and parameters of light.

There is something elusive about light. At best, you can say it is warm or cold, diffused or direct, fragmented or soft. Just as there is no geometry to a cloud, the nearest that lighting comes to being scientifically measured is with scale. A certain quantity of light equals a certain number of lux or candle power. A higher wattage gives a bright light.

Perversely, as lighting gets more technically proficient with complicated controls, it looks more beautiful. Flick back over lighting books of the last century and they bristle with more moving spots on tracks than a contemporary theater, or ceilings punctured with recessed halogen spots hiding black box transformers. New lights loosen up in form, and performance, to soften the light source. Diffuse, rather than direct, is the lighting goal as the West looks to the East for

ABOVE Layered sheets of Nomex, a new aramidic fiber by DuPont™, on "One by One," designed by Steve Lechot for Belux, are just like a paper lantern, but tear-free, durable and fireproof. The fluorescent lamp can be dimmed. Its sculptural presence is finely balanced between being substantial and insubstantial.

inspiration. Lanterns raised high, or stacked in sheaves as floor lamps, are made in silicone or polyester to outperform paper, while keeping the same soft, even glow. Lighting genius Ingo Maurer pastes onto his chandelier fragments of Japanese paper digitally printed with images of porcelain figures he found on a trip to China, "a must-have not just because they have an erotic content and delicate beauty, no, because I knew at once I would integrate their expression in a new work. I was tremendously inspired and this became 'Blushing Zettel'z'."

Beauty is not a word normally associated with lighting designs but these lights, even though made in commonplace materials, are beautiful. "Clouds," designed by the celebrated architect Frank Gehry, began as squashed-up polystyrene coffee cups, the kind found in vending machines, stapled together in homage to the sculptor Isamu Noguchi (1904–88). Like Noguchi, Gehry sought the handcrafted appeal of a light that could be mass-produced and packed flat into an envelope. Belux ingeniously realized his prototype in polyester that looks and feels like strong fibrous paper. Another famous Pritzker Prize-winning architect, Zaha Hadid, turns prosaic materials into a light swirl made with fiberglass, acrylics, and car paints concealing high-pressure LEDs by Zumtobel. She calls it "Vortex" which precisely describes the whirling motion of a fluid forming a cavity in the center, drawing in the onlooker.

After a period of about 50 years when functional and task lighting ruled the day, interest again focuses on the central light source, almost as an anchor to which furnishings can relate. Architect Alessandro Mendini made an architectural statement when he hung huge Murano glass chandeliers made by Barovier & Toso in the 18th-century villa in Verona that opened as the Byblos Art Hotel. The hotel showcases modern art and design classics, curated and listed just as in a design museum. Guests snack at Frank Lloyd Wright tables, check emails from a Philippe Starck chair, lounge on Salvador Dali's lips sofa, put their feet up on a mosaic

LEFT Ingo Maurer gracefully implodes the Japanese lantern. Trembling paper lampshades effortlessly hide sophisticated lighting technology. In a special edition, his "Blushing Zettel'z" modestly conceals, behind 80 Japanese paper sheets digitally printed with images of 9 Chinese porcelain figurines, a light touch dimmer, transformer, and halogen light bulbs.

BELOW LEFT The Japanese word for light implies weightlessness. Isamu Noguchi married these two qualities in his magical "Akari" lamps. Handcrafted in *washi* paper made from the bark of the mulberry tree and shaped on a bamboo frame, it is marvellous to think that lights with such presence could be folded and put into an envelope. Today they are mass produced.

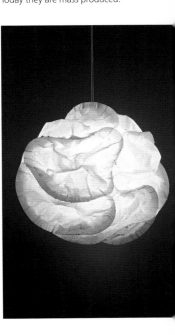

pebble by Marcel Wanders, and retrieve peanuts from Anna Gili's colourful mini-bar, all under the sparkle of these beautiful Murano glass chandeliers.

Quick to spot – or set – a trend, Swarovski commissioned fashion and theater designers to use crystals and create contemporary chandeliers. Inventor Gaetano Pesco made "Mediterraneo" pulsate with life – with thousands of crystals illuminated by LED upon threads. There are now more chandeliers in public places than there were in private residences in the 18th century but that does not mean the look will not filter down into homes. When Tom Dixon, head of retail design at Habitat in Britain, and designer of the "Mini-Ball" in the Swarovski 2005 collection, predicts the comeback of chandeliers, it means that this particular trend is happening in a high-street store near you.

So what has brought about this change of attitude?

ABOVE Frank Gehry's homage to Isamu Noguchi, the "Cloud" is made by Belux in polyester sheets which feel and look like strong fibrous paper. Polyester stiffened with a transparent polycarbonate ring and clipped together pack flat to simply spring back into shape on a filigree wire shade holder.

LEFT Sculptor Isamu Noguchi at his Long Island city studio, now the Noguchi Garden Museum for his sculptures and lanterns, with "Akari" sculptures in the 1960s. The name *akari*, which in Japanese also means light as illumination, suggests lightness as opposed to weight.

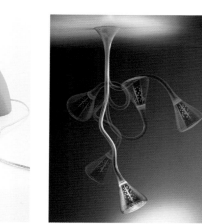

LEFT "Sticky" lamp made of PVC by Chris Kabel for Droog 2002 climbs walls like Batman. "Sticky" uses the malleable qualities of rubbery PVC to push outwards a bulbous form that shields the 6W neon light.

RIGHT Detached from its double-jointed spring-loaded arm, the Anglepoise designed as a table lamp in 1933 by George Cawardine turns into a workmanlike pendant lamp shade. Extra outsize, the encircling warm glow from its incandescent bulb casts a wide beam of light below.

LEFT Made of supple silicon rubber, soft to touch and shatterproof, the Foscarini "Uto" lamp by LaGranja Design is totally flexible in every detail. On the floor, ceiling, or wall-mounted on a hook, the lamp goes anywhere, even following the individual from room to room. Safe out of doors, its bell with a polycarbonate screen protects and insulates either an incandescent or fluorescent light source while allowing the passage of direct light.

BELOW LEFT Karim Rashid calls his designs "techno organic." Soft, rounded, playful, curling shapes include "Blob" for Foscarini. Made in white or yellow with a molded polyethylene diffuser, the curvy shapes may look simple but when Rashid designed a swimming pool for his weekend house in upstate New York, its odd shape was minutely calculated to ensure that the sun tracks the water.

BELOW RIGHT Darlings of the art world, architectural Swiss duo Jacques Herzog and Pierre de Meuron designed the "Pipe" for Artemide. Its light source is a 32W fluorescent lamp enclosed in a nozzle with a long loopy flexible 1.38m (4ft 5in) fitting to twist, unravel, loop, or move like a microphone in any direction needed.

The new light source of light-emitting diodes for a start. LEDs are tiny devices made of semi-conductor material that allows an electric current to travel in only one direction and produce light as a by-product of current flow. They are very bright at a single point, handy for showing the mobile telephone is charged but a drawback to filling rooms with light. Without filaments like fluorescents, they run cooler and last longer. That is why the one-bedroom Vos Pad™ in London has over 360 LED arrays and about 20 yards of plastic ribbons embedded with glowing semi-conductors.

Secondly, the low-energy compact fluorescents. At first, like all new technologies, low-energy fluorescent bulbs suffered from being expensive. Back when fluorescent lights were called neons, they flickered. Now they do not. Colour rendered, they are graded not just for wattage but for colour rendering, and colour temperature for warm or cold light. The Building Research Establishment estimates that if every light bulb in a house was replaced with its low-energy equivalent, the average electricity bill would be cut by half. These bulbs operate at 8,000 to 10,000 hours, around ten times the life of a traditional bulb.

In the late 20th century, a fundamental shift occurred in the role of light as the symbol of enlightenment. Ever since the 17th century, light has been seen as the

triumph of reason over ignorance. In the West we still say we have "seen the light." Now that we need shadows to read the information transmitted onto screens, shade is more important than bright light. This has brought back an interest in the different light cultures of the ancient shoji culture of Japan where a gentle illumination is transmitted through panels of rice paper. Twenty-first-century architects like Frank Gehry, and Swiss duo Jacques Herzog and Pierre de Meuron, pay tribute to that shielding tradition, by using modern light sources. The new lanterns hide their lights behind polyprolene shades, silicon, pleated Plexiglas, paper-thin metal folded like origami, opalescent glass... anything but paper. Unless it is Bernhard Dessecker's crumpled paper shading low-energy compact flouresents in a carbon fiber cage. Floor, wall, and table lamps break out of their industrial packaging to hide their superior performance in playful shapes.

Lights strung up through a tree are festive: floodlights beamed from a security fence are not. Light can cure and heal, yet it can be an instrument for torture. Light, and its absence, depends on how it is perceived by the individual. Never formulaic, the magical ability that light possesses for wellbeing as well as its ability to shape and define space cannot be quantified. That is its power.

ABOVE LEFT Light levels drop in the digital age to read the information that is transmitted in pixels of lights onto our screens, as Erco shows. In the USA the 1500 lux (the level measurement of light) specified for working environments dropped in a decade by mid 1990 to 800 lux, in the UK from 750 to 500.

ABOVE RIGHT Bathed in unearthly pink light, this living room in the Vos Pad™ changes on a computerized program to be suffused in ethereal green, or blue. LEDs with over 16 million colours, and 120 floor fittings light Marcel Jean Vos's Vos Pad™.

RIGHT Already in the permanent collection at the Guggenheim in New York is "Repose" by fashion designer Hussein Chalayan for the Swarovski 2006 "Crystal Palace" collection. His conceptual art installation piece includes an airplane wing balanced against a wall, its large wing flap moving slowly up and down, revealing a long strip of Swarovski crystals, illuminated from behind by LEDs.

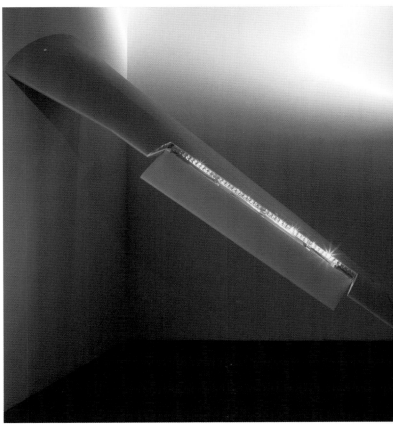

lighting/in praise of shadows

Postgraduates lighting designers at the Domus Academy in Milan are introduced to an eloquent essay on the Japanese sense of beauty, *In Praise of Shadows* by Jun'ichiro Tanizaki. The author believes that, "A Japanese room might be likened to an inkwash painting, the paper panelled shoji being the expanse where the ink is thinnest, and the alcove where it is darkest. Whenever I see the alcove of a tastefully built Japanese room, I marvel at our comprehension of the secrets of shadows, our sensitive use of shadow and light."

The book is currently achieving a cult status because it addresses a worldwide phenomenon in the digital age. To read information transmitted in pixels of light onto our computers and television, we need more shadows. Light levels measured in lux fell dramatically from the 1500 lux specified for offices in the 1980s in the USA to 800 lux in a decade, and in the UK from 750 to 500. At home we pull down the shutters and switch off the lamps to read our screens.

Designers' response is to dim down the low-energy compact fluorescents or LEDs lights, not just with controls, but by diffusing the source. Shades made of silicon, opalescent glass, transparent and opaque plastic, crumpled tissue paper, even vending machine cups for Frank Gehry's "Cloud," his homage to sculptor Isamu Noguchi, herald the new age of enlightenment.

1

2

3

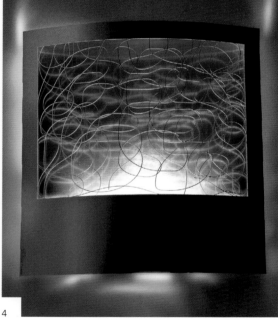

4

Viewed from every angle,
1   the strong profile of this laser-cut wooden "Helio Spa" light sparkles from the cluster of seven 60W incandescent lamps within, designed by Manel Ybarguengoitia. Spanish company B.Lux also makes an aluminum version in two sizes, 900 or 600mm (36 or 24in).

Crumpling white paper
2   and shooting it into the basket, an act excelled in by many executives, creates the "Knüller" – a floor lamp like a netball goal on a thin stand by Bernhard Dessecker for Ingo Maurer. In German, "Knuller" has two meanings – to scoop or to crumple. Energy-saving light bulbs in the center of the carbon fiber basket are shielded by several layers of tissue paper and pleats.

Raise high the white
3   lantern with Foscarini's best-seller, the "Havana" by Jozeph Forakis. This floor and table lamp, using either an incandescent or fluorescent bulb in a white or cream polyethylene diffuser to a height of 4m (13ft), moves outdoors to light huge areas like paths, drives, and fields. New York's Museum of Modern Art has chosen it for its permanent design collection.

Origami is the Japanese
4   art of paper folding which Liat Poysner, an Israeli designer, brings to her metallic collection of lights for Baldinger®. The quality of light diffused through the screen on this wall light ripples across the surface. Upturned and suspended from wires, the fitting becomes a pendant light. Each time the source is hidden.

A conch shell made of
5   plastic, the Tecnolumen® "Pearl" table lamp by Nico Hellmann enfolds a standard incandescent supermarket bulb. Shaped from rigidly pleated yet flexible Plexiglas, the heat-resistant table light collection of "Pearl," the convoluted "Snail," and rounded "My Heart" achieves curves and volumes impossible in any other material.

The Far Eastern equivalent
6   of a takeout, the tiffin box is round and squat like the "Medusa" for Leucos. Light from its transparent base is brighter than that filtered through its opaque lid.

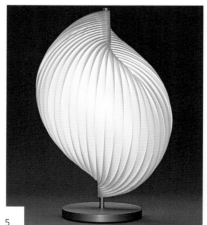

5

6

Herzog and de Meuron
7   hang their teardrop
suspension lamp made in
silicon in their architectural
practice in Basel. Light from
the transparent "Jingzi,"
in production with Belux,
is activated by touching
its thin-walled casing.

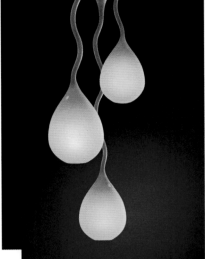

7

8

The "Olla," designed
8   by Asahara Sigeaki
for Lucitalia, can take an
off-center overhead swing if
the decentralizer support
fitting is attached. Its blown,
acid-etched, opal glass diffuser
filters the glow through a
silvery matt gray finish.

9

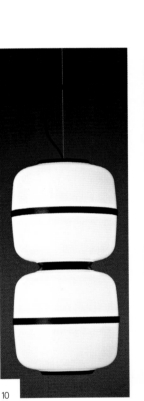

10

11

12

Reminiscent of the
10   traditional Chinese paper
lantern, two identically shaped
bowls girdled by a black ring
softly glow through plastic.
Stacked one upon the other,
"Lantern" by young French
designers Ronan & Erwan
Bouroullec for Belux is also
made in red or black injection-
molded plastic. At each open
end, smaller black rings serve to
hold the light source and
weight the suspension.

No shadows at all are cast
9   from the "Glo-Ball" by
Jasper Morrison for Flos. Lit, the
softly glowing flattened globe
appears to be two-dimensional,
with no hint of its source, an
incandescent bulb. Like all of
Morrison's understated designs,
it combines technical brilliance
with simplicity.

This pendant above a
11   dining table is a mosaic of
refractions. Brilliantly multi-
faceted, softened to sparkle
rather than dazzle, "Caboche"
by Patricia Urquiola and Eliana
Gerotto for Foscarini surrounds
a halogen source with 189

polymethylmetacrylate balls.
A hidden matt white glass
screen on top diffuses light
upwards to reflect off the
ceiling, while a concave screen
at the base prevents too much
light escaping.

Reminiscent of lanterns
12   hung on coastal houses in
Spain to signal returning ships,
the "Cesta" lantern was
designed in 1964 by Miguel
Mila, made in plastic and
framed in Manila cane. Now
Santa & Cole make it in heat-
curved cherrywood holding an
opal crystal ball on a dimmer.

lighting/decorative

Decorative is not a word associated with the skill of lighting designers, or architects. But it makes a comeback in the world of lighting. Decorative lighting concerns the quality of light and the way in which it falls as well as the form it takes. Inspired by sunlight through trees, Louise Campbell laser cut leafy shapes across three acrylic lampshades, and stacked them in a shade to get the same dappled light and shade effect that theater designers recreate with filters and Gobo lights. Also looking to nature, and at the agave plant that grows like aloes in Spain, Antoni Arola wrapped his light for Santa & Cole in its leaves replicated in balsa wood.

Since being banished by starburst ceilings of low voltage halogens, pendant lights – only designers call them suspension lamps – make a comeback. And the chandelier returns. As head of retail design for Habitat and internationally acclaimed designer Tom Dixon observes: "It is so loaded with history and decoration that I wanted to create the most pure shape I could think of. I wanted to do the bare minimum to make a chandelier. I had a vision of a meteorite flying through space like a luminous object." His glittering chandelier is made by Swarovski, who launched its annual "Crystal Palace" collection in 2002 to introduce internationally acclaimed fashion and theater designers as well as industrial product designers to the beauty of crystals.

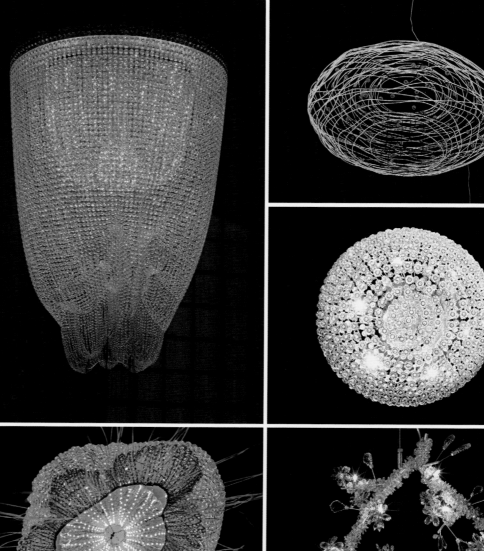

1

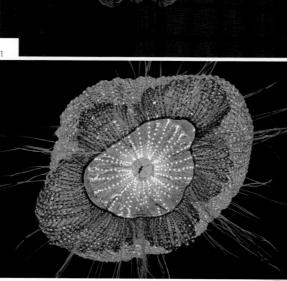

Since 2002 the Swarovski
1   "Crystal Palace" collections have aimed to reinvent the traditional crystal chandelier. Left: "Science and Fiction" by the fashion designers Basso & Brooke. Marie Therese's baroque museum piece inspired a traditional chandelier made out of metal festooned with multiple tiers of the classic

Swarovski pendular clear crystals, each engraved with intricate fashion designs. The shadow it casts below is like the Sputnik spacecraft of the mid 20th century. Above (with detail below): the showstopper of the Milan fair 2006 was this chandelier for Swarovski by Gaetano Pesce. Like a giant shimmering jellyfish, "Mediterraneo" squeezes

up its 140 crystal strands lit by LEDs programed to change colour from squid ink blue to red and silver, bunches them (detail below) releasing fine thread fronds and then slowly pulsates and balloons out (above). Top, three more from the Swarovski "Crystal Palace" collection: (top right) "Cosmos" by Naoto Fukasawa looks like the after-image that

remains in your eyes after drawing circles in the air with a powerful flashlight beam. Tom Dixon's design for "Mini-Ball" (middle right) suspends hundreds of pieces of crystal on threads to form a sphere. Tord Boontje's "Mini Blossom" (bottom right) throws out exquisite bejeweled blossom branches entwined with fiber optics.

2

3

4

A light that doubles as an art installation, Danilo De Rossi's light-emitting glass droplet "Glo" is handblown by Leucos in the old tradition of Murano glass. Available in transparent crystal, cobalt blue, or crimson as shown, with a glass plate placed below the droplet like a puddle.

Every artistic installation needs good lighting control, which can be as dramatic as the fixture. Lutron's range of dimming controls will transform a room from a bright welcoming space by day (left) to the more mysterious lighting at night (right) for a dinner party. "Lyneo" is Lutron's simplest dimmer which can be pre-set so LED controls can alter lighting and create subtle changes at the touch of a button.

Inspired by the dappled sunlight through trees, Louise Campbell captured the same interplay between light and shadow in her design, "Collage" for Louis Poulsen Lighting. She used laser-cut patterns of leaves in three acrylic shades overlaid on each other to behave like foliage, shading the light source to prevent glare.

⬇ ALSO SEE

walls and ceilings p.32

lighting/decorative

According to Stephen Hawking, 2kg (4lb 4oz) of matter hurtling through the void exploded with a big bang that sent planet earth bucketing through space with the rest of the constellations. The "Big Bang" by Enrico Franzolini and Vicente Garcia Jimenez has methacrylic planes escaping the central core of luminous halogen in this ceiling lamp by Foscarini.

"Enigma" from Japanese designer Shoichi Uchiyama poses the question: How does he achieve such powerful light in such a minimalist piece? "Enigma" weighs only 1kg (2lb) yet its aluminum cone, housing the halogen reflector lamp, and four hovering rings on ultra-thin steel wires both indirectly reflect light from their polished underside, and emit direct light as the shades diffuse it. Made by Louis Poulsen Lighting who won the IF Design Award for it in 2004.

5

"Quite a lot of the time we all take light for granted, but there are many times when our inner nature cannot help but make us respond to light.

"In the natural world it could be the shafts of sunlight breaking through the darkening clouds, the colour and beauty of the sun setting behind a mountain range, or the violent burst of energy associated with lightning.

"In the world of artificial light it could be the intimate glow of a candlelit dinner, the brash white light of a brightly-lit convenience store, or the brilliant burst of fireworks on New Year's Eve. The acid test is to give a kid a flashlight, turn it on and watch what they do."

Mark Major with Jonathan Speirs in conversation with Anthony Tischhauser in *Made of Light: The Art of Light and Architecture*

⬆ **DESIGN INFLUENCE**

6

Wooden strips ribboned around a steel frame tie up a powerful source of light in "Leonardo" from Barcelona designer Antoni Arola for Santa & Cole. Inspired by agave plant leaves, the ribbons of variable transparency wrapped around the light strips have the Mediterranean freshness of a bowl of tagliatelle.

7

lighting/architectural

An architectural approach to lighting seeks to quantify the expressive and emotive quality of light. Lighting designers Jonathan Speirs and Mark Major, in *Made of Light: The Art of Light and Architecture*, use the seven parameters of Western music notation as a model to describe light, that intangible, sometimes invisible, disappearing act that so powerfully affects us.

Pitch they equate to Colour Temperature (effects, not heat); Dynamic to Intensity, the scale of brightness; Articulation to Texture (wash, diffuse, back-lit); Duration to Time (how long the source lasts; Tempo to Control (dim up and down); Silence to Darkness; and Timbre to Ambience, that mood-enhancing quality of light sought by all designers.

This scale is made visible in the coloured kinetic light show staged at an old power station in Edinburgh by Speirs and Major. A once threatening industrial plant painted battleship gray turns into a light show, bathed red on Valentines Day, with the blue and white flag on St Andrew's Day. Moving indoors, the computerized colour-change light show is possible on a small domestic scale with RGB (colour changing LED in the industry) Light Emitting Diodes. After decades of bathing space in white light, coloured light returns to the architectural palette.

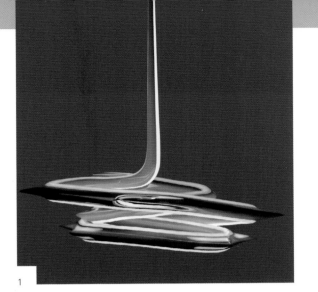

1

2

3

"LedPlus" by Jean Michel
2   Wilmotte is a new tool in technical lighting, both indoors and out, by iGuzzini. Recessed lights, round or square, and available in floor and wall-mounted fittings, are very thin yet have a load resistance of up to 500kg (½ton). Light colour changes are made with built-in equalizers managed by a double control panel and the light source is either LEDs or the LED RGB Colourmix by Osram.

An outdoor light that
3   requires no electrical wiring, the "Solar Bud" by Ross Lovegrove for Luceplan collects solar energy by a polycrystalline silicon photovoltaic cell to power two rechargeable nickel cadmium batteries. At sunset the energy from the sun spontaneously turns on the light-efficient LEDs. The duration of the light when fully charged is between 13 and 15 hours. Sun exposure time to reload energy expended after 13 hours of lighting is about 5 hours.

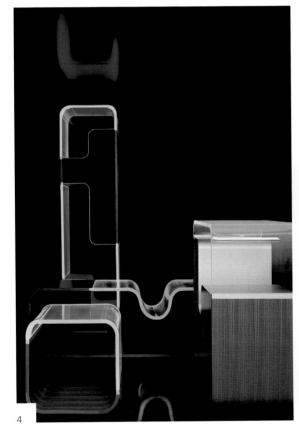

4

Like molten glass swirled
1   capriciously from a slender stem, the "Vortexx" makes light fluid even as it captures it. Made with fiberglass, acrylic, automotive paint, and high pressure LEDs, "Vortexx" is designed by Zaha Hadid with Patrick Schumacher. It is made in limited edition by Sawaya & Moroni in collaboration with Zumtobel.

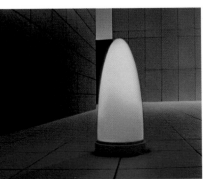

5

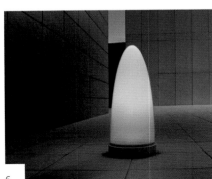

6

Glass or acrylic panels for
4   walls, ceilings, floors, and stairs, as well as furniture and product design, from emdelight® by Thomas Emde can produce all the colours in the RGB spectrum and change them, as well as varying the intensity of the colour. Lighting becomes an integral part of the architecture and interior design rather than an add-on item.

"Globolus" by Watanabe
5   & Tanaka for O Luce can drift about the room, brightened or dimmed and changing colour. Using LE source with a RGB (colour change) system, the stripes on "Globolus" emit light-changing colour in a cycle, starting from one primary colour and shading into the next colour. The cycle can be stopped at anytime.

"OFU" by Alvaro Siza for
6   Reggiani changes colour with the LED RGB colour change system. The die-cast aluminum base houses the control gear and the light source is softly diffused by the opal or transparent methacrylate diffuser.

⬇ **ALSO SEE**

walls and ceilings p.40
heating and cooling p.110

lighting/architectural applications

Early in the 20th century, Le Corbusier beamed down light through polychromatic light wells to create changing patterns of light that tracked the sun upon stone floors in the chapel at Ronchamps. As he famously explained: "Architecture is the masterly, correct and magnificent play of masses brought together in light." Now in production are two light fittings based on original sketches, and the remake of existing fittings, which began in 1999 between the Le Corbusier Foundation and Italian manufacturer, iGuzzini on the refurbishment of the Maison du Bresil in France,

designed by Le Corbusier in 1954 with Lucio Costa. Lights designed by architects for specific interiors and subsequently put into mass production include a collection by Baldinger® of Michael Graves' designs and Finnish architect Alvar Aalto's designs, as relevant today as they were in the 1950s, still made by Artek (and marketed in the USA by Baldinger®). Some lights are designed to become part of the architecture itself, like Ingo Maurer's "Schlitz Up" and "Light Cone" ceiling lights, or Kreon's "Cadre" which casts a narrow band of intense light.

4

French designer Andrée
1   Putman has put her poised, elegant style on hotels, interiors, furniture, and now, lights for Baldinger® with a pendant (far right) and wall sconce (right). A modernist, she explains: "To me modernity doesn't mean contemporaneity. Modernity is a pastiche of time and style. It has a classical purity of image that doesn't age. It's discreet and indefinable."

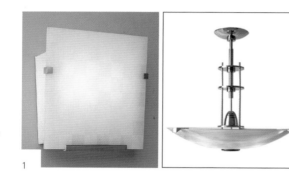

1

"Slim" by Christoph
4   Steinemann for Belux is a modular light aimed at architects. It packs its electronic ballast units into a slender fitting for easy wall or ceiling mounts, either individually or in a chain as shown. It can also be a suspension light. Different covers and films can be applied for individual light direction and glare protection.

5

Made-to-measure
5   light by the meter won the IF Product Design Award for Belux. "Meter by Meter" by Matteo Thun can run up or across the wall, doubling as a direct light source or, with a cover of either aluminum or satinized glass, as an indirect source, or a combination of the two. It can frame mirrors, doors, and passageways.

Picture lights were
6   never so unobtrusive as the "Pausa" by Mario Ruiz for Blauet which travels the world from Europe to the USA, Japan, Asia, and Australia. Even its finish in neutral colours of gray metal, satin nickel, or beige, are designed to put this light into the background as its task is to light up what is displayed beneath it.

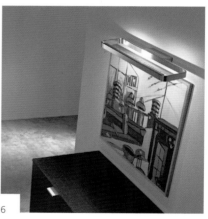

6

Designing houses, architect
2   Michael Graves customized lighting fixtures. His pendant lights (left), wall sconces (right), and chandelier (center) are made in the States by Baldinger®. Frosted glass and bronze contrast with the

recessed can lights and fluorescent tubes of the 1980s, when Graves designed them.

Richard Meier established
3   his architectural practice in NYC in 1963. During his training in the 1950s, he was influenced

by the concept of "architecture as art" to push the boundaries of design and harmoniously combine form and function. His wall sconces (left and right) and ceiling pendant (center) for Baldinger® embody simplicity with purity of form.

The "Q.BO" (as in cubo)
7   freestanding light box evenly distributes light within a cube. Designed by Carlos Serra and Antonio Herrero for B.Lux, it can sit alone or in a cluster; its base is weighted to stop it from sliding. The polycarbonate finish, textured like fine sand, diffuses the 18W compact fluorescent, taking away any harshness to warm it up and glow.

7

8

With "Slot" for
9   FontanaArte British
architect David Chipperfield
gives minimal architecture
the monumental lighting
experience, delineating
architectural planes with
a fine line of light in corridors
or meeting rooms.

Finnish architect Alvar
10   Aalto's warm, sensuous,
organic designs for libraries,
sanatariums, and homes earned
him a place in the panoply of
great architects of the 20th
century. From his lighting
collection, still made by Artek,
two of his best-known designs:
the pendant lamp A331 (far
left) designed in 1953–4, in
white-painted aluminum with
polished brass rings, and the
A440 (left), in sandblasted
opal glass with white-painted
fittings, designed in 1954.

"La Roche" is a new
11   edition by SirrahiGuzzini
in collaboration with the Le
Corbusier Foundation. Of a
metal tubular wall light, is an
original design by Le Corbusier
from the late 1920s. Made in
techno-polymer with a Pyrex
glass screen, the colour of the
finish is taken from the original.

Two lights by Roberto
13   Pamio for iGuzzini.
Top: "iBlock" designed as a
glass frame that looks both
solid and lightweight at the
same time. It diffuses light
from mains voltage halogen
lamps, called Halopin.
Bottom: "Cup," made of thick
transparent glass, conceals the
light source for accent lighting
from either Halopin or compact
fluorescent lamps.

9

11

10

At the Isola restaurant in
8   Antwerp, Belgium, the
"Cadre" lights tables as it
frames a view of matt gray
walls. Unlike traditional
pendants, Kreon's "Cadre,"
designed by Kristof Pycke,
does not float in space, but
structurally becomes part of it.
"Cadre" echoes the thinness
of the fluorescent tube. Two
identical aluminum extrusions
connected with an aluminum
adjustable suspension system.

A new twist on ordinary
12   downlights. Ingo Maurer
produces two alternatives:
"Light Cone" (right) and
"Schlitz Up" (far right). This
duo of flush-mounted ceiling
lamps can be used to illuminate
large surfaces. Its unusual form
makes spaces more exciting.
Both can be angled from
8 degrees to 45 degrees.

12

13

lighting/classics

Fast forward over a hundred years of lighting, with just a single light chosen for each decade, and it will show up some of the design preoccupations of the 20th century with an optimistic start to the 21st.

In the beginning, there was Edison's light bulb with a bamboo sliver where the tungsten filament now burns, when Austrian architect Josef Hoffmann's rationalist ideas on construction set modernism in action. The Bauhaus program in the 1920s revealed function in every form so that electric cables are visible inside glass shafts. As electricity lit up the world, ergonomics crept back with the engineer George Cawardine adapting the joints of the human arm into his 1933 Anglepoise to throw light just where it was needed. Scandinavians Hans J Wegner and Alvar Aalto encapsulated warm light with low illumination in a series of friendly lights until the playful explosion of Pop Art and plastics in the 1960s introduced Italian exuberance. The review ends with Ingo Maurer's tribute to Thomas Edison's invention that changed the world, and its next generation of lights as a hologram with "Eddy's Son" (2005) and Patricia Urquiola's fashionable "Bague" (2005) that totes the world's first light bulb, Edison's incandescent.

1

A table lamp that could take its place on a desktop as easily today as in 1903 when architect Josef Hoffmann designed it. It is still handmade in brass or nickel, with opalescent glass shading a pair of incandescent lamps by Woka in Vienna. Weiner Werkstatte founder Josef Hoffmann rejected historicism to pioneer the use of simple, geometric forms.

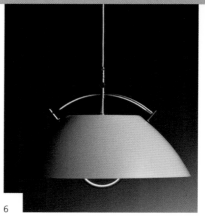

6

Mid 20th-century classic, the "Wegner" by Danish designer Hans J Wegner for Pandul in 1962, when Scandinavian design was at its most influential, is a ceiling light in stainless steel and aluminum fitted with a standard incandescent bulb. Height adjustable on a cable lift, it has a separate adjustable shade.

3

A 1926 ceiling lamp from Marianne Brandt, one of the most talented members of the Bauhaus metal workshop in the 1920s. It is stamped with the Bauhaus logo by Tecnolumen® who make re-editions of the original in brass with an opalescent glass globe and an incandescent bulb. Her lamps, inspired by elementary geometric forms, remain among the best of the Bauhaus products.

2

Fashion and theater designer Mario Fortuny's 1907 table lamp version of his photographer's studio light on a tripod with a huge circular shade, downsized and suspended from an arc by Alivar.

4

The celebrated Anglepoise lamp, designed in 1933 by automobile engineer George Cawardine, with its spring-tensioned parts based on the human arm, is far from showing creaky joints.

5

On steroids in the early part of the 21st century, the Anglepoise grows to enormous size as a freestanding floor lamp to tower over its original model, but it is just as easy to swivel or rotate the head and position the arm.

8

9

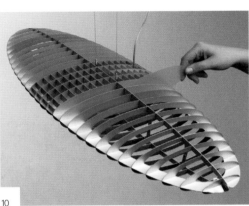

10

11

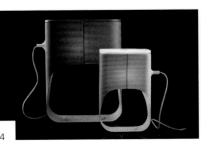

14

13

12

7

"Archimoon Classic," by
12 Philippe Starck in 1998 for Flos, is the head of a family of table lights that address three main light sources: halogen, incandescent, and compact fluorescent. Attached to the same skeletal body, the head (or shade) changes to reflect the light source. The "Classic" houses the bigger incandescent. Starck believes designers must pare down materials to make the most of what is available.

Ingo Maurer's tribute
13 to Thomas Edison, "Eddy's Son" does not use the incandescent as a light source but makes it a virtual light as a hologram. Above it, the halogen source is hidden in a profiled fitting. "Eddy's Son" 2005 is a scaled-down version of the "Where are you Edison?" hologram created in 1997, the year that Ingo Maurer's light installations were shown at MOMA in New York.

Patricia Urquiola names her
14 lights designed in 2005 after fashion accessories: first the "Caboche" and now the "Bague" table lamp in three sizes: large and small, which take the 100W incandescent; and mini, which takes the tiny 40W incandescent. Metallic mesh is coloured in white, black, or aluminum and covered with silicone, then given a frosted shade screen by Foscarini.

The "Arco" floor lamp in
7 metal with a marble base, by Achille and Pier Giacomo Castiglioni in 1962 for Flos, is as fashionable in contemporary interiors as it was then. Anchored in a heavy marble base, the tensile, arching steel suspension arm supports the semi-circular shade, which is pierced to allow light to escape upwards as well as down.

Almost a hood made of
8 one pressed plastic sheet for a protected light, the "Dalu" by Vico Magistretti in the 1960s re-issued in transparent orange or red, with opaque versions in white or black, polycarbonate by Artemide.

Its beaky presence on
9 scaffolding makes the "Tizio" light by Richard Sapper (1972) for Artemide one of the best-known lights of the 20th century. But it was not the anthropomorphic styling that won the coveted Compasso d'Oro in 1979 so much as its brilliant technology. No wires or cables appear to power the halogen bulb in the head, shielded with a small reflector. The electric connection is hidden within the fully adjustable jointed parts.

"Titania," by Alberto Meda
10 and Paolo Rizzatto in 1989 for Luceplan, is a suspension lamp in aluminum lamellar shell like ribs. Removable coloured filters slide into the casing over the halogen source which change the body colour of the fitting without affecting the white light emitted from it.

The "Tolomeo," by Michele
11 de Lucchi and Giancarlo Fassina (1987), is such a world-wide success that Artemide has re-issued variants on it twice. In 1999 the "Micro" version downsized the table light. Now a limited re-edition of it in all the colours of the rainbow is made as a cantilevered desk lamp and a neat clip lamp.

bathrooms

ABOVE LEFT "Moody" glass washstand, designed by Ambrogio Rossari for Even, is shown as an aquarium, but could also display a terrarium or a Zen pebble garden.

ABOVE CENTER Kaldewei's "Vivo Turbo" jet, patented worldwide, has silent mini turbines fitted in each jet in the whirlpool bath.

ABOVE RIGHT The angular, square "Monoblock" sink mixer from the "Plano" collection, designed by Angeletti Ruzza for Fantini, with an interchangeable wenge wood handle.

LEFT Philippe Starck's freestanding oval bathtub for Axor, fitted with his freestanding bathtub and shower mixer faucet. The world-famous designer told Lloyd Morgan: "In no case do I create for the sake of creating. I prefer to take everyday things we all have to do, like washing or keeping out of the rain, and to give these simple necessities a fifth dimension, a depth that gives an ordinary object the opportunity to speak of other things. It's part of a simple proposition to make people happier by making their everyday lives better."

Baths no longer hide behind closed doors in the smallest room in the house. Demographics show that more money is now spent on bathrooms than on any other single room in the house. Ideal Standard, the largest manufacturer of sanitaryware in the world, has seen consumer spending on bathrooms increase by 30 per cent in one year. First it was the kitchen that broke out of bounds to take over the house as a dining, living, and entertaining area. Now the bathroom is starting to move into the bedroom to gain more space.

Michael Sieger, bathroom designer for two worldwide German brands, Dornbracht and Duravit, teaches at Pforzheim University where a project called "Redefining the Bathroom" showed that architectural students are as uninhibited about showering and bathing in open spaces as were the Victorians, who were obliged to put a cast-iron tub to warm in front of the coal fire once a week.

The trend for placing a freestanding bathtub in the bedroom space behind a single, frosted-glass panel or setting the bathtub at the foot of the bed where the ottoman would once have stood, began in hotels. Antonio Citterio, who designed the Hotel Bulgari in

Milan, where precious materials can be found all over the hotel as befits a fashionable jewelry house, designed bathing areas clearly visible within each bedroom. He describes these ensuite bedrooms as "rooms for water and the space for living" with two distinct areas he calls "needs" (the toilet) and "wellbeing" (shower and bathtub).

Hotels also set the trend for designer bathrooms with famous architects and design studios blueprinting baths and sinks, bidets, and toilets. Because bathroom sanitaryware is essentially sculptural, designers and architects are able to put their signature to it more easily than they can to a kitchen range. Now property developers market residential properties as having a "Philippe Starck bathroom," for example.

Travel has brought the industry closer to new worlds and new bathing rituals. Whichever part of the world you inhabit, you can now buy and install at home, simply and efficiently, a Turkish bath, Scandinavian sauna, Japanese hot tub, or German spa shower-and-steam cabinet that is designed to look good too.

Not for today's savvy traveler the uninviting, orange-colored pine-log cabin with hot coals in a corner

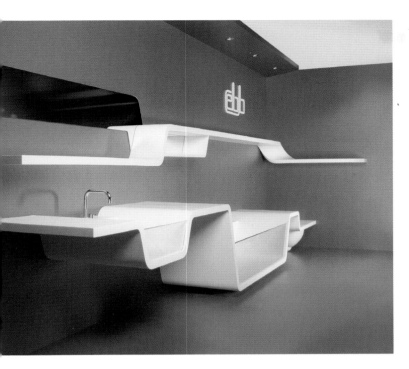

OPPOSITE PAGE LEFT Hotels introduced travelers to contemporary design, then manufacturers made it possible to get the look at home. Designer Marcel Wanders and restaurateur Peter Lute created different hotel suites in seven different houses dating from 1740 in Amstel, near Schiphol Airport in the Netherlands. Against a wall of Bisazza mosaics, Marcel Wanders' steel "Pipe" shower system with crimson controls stands 2.3m (7ft 6in) high, dwarfing his squared "Gobi" sink.

OPPOSITE PAGE BELOW The "Soap Tub" by Marcel Wanders installed in one of the Lute Suites with a matching collection of sink, bidet, and toilet.

LEFT New materials are revolutionizing bathroom design, making loadbearing spans and customized shapes possible. The "Ebb" bathroom by Tretzo integrates a glass-fronted sink and bathtub with open shelving in one single fluid piece. Designers Jack Woolley and Alan Marks used durable, stain-resistant, LG Hi-Macs acrylic, which allows seamless

joins and spans that plunge into a deep bathtub and unfurl like a ribbon into shelving that turns the corner gracefully.

BELOW In black Durat®, this sink unit with under-the-counter storage was specified by architect David Chipperfield for the white marble ensuite bathroom he designed at the Hotel Silken Puerta América in Madrid. Durat®, made from recycled plastic to form a solid polyester-based material, is used in public and private interiors to provide custom-made, seamless surfaces tens of meters in length.

advertising itself as a sauna or the shared hot tub of the 1970s – so last century! Twenty-first-century bathrooms are as inviting as spas. They feature plunge pools designed to overflow with water rippling over the edge like the infinity pools on the Indonesian horizon, Roman laconiums, steam cabins with ice-cold water piped in, dry rock heat saunas, electronic rain curtains programmed to provide a downpour or a gentle mist, whirlpool baths, or showers with wall panels positioned to deliver shiatsu-massage jets along the body. Bathrooms turn into wellbeing centers as the therapeutic benefits of water therapies become widely recognized.

"Multifunctional" is the prosaic marketing term used by bathroom manufacturers to describe the powerful equipment scaled down for domestic bathrooms that delivers these water therapies. By expertly controlling the movement of water, such equipment offers the healthy benefits of hydrotherapy. Whirlpool systems send water pulsing around baths, with hidden air-injection systems to aerate the water and keyboard controls to change the massage effect from gentle to intense. Showers do more than splash water from overhead: the waterfall or flood shower helps soothe muscular tension with a neck and

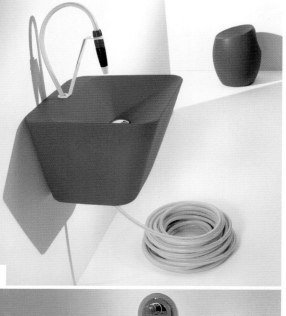

New materials revolutionize bathroom design and the shape of fittings:

1 The "Roto" design by Benedini Associati for Agape is an elliptical sink produced by rotational molding of a single polyethylene piece. Shown here in lime green, it is also available in white or orange.

2 This "Travertine" bathtub is made from one block of treated, polished stone, sourced from quarries near Siena in Tuscany, Italy, and skilfully carved by Boxart. Travertine's naturally formed layers are the result of minerals deposited underground by hot springs. The interiors of these baths – and of the matching sinks – are treated with a polyester-based resin to create a silky finish. The solid stone bathtub is so heavy that floors must be surveyed to ensure that they are able to support the weight before the bathtub is installed.

3 Entirely recyclable, and made from recycled polyethylene with the rigidity of plastic traffic cones, the "Pharos" tub by Jan Puylaert for WET is lit by an LED light.

4 Everything – including the kitchen sink – with the portable Cosmic "Simplex" by Spanish designers, que. It is sold with a garden house and a container stool to hold the 500 x 500mm (20 x 20in) polyethylene sink, which is shaped by rotational molding and is tough enough to withstand knocks. Fixings and the water inlet and outlet pipes are hidden within the sink.

5 "Alpha" sink by Francesco Lucchese made by Respect. Shown here in the color called "sun," the sink is made from light-diffusing, waterproof DuPont Corian®.

6 Ceramica Flaminia "IO:SI" by Alexander Duringer and Stefano Rosini is a new bathroom concept, which includes a bathtub and a sink in three sizes, a toilet, and a bidet. The "IO" collection is fitted with faucets inspired by waterfalls from the "SI" collection. Fluid, rounded shapes in ceramic are contrasted by the stark geometry of the benches, shelves, and vanity tops in wood or colored-lacquer finishes. Both the sink and bathtub can be encased in very thick shelves or panels, "dressed" (top), or "undressed" (below).

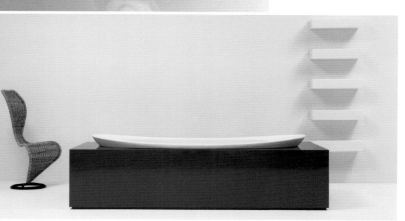

RIGHT Design-conscious consumers can create wet zones, like those of a health club, at home by waterproofing an area and installing showerheads. "Boiserie" is the slatted wood-and-resin wall-and-floor wet zone surfacing by Merati. Fully waterproofed and bought in a roll, like wallpaper, "Boiserie" never absorbs humidity, which makes it the perfect material for a shower area. It is nonslip, too. The "Waterblade" faucet by Ritmonio powers this shower behind glass walls designed by Theo Williams for Merati.

shoulders massage; the overhead shower trickles softly from above; and the hand shower, with variable jet strengths from soft to normal to powerful, can be attuned to personal showering preferences.

Many baths and cabinets are fitted with LED lights programmed to change color. Every skin cell in the body is receptive to colored light, so American bathroom manufacturers Kohler claim that immersion in a chromatherapy bathtub benefits the whole body, "even if your eyes are closed." Scent stimulates different emotions and induces a feeling of wellbeing, which is why steam cabinets are also fitted with essential oil dispensers for herbal or floral extracts. Loudspeakers resistant to steam and water are fitted so that music can be played in the shower, as can television.

Jacuzzi®, who pioneered the whirlpool system in the mid 20th century, have also designed the whirlpool tub of the future, "La Scala," which features a 1.07m (3ft 6in) high-definition plasma monitor and state-of-the-art surround-sound system, with a floating keypad that gives access to the internet and a waterproof remote control that allows video monitoring for the home security system.

It is not just the top end of the market that spends more on reinventing bathrooms, however. In Britain, the most expensive shower-and-steam cabinet at popular mass-market home store B&Q has seen an increase in sales in one year of more than 40 per cent.

LEFT A spa experience at home with the "Sōk" infinity bathtub from Kohler. Soaking in the ultra-deep bathtub to the sound of cascading water is enhanced by chromatherapy, which promotes physical wellbeing by using colored lights that affect the emotions. At the touch of a button, water moves through a spectrum of eight colors, from relaxing to stimulating, while champagne-like bubbles are injected into the water.

BELOW The Pharo "WellSpring" shower-and-steam cabin provides colored light therapy, aromatherapy, and music. Blue is calming and soothes both mental and physical agitation, consequently helping to lower blood pressure and aiding more even breathing.

The unsung heroes of the industry are not the designers of all these shapely, forceful fittings, however, but the faucet manufacturers who recognize the preciousness of water. An essential resource, water must never be wasted, and a lot of thought has gone into the design of faucets with hidden controls. Plumbing is hardly the most glamorous aspect of bathing, but the harnessing and control of water is taken very seriously by European and American faucet manufacturers. Poisonous residues from the faucet industry had poured into rivers for years, but the new millennium was heralded by faucet manufacturers on the shores of Lake Orta in Italy taking a press party boating to illustrate the life-giving changes that cleaning up their act had instigated. Ethics in the industry are as important as esthetics, and ethical policies now govern production, distribution, design, and management.

Furniture is particularly important when bathrooms occupy space that is also used for sleeping. Now that freestanding baths, shower-and-steam cabinets, and stand-alone sculptural sinks do not require furniture to play a supporting role, designers have created bathroom storage ranges that could move into the living room. Library stacks rather than shelves for towels, huge mirrors propped against the wall like artists' canvases, chaises-longues, and accessories designed like jewelry all enhance the bathroom. Even big storage items such as cupboards and drawers are designed to free wall- and floorspaces to soften the perimeters.

Minimalism in the bathroom is out. The day of a single faucet with a freestanding sink has gone. New technology and new materials have introduced color, pattern, movement, light, and life to the experience of bathing.

ABOVE Kohler brings together a range of bathroom products, which it claims are no longer limited to the bathroom, thanks to their beauty and diversity. The bedroom benefits from the addition of a stylish shower, the "Presqu'ile" quadrant enclosure and low profile tray.

RIGHT A tropical downpour upon rising or a soft mist at night from an electronic rain curtain. "RainSky" by Sieger Design for Dornbracht is a ceiling panel with a fine mist spray, head and body spray, and a rain curtain like a water wall. All three zones deliver 52 liters (14 US gallons) of water per minute, at a three-bar pressure, so waste pipes need to be bigger than normal. Simplified electronic controls deliver light and sound as well as water.

bathrooms/baths

As baths move center stage to take over more space, mainstream architects and designers take time off from designing world-famous buildings and interiors to put their signature on mass-produced bathtub collections. Norman Foster, David Chipperfield, Philippe Starck, and Andrée Putman design bridges, buildings, and hotels as well as household products such as baths, sinks, and bidets. What can an architect bring to the design of baths already perfected by the Ancient Egyptians? Firstly, the tub assumes a strong presence within its allocated space. Architects' baths are not always monumental – although some are, such as Michael Graves' "Dreamscape." David Chipperfield's "White & Silver" collection is designed to fit into compact spaces. Whether freestanding or tucked into a corner, they are always sculptural.

Ceramic is the most difficult material to mold into rigorous geometrical shapes and so many of the most shapely architectural baths are molded in new resins that allow more fluid lines, whether egg-shaped, oval, round, or rectangular. Ergonomics plays a role – the study of the human form in relation to the working environment is particularly pertinent to bathrooms. This results in inner linings of the bathtub differing from the outside form: a keyhole-shaped bathtub may be contained within a simple rectangular shape, for example.

Architects design complete bathroom suites – with bath, sink, bidet, and toilet skilfully styled to fit together – rather than ensuite bathrooms, to prevent purchasers ruining the original design with different products collaged within the same space.

3

1

2

4

Beneath brushed-steel
2   panelling, Andrée Putman's "Edition" bathtub for Hoesch has deep-seated dips, generously rounded at either end to make sinking into a hot tub pleasurable. The designer of Concorde interiors, film sets for Peter Greenaway, furniture collections, and hip hotels, Andrée Putman believes that true luxury has to do with simplicity.

World-famous architect
3   Norman Foster retains an interest in the design of everyday household objects. The oval "Foster" bathtub made by Hoesch can be freestanding or built in flush to the wall. The bath, which is studded with 16 tiny water jets, is narrowly rimmed on three sides of its circumference, while the side nearest the wall broadens to conceal plumbing.

Already a household name
1   for everyday objects, from ice tongs to kettles, in use all over the world, Alessi's first venture into large-scale production is the "Il Bagno Alessi" bathtub designed by Stefano Giovannoni. Made by Laufen with faucets by Oras, the collection includes bath, sink, bidet, and toilet, along with bathroom furniture.

Based on an egg, the
4   "Aveo" ceramic bathtub is made by Villeroy & Boch and designed by Conran & Partners, who claim there are similarities in the performance of the shell of an egg and bathroom ceramics. Sliced in half for the wall-mounted bidet and toilet, the shape also downsizes into a sink. Source faucets are made by Dornbracht.

The "White & Silver"
5   bathtub collection by David
Chipperfield for Ideal Standard
is so called because silvered
chrome faucets let water fall into
white vessel sinks styled to
look like substantial stone. The
architect of the Neues Museum
extension in Berlin, Chipperfield
chose to play with different
geometries in the design of
this collection, setting a round
shallow sink on a slab beside the
rectangular bath.

Ideal Standard was the first
6   bathroom manufacturer to
link up with named designers
when it collaborated with Italian
design genius Gio Ponti in 1954.
The "Newson Suite" by Marc
Newson for Ideal Standard
won the best bathroom
product design in the Design
& Decoration Awards in 2004.
Newson's furniture designs are
in the collections of the Museum
of Modern Art in New York,
the Design Museum in London,
and the Musée des Arts
Decoratifs in Paris.

American architect Michael
7   Graves' "Dreamscape"
bath, exclusive to Hoesch, stands
on streamlined, solid legs
sculpted out of the elliptical
form. Graves' worldwide fan
club began after he put Mickey
Mouse ears on the Disney
headquarters building in
Orlando, Florida. Inspired by Art
Deco, American Pop, pre-
Colombian culture, and the
language of cartoons, Graves
believes that American Design is
softer, less intellectual, closer to
the taste of the average public,
which is why this master of
populist post-modernism
designs household appliances
for the mass-market Target
stores in the United States.

5

6

7

The extra large "UFO" stainless-steel bathtub designed by Benedini Associati for Agape measures 2m (6ft 7in) in diameter and holds 880 liters (232 US gallons) of water. Draped over its sides is a backrest molded in silky smooth white Exmar. This bathtub needs a structural engineer's report on the loadbearing capacity of floors before installation.

8

"England's only hot springs spew 250,000 gallons a day into pools in Bath, an ancient Roman city built around the bathing tradition. Modern excavations have uncovered very elaborate and sophisticated chambers that featured three different types of baths for different water temperatures – the chilly frigidarium, the lukewarm tepidarium, and the steaming caldarium."

Charles W Moore and Jane Litz, Water + Architecture

⬆ DESIGN INFLUENCE

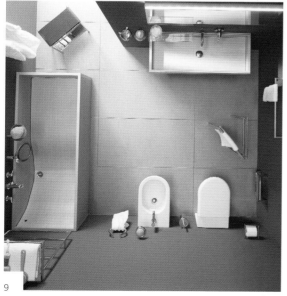

Japanese in style and made from plywood with a birch or wenge wood finish, the "WoodlineV" bathtub by Benedini Associati for Agape features a reclining liner for comfort and to speed up drainage. It is shown here with Agape's "OLC" accessory ranges.

9

Measuring 2.1 x 1.2m (7 x 4ft), the "Cubic" bathtub is carved from a single piece of black basalt by the LimeStone Gallery. Custom-made, sloped interiors can figure-hug the bather. The bathtub has to be craned into position and the floor able to support 1.5 tons.

10

⬇ **ALSO SEE**

flooring p.46
heating and cooling p.116
lighting p.143

11

12

13

The capacious yet slim-walled "Baia" bathtub by Carlo Colombo for Antonio Lupi is molded in Cristalplant, an acrylic resin that makes uniform, silky smooth surfaces. Shown here in the stone finish, the bathtub is seemingly sculpted from a single block of granite. The freestanding faucet is the famous "Blok," also designed by Colombo.

The "Mini" tub, designed by Matteo Thun for Rapsel, is made in opaque white Cristalplant and is shown here with "Wellcome" wall-mounted sanitaryware, also designed by Thun. "Lay-up" stackable glass cubes designed by Studio Saba support the coral "Momy" table lamp by Georges Adatte.

Clear, precise lines define the "Subway" collection in ceramic from Villeroy & Boch. Compact rectangular sinks, floor- or wall- mounted toilets, bidets, small washstands, and bathtubs that fit around consoles and floor-mounted cupboard units are designed for the smaller bathroom.

14

15

Adolf Babel, who designed the "Free" bathtub in a transparent acrylic patented by Hoesch and supported on teak legs, says, "Every object linked with water brings with it the desire for transparency. The idea of being able to make a bathtub that looks like a spring of fresh water represents an archetypal model for everyone."

At last, a bathtub designed to overflow. The "Starck X" bathtub for Duravit, named X as in the unknown in mathematical equations, and designed by Philippe Starck, overflows into a pebbled base angled to drain away. The bathtub is sold with a bag of Carrara white marble pebbles. Inside the platform base, LED lights are programmed to change color.

Monolithic and self supporting, freestanding sinks are like small sculptures for the home. Molded in glass, stone, and ceramic, as well as other new materials such as Cristalplant, which is pliant, compact, and nonporous, sinks are no longer put on a pedestal but are treated as works of art on tabletops. New materials, such as Cor-Ten steel, used by Ritmonio for the curvaceous support of an enameled aluminum sink (picture 6 opposite), and the revival of DuPont Corian® by Respect (see page 148) and others in sinuous new shapes, bring sinks out of the woodwork of the old-fashioned vanity unit and into focus in the bathroom.

The shape of contemporary sinks makes the most of the materials from which they are made. Stone washstands are characterized by their rounded or squared form, revealing the thickness of the material. Glass sinks balloon in volume, exploiting the transparency and associated fragility of the material in robust shapes. Even wood, which does not easily lose its straight edges, sinuously transforms sinks into shapes that are anything but wooden. Enamel, aluminum, and recycled plastics spring into cylindrical shapes, leap from the walls in an exaggerated spring, or turn up their edges like paper airplanes to swoop into bathrooms. Sometimes the shape within the sink is not the same as the slab that contains it. The island of Samoa inspires the shape of Matteo Thun's sink (see page 160, picture 16), changing the depth of water it holds within its contoured outline. Designer Roberto Palomba likens his sinks for Laufen to pebbles shaped and smoothed by waves.

Ingenious ways of getting water to flow into these objects of beauty include sensors installed within the sink rather than faucets. In the "Magic" sink by Villeroy & Boch (picture 11 on page 176), water flows from a seemingly unknown source, its flow and temperature controlled by an integral sensor that is activated by positioning hands within the sink. Move hands to the left and water warms, to the right and the water gets colder. Remove the hands from the sink and the flow stops altogether.

1

"The twentieth century would not exist without the plumber. He has become its emblem and for us has become indispensable... Now the plumber is exactly the pioneer required for this campaign for cleanliness. He is the most precious artisan in the country, a yeoman of culture, that culture which is so decisive today. Each British sink with faucets and drains is proof of progress."

Adolf Loos, *Spoken into the Void*

⬆ DESIGN INFLUENCE

1   A glass top with an integral sink called "Space" by Altamarea offers just that, a space-saving, transparent sink and worktop that appears to float in this luminous bathroom. A frosted-glass panel separates the sink and shaving/make-up area from the shower, and a bathroom storage cabinet on wheels frees floorspace.

2

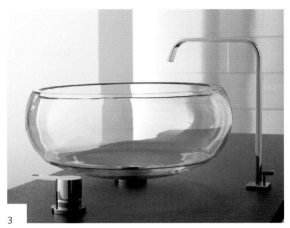

3

4

Soft, flexible, translucent,
2   the "Foglio" ("leaf" in
Italian) sink by Agape is made
from a sheet of scored, folded
PVC. It rests on a wall-mounted,
stainless-steel ring, which also
supports the monoblock faucet.
The leaves are colorful, available
in orange, gray, or violet.

The softly shaped "Bubble"
3   sink in handcrafted blown
glass by Carlo Colombo in the
Materia line from Antonio Lupi
appears light as a soap bubble,
its thickness varying from 15 to
20mm (⅝–¾in). Upraised on a
slender stem, the sink can be
mounted on the "Easy" box
surfaces made of plywood with
an oak veneer. Other container
modules in the same "Easy" line
can be installed beneath the
counter-top to build up the
bathroom cabinet range.

The "Simbiosi" sink
4   designed by Davide Vercelli
for Ritmonio. Sea-grass green
enamel coats the aluminum
sink, which is set upon a
waterproofed table made
from Cor-Ten steel.

6

5

Pearwood covers the
5   sinuously shaped ceramic
sink and accompanying bidet
and toilet designed by Patricia
Urquiola for Agape.

The apparent fragility
6   of the "Vedo" glass
sink designed by Bertocci is
anchored by the nickel-coated,
solid-brass mixer "Mercurio"
faucet, both by Rubinetterie
Toscane Ponsi. The faucet
conceals within its streamlined
form ceramic disk cartridges,
which control water pressure
and flow, and flexible, water-
induction tubes which increase
water power.

Regia developed a resin
7   that they call frosted
glass, or "Vetro Ghiaccio,"
for brilliantly colored, semi-
transparent sinks in amber, blue,
apple green, and red in the
"Gloss" range by designer
Bruna Rapisarda.

7

bathrooms/sinks

These appropriately named "Ciottolo" sinks (*ciotto* means pebble in Italian) are produced by Sieger Design for Duravit. The 500mm (20in) diameter sink has smoothly rounded edges made of ceramic, which in one version (below) is presented in a white gloss finish atop a birch shelf, while in another (left) it is finished in platinum on rosewood.

8

The cylindrical "TwinSet" sink is smaller overall than the average round sink but has been cleverly designed by Giulio Cappellini and Ludovica and Roberto Palomba for Ceramica Flaminia to feature a bowl that is both deeper and wider than most. The "TwinSet" is available in two sizes, 420 or 525mm (16½ or 20½in), freestanding, wall-mounted, semi or fully inset into a work surface, or mounted on top of one. Pull-out linen hampers fit neatly underneath.

9

9

8

"Tiber" ceramic sink from the Spanish company Porcelanosa, whose line of tiles and bathroom fittings in graceful geometric forms combines materials from glass to stone and ceramic. Linear wenge wood shelves support the elongated oval sink.

10

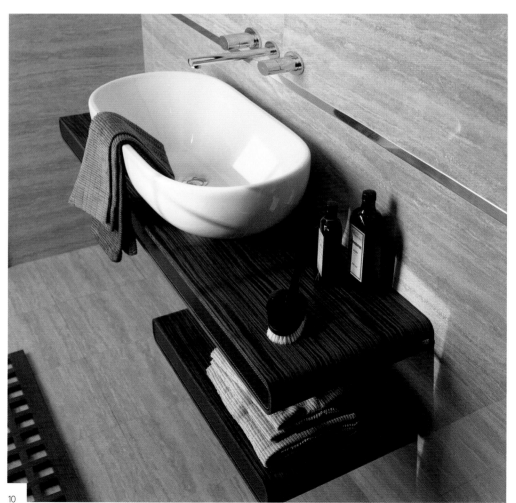

10

The "Torno" sink and
11 child-sized "Torno Mini,"
designed by Mick Brundle of
Arup Associates, are made from
durable Durat®. This solid
polyester-based material
containing recycled plastics is
itself recyclable. Used for
custom-made surfaces, or
freestanding design pieces such
as these sinks set atop steel
cylinders, the material is both
silky and warm to touch and
sufficiently resilient to be buffed
up with a slight sanding.

The organically shaped
12 "Istanbul" sink, like a drop
of water on a fluid stem,
is just one of more than 100
bathroom items designed
by Ross Lovegrove for the
international bathroom brand
VitrA. Inspired by the flow and
liquidity of water, his sculptural,
fluid shapes are slip-cast in
ceramic. Eau-de-nil wall tiles are
decorated with digital images
of water, and white floor tiles
have subtle wavy surfaces.
Showerhead fittings reveal
hexagonal patterns overhead,
inspired by Ottoman friezes.

12

11

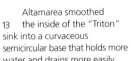

Altamarea smoothed
13 the inside of the "Triton"
sink into a curvaceous
semicircular base that holds more
water and drains more easily.

The "Cube" sink
14 is designed by Benedini
Associati for Agape to
accompany the high-sided
vertical lines of the "Woodline"
bathtub (picture 9 on page
154), inspired by Japanese
hot-tub bathing (or *onsen*).
The drainage is concealed
in the lower part of the tall,
slim, oak box.

13

14

15

Altamarea specializes in
15   bathroom furniture with
integral sinks. Its long "Reef" of
modular wall-mounted
cupboards with rounded
corners and sinks includes a
more compact version, this
"Atolla" sink, which neatly tops
the slender column of
cupboards.

The island of Samoa
16   contours the sink cut
out of a square ceramic slab
designed by Matteo Thun for
Catalano Ceramiche. Sink
shapes no longer have to mirror
the modular unit they are set
in, and depths can vary like
rockpools within a single sink.

16

17

"Lito I" is the first of
17   a collection of three
freestanding sinks designed by
the architect and urban planner
Angelo Mangiarotti for Agape.
All three lean away from the
wall, poised as if to spring. "Lito
I," shown here, is essentially an
inverted "L," the soft shape of
the hollowed-out sink carved
from a single block of white
Carrara marble. "Lito 2" is a
sloping block with curved
edges, while "Lito 3," more
angular than the other two,
has a sink that slopes at the
front. All three require wall-
mounted faucets.

Like a spring of clear water,
18   "Mylos," designed by
Marco Piva for Rapsel, is made in
Cristalplant, a pliant, compact,
nonporous material that lends
itself to these fluid, cloudlike
shapes in a way that would be
hard to achieve in stone. Faucets
are from the "Vola" series.

18

⬇ ALSO SEE

kitchens p.198

Inside the "Duomo" sink,
19   carved out of Blanco Almeria marble by the Spanish company Porcelanosa, the gentle incline from the front to the deeper trough at the back makes for better drainage and a more tactile approach.

Larger than most, this
21   600mm (24in) sink in anthracite ceramic holds a lot of water, hence its name, the "Acquagrande." Launched in 1997 as part of the Ceramica Flaminia "Work in Progress" collection, it was designed to seek challenges in mass-production sanitaryware in ceramic, a material recognized as being difficult to mold into rigorous geometric shapes.

19

20

21

22

The elliptical "Crucible"
20   sink in Kohler's "Vessels" collection tilts its face toward the user. The white sink is available with colored linings in blue, biscuit, lemon, and a watery green they call sea-grass. "Stillness" mixer faucets and the central "Falling Water" faucet are all by Kohler.

Duravit called its new
22   collection by Sieger Design the "Happy D" because its graphic shape is based on that letter of the alphabet, the angular corners of the "D" softened as shown. Pieces can stand alone or on furniture – this wall-mounted sink has a zebrano cupboard beneath it. The range includes shelves, cupboards, and cabinets on wheels.

bathrooms/showers

Showers no longer need to be taken in Tardis-like boxes or behind a shower curtain while standing in the bath. The contemporary shower is streamlined to be little more than a jet-powered column, a floor area hiding pumps and drainage systems, and the surrounding walls siliconed to rebuff even a drop of water. The creation of a wet zone – known as "tanking up" in plumbing terms – makes it possible to customize shower corners.

Large flat showerheads the size of watering-can spouts installed in an arch overhead or on the ceiling combine air-injection systems, which blend water and air, and vary the water jet from Scotch-mist softness to monsoon-like pounding rain. Handheld showerheads as slim as microphones on fixed or height-adjustable supports, or fitted to wall panels like the wave-shaped Teuco "Evolution," increase the volume of water. Size no longer indicates water jet power. Anti-limescale surfaces simplify maintenance, while more ergonomic and functional handles and mixers vary the water pressure.

Competition from these wet-zone fittings has made the conventional shower cabinet work harder. Wired for sound and light, shower cabinets can double as steam rooms and hydrotherapy centers. Strategically placed jets are positioned along the walls on the path of shiatsu massage. Changing lights in the cabin enhance mood according to chromatherapy principles and essential oils can be beamed into the cabin on an aromatherapy program electronically operated from a remote control.

The result is a new way to take a shower that transforms a healthy and hygienic habit into a moment of great wellbeing: showers are capable of reawakening not only the body but also the mind.

1   Roberto and Ludovica Palomba remodeled the Japanese tatami mat to make a nonslip shower base doubling as a floor, called "Tatami" for Ceramica Flaminia. A mounted showerhead, a handheld shower, and wet-room wall coverings transform the zone into a showering area behind a frosted-glass panel. The "Dip" sink is also made by Ceramica Flaminia.

2   Matki's "Eau Zone" 2m (6ft 7in) shower looks and feels like a spa wet room but avoids the complication and expense of tanking existing bathroom floors. The special shower floor slab is recessed into an existing floor, partially surrounded by high glass walls accessed at either end for a seamless transition from bathroom to shower zone. The chromed shower column, which supports the glass walls, fits onto the floor slab and holds the "Deluge" showerhead, a handset, and six separately controlled body-zone jets.

3   A wet room designed by Milledue behind a frosted-glass shower enclosure to showcase lacquerware. "Symi Y47" lacquered shelf system is designed by Lino Codato.

1

2

3

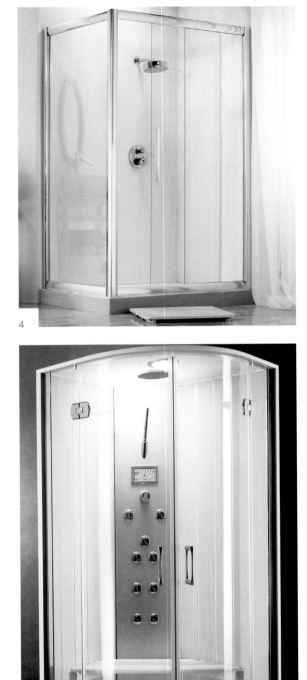

Installation of the "Fresca"
4   by Flair is made easier because profiles at either side of the panels are adjustable to allow for out-of-line walls. Sized for a larger bathroom, the slide-away door and side panel are power-shower proof to prevent any leaks under the doors.

An open entrance space
5   with curved glass walls wrapping around a teak foot board invites showering in "Logic Active" by Piet Billekens for Cesana. Electronic controls for water temperature, flow, and time can be set before showering, outside the wet area near the slatted towel-dry area. The integrated water-control column has a vigorous hydro-massage system.

Designed by Takahide Sano
6   for Titan, the "Genesi" shower cabinet, with bleached oak back and glass surrounds, turns into a Turkish steam bath. Chromatherapy, aromatherapy programs, and water-jet nozzles at the shiatsu points increase the relaxing and toning effects of showering.

The "Tara" shower fitting
7   by Sieger Design for Dornbracht turns an area anywhere in the house into a wet room, provided there is a pump, underfloor drainage, and a waterproofed wall. A fixed shower mixer combines with the handheld shower fitting for powerful water massage.

"Evolution," designed by
8   Lenci Design for Teuco, is a multifunctional shower cabinet with electronic controls to operate a chromatherapy program, hi-fi speakers, and an aromatic herb dispenser as well as water flow. It is fitted with a central showerhead, handheld shower, thermostatic mixer, and four jets of vertical massage, with a sauna steam inlet by Dornbracht.

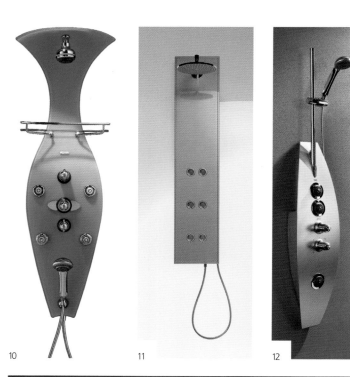

10   11   12

A shapely shower column
10 called "Evolution" by
Teuco is equipped with four
vertical massage jets, an
overhead flexible showerhead,
a handheld shower, and a
thermostatic mixer. Made
in semi-transparent, tinted
Duralight® or aluminum, the
panel curls away from the wall
just like a wave.

Fitted in the British Airways
11 shower rooms in passenger
lounges around the world, the
"Starck X" waterfall designed
by Philippe Starck for Axor
contains six body jets, an
overhead "Raindance"
showerhead, and a handheld
shower styled like a microphone
within a single slim panel.
Standing away from the wall to
hide the plumbing, the panel
has shelves at the sides where
controls are housed.

The elliptical Grohe
12 "AquaTower 2000"
shower looks like a sail under
wind and can turn an everyday
bathroom into a wellbeing
center. Twelve multi-jet side
showers hinging in a 30 degree
swivel-joint fluctuate between
soft and vigorous, keeping the
selected water temperature
steady. The smaller 1000 model
has a slightly curved vertical bar
like a wristband, which holds
the fitting to the wall.

9

The self-contained
9 "Solitude" shower by
Dornbracht contains every
fitting required for power
showering anywhere in the
house. All that is needed to set
up this easy-to-install shower
column is access to water and
electricity supplies.

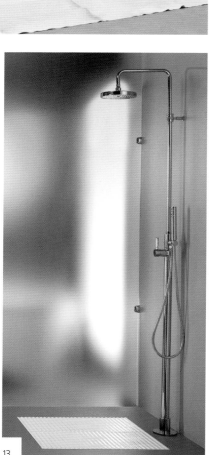

The floor-standing shower
13 mixer from the "Floor"
collection of freestanding mixers
for sink, bath, and shower made
by Rubinetterie Toscane Ponsi
throws out a volume
of water from its wide spout
despite its slender profile.

13

14

"Water Wall," designed by
14 Ludovica and Roberto
Palomba for the "Floyd" project
by Kos, has a wall-mounted
panel with mixer controls and a
seat behind the waterfall. The
broad showerhead, which sends
water splashing onto the wet
zone, is fitted with a valve to
regulate the jet.

Having produced the "Wet
15   Light" bathtub in a single
shell of polyethylene recycled
plastic, Wet introduced a
handheld shower that is flexible
and colorful, ergonomically
sound and functional. Available
in various colors, the hand
shower can be fixed on height-
adjustable supports.

Watering-can showerheads
16   permit multi-jets across
large surfaces. Rubinetterie
Toscane Ponsi fits its ones
with an air-injection system
to aerate the water as well
as an anti-limescale system.

15

16

17

The "Signorini" square
17   showerhead from
Colorwash is also designed as a
circle. The ceiling-mounted
Italian fitting has a self-cleaning
feature – each hole is fitted
with a rubber nozzle that
can be rubbed to break
down limescale.

18

A suspended showerhead
18   with wall-mounted, single-
control mixer from the "Blok"
collection designed by Carlo
Colombo for Antonio Lupi, who
also designs made-to-measure
shower cabins called "Slab" in
collaboration with Italian glass
and marble suppliers.

**"Everything we need to remain in good health is provided
in abundance by nature itself,"** wrote Sebastian Kneipp,
19th-century Bavarian author of *My Water Cure*. The
book is enjoying a revival in Germany, where Kneipp's
ideas on the efficacy of hydrotherapy to promote good
health are being exploited in shower-and-steam cabinets
by Duravit. Regular sessions of alternating hot and cold
showers apparently raise the activity of immunological
systems and thus strengthen the body's inherent defences
while improving circulation and relaxing muscles.

⬆ **DESIGN INFLUENCE**

19

Shower in water and light
19   beneath a downpour from
the Ondine "ELS Chrome." The
showerhead holds 270 no-clog
spray channels and fiber optic
lights illuminated by a special
halogen light source, which
delivers light in yellow, green,
and blue. Aerated jets of water,
which vary from mist to rain to
a downpour, are controlled by
an electronic touch panel.

Simplicity and strength in
22   the arching water carrier,
the "ShowerArc" by Pharo.
Fitted with the "Raindance"
showerhead, handheld
shower, and six thermostatically
controlled jets on either side
of the arc, it provides 3D
showering from every angle.

A favorite with architects
20   and interior designers, the
"Dada"showerhead and handheld shower with thermostat
from faucet manufacturer
Zazzeri, is easy to use and
powerful in action while clean
cut and minimal in line.

The "Café" showerhead by
21   Davide Mercatali for Fantini
can be wall-mounted on an
extended curved arm. Italian
company Fantini's collaboration
with architect Davide Mercatali
goes back to the 1980s when he
designed their classic bathtub
faucet and shower system,
"Calibro."

20

21

22

bathrooms/spas

As the world shrinks in the slipstream of airliners, travelers are introduced to different bathing rituals. Cedarwood tubs in Japan, Scandinavian dry-heat rock saunas, Turkish steam baths called "hammams" – an Arabic word meaning "spreader of warm" – and hydrotherapy baths and showers known to have therapeutic qualities spring up all over the world.

To experience any one of these spa treatments, it is no longer necessary to leave home: designers and bathroom manufacturers have scaled down spa equipment for home installation. Baths offer whirlpool massages, showers have body jets leveled at shiatsu points. It is even possible for the armchair traveler to enjoy a plunge pool fed by a wide-mouthed spout. Faucets are as important as bathtubs and showers in the home spa. Steam or sauna areas can be installed in a closet, the plumbing hidden beneath floors and wall panels to take away condensation as efficiently as the laundry clothes dryer.

International designer Ross Lovegrove, who immersed himself in Turkish hammams when he designed his "Istanbul" range for VitrA, observes that "Hammams are sanctuaries but that does not mean they have to be big, just well organized. Lighting is as important as fragrance for creating an atmosphere."

Light-changing chromatherapy sessions, along with aromatherapy systems and stereo sound, make bathing in sound and light as easy as tapping an electronic button on the remote control. Chromatherapy is just a smart term for color therapy, the beneficial effect that colored lights can stimulate, acting upon our emotions and enhancing our physical wellbeing.

1

Light falling through the Islamic screen complements the patterned overflow grille around the rim of the "Nara" infinity bathtub (1.8 x 1.4m/6ft x 4ft 7in). Fitted with a whirlpool and air-injection system to aerate the water, and the "Nara" waterfall spout, the bathtub was chosen by interior designer Ann Boyd for the flagship store of Bathrooms International in London.

2   An illuminated waterfall running the entire length on one side, and fitted with an air-injection system, fills "Seaside," a sizeable tub (2.15 x 2m/7ft x 6ft 7in) by Talocci Design for Teuco. There is a raised and cushioned zone for soaking around the plunge pool encircled by a beam of light. Faucets as well as electronic controls are hidden.

3   With its new flat, wide spout, the waterfall faucet in the "MEM" collection by Sieger Design for Dornbracht adds an elementary aspect to faucet fittings. Its minimalist design conceals high-performance technology that causes water to surge, just as in a spring, without an aerator. It creates a controlled waterfall, as opposed to a jet or a trickle.

2

3

4

Every color in the spectrum is assigned particular curative properties in the Duravit multifunctional shower by Jochen Schmiddem. Fitted with showers and body jets, steam and aromatherapy, speakers, and LED lights on an electronic chromatherapy program, it changes color to stimulate wellbeing. Green light brings equilibrium, red increases circulation and physical energy, orange stimulates enthusiasm and helps to combat SAD syndrome, while blue calms as it lowers blood pressure.

5 Made from glass and aluminum rather than acrylic, the Pharo "Shower Temple" by Phoenix Design will accommodate one person or two and fits into a corner. It offers steam, chromatherapy, and aromatherapy, and is piped for sound.

7 Modeled on Finnish saunas, the "Logica" sauna combined with a shower cubicle, designed by Giovanna Talocci and made by Effegibi for home installation, fits into a space of 2.3 x 2.3 x 2m (7ft 6in x 7ft 6in x 6ft 7in). Inside the sauna are dry heat and ice-cold water, music, and color therapy. Outside there are controls and a place to hang bathrobes behind a door, which, when opened, creates a screen to isolate the adjoining shower.

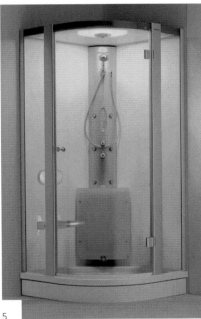

5

7

6 "Hammam" is a steam bath without condensation or evaporation problems especially designed for private houses by Giovanna Talocci with Effegibi. Fitted into masonry walls, steam generators on different power levels are hidden behind tiled panels, with wooden or leather seats, tables, tubs, and ladles.

6

8 "Kosmic" from Kos is a revolutionary steam-and-shower cabin, available as a corner installation and fitted with one or two seats. It has color therapy with fiber optic lights, aromatherapy, steam, and both body and massage jets.

9 "Steam'In Solo," made from acrylic reinforced with polyester and glass fiber by Villeroy & Boch, fits into a corner or an alcove. Three steam cabins in the collection come in three sizes: Solo, Duo, and Family. Behind the safety-glass door is seating, lighting, and aromatherapy, and a handheld shower on a sliding rod to vary spray intensity.

8

9

10   "Kaos" freestanding whirlpool bath from Kos is lit by LEDs in eight mood-enhancing colors and sits on a metal frame so that the bathtub appears to be suspended in air. Its unique internal shape is designed to be more comfortable for the bather.

11   Three bathtubs from Frog Design for Teuco – oval, rectangular, and corner – all use "Hydrosonic," the only hydromassage with ultrasound in the world, patented by Teuco to provide a subcutaneous micro-massage that improves skin elasticity and removes skin blemishes. In this freestanding oval "Noovalis" tub, separate ultrasound and whirlpool jet bosses are operated by a remote control linked to a screen built into the contour of the tub below the "Flow" faucets. Two back and headrests provide bathers with soft support.

12   Kaldewei makes the enamels that line its steel bathtubs to a secret recipe. This "Centro Duo" whirlpool tub operates on a turbine system patented worldwide (*see* page 145). Most whirlpool baths sound as though a lawnmower has been switched on as water is pumped noisily through pipes connected to jets. This silent system has a mini turbine within each jet that sucks in water and jets it out.

Defined by Kohler, chromatherapy colored light washing over the bather can stimulate, calm, or harmonize energies, depending on the color spectrum:
Red: courageous/energizing
Orange: joyful/spontaneous
Yellow: hopeful/illuminating
Green: harmonious/balancing
Blue: calming
Indigo: serene/peaceful
Violet: inspiring/creative
White light is for purification, like the Zen white flash.

↑   **DESIGN INFLUENCE**

Pharo's "Whirlpool 375" by Phoenix Product Design is a streamlined, elliptical, two-seater tub with soft waterproof headrests at either end and a full whirlpool system built into the contours. It can be either freestanding or positioned against the wall (shown), where it is fitted with wall-mounted Hansgrohe "Axor Starck" bathtub mixer faucets.

13

The "Alpha" bathtub in the "Morphosis" series designed by Pininfarina for Jacuzzi® gives the bather two distinct hydromassages from the classic Jacuzzi® jets and penetrating back massage with extra rotating micro-jets. Cromodream® technology glows within the arches of the bathtub canopy and beneath the water in five different colors. A bathtubside mounting for the remote control recharges the lithium battery by induction.

14

14

The 200 series from Pharo's "WellBeing" range are in the lower price bracket. The "Whirlpool 290" corner bathtub has a cloud-shaped, curvaceous interior within the wedge shape. An acrylic panel across the front further enhances its fluid lines.

15

"La Scala" plasma screen whirlpool bath from Jacuzzi® was launched in 2004 at the Kitchen and Bathroom Fair in Florida in limited edition for the American market – the TV operates on the PAL system. It features a 1.07m (42in) high-definition plasma monitor and a state-of-the-art surround-sound system, a floating keyboard that gives access to the internet, and a waterproof remote control that allows video monitoring of the home security system.

16

15

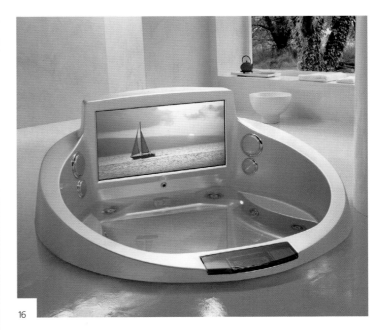

16

↓ **ALSO SEE**

walls and ceilings p.32
flooring p.57

bathrooms/faucets

Clean water is a universal right, yet 20 per cent of the world's population consumes 88 per cent of available water. By 2020 there could be 3 billion people without access to drinking water. The bathroom industry, and faucet manufacturers in particular, seek to respond to this problem with new designs to control water without waste. Not all are beautiful. Some, such as the "Grippa" design by Isis – chosen by the Design Council as one of the best British designs for the 21st century – are hidden underground. "Grippa" stops water mains springing a leak with a plastic pipeline adaptor in 3 sizes to link all households to the water mains supply. Variations in mains water connections in Britain mean that plumbers have to carry 20 different fittings.

Good design combined with intelligent technology produces efficient faucets. Manufacturer Hansgrohe's guidelines are "avoiding, reducing, recovering."

Of course, the job of a faucet is to emit water, but what kind of water and how much of it? Modern faucets are fitted with filters to stop the build up of limescale, and ceramic disk cartridges must meet industry regulations. Grohe's dual-flush "Beta" system allows the toilet to be flushed with two different volumes of water. Under-the-counter valves make it possible to redesign faucets purely to convey water, rather than to mix hot and cold water from separate pipes within the faucet. Hidden sensors activate water at the shake of a hand. Peter Jamieson's "Waterblade" is a bathroom shelf with water falling from its slim profile. The "Isy*" faucet by Matteo Thun for Rapsel conceals all the technical parts within a slender faucet, while Antonio Citterio's new faucet for Axor heralds the style of a tube no longer based on a round or oval section but rectangular, obtained with a sophisticated welding system that reduces the width of the faucet to become very flat.

1

The "Hansa Murano" sink
1   mixer faucet from a range designed by Bruno Sacco and Reinhard Zetsche for German manufacturer Hansa allows water to flow freely from the tilted Murano glass disk into the sink.

A faucet for the GameBoy/
2   Playstation joystick generation, the "Hovo" by Rubinetterie Toscane Ponsi loses any minimalist lines to balloon out and sport colorful operating levers.

"Hey Joe!," designed by
3   Maurizio Duranti for IB Rubinetterie, is a range of faucet fixings comprising 20 different items. A traditional cartridge system is used while the body is pressure die-cast. As well as the sink mixer on which the series is based, there is a flat, wall-mounted shower unit hinged to angle the water jet, completed by a manual head.

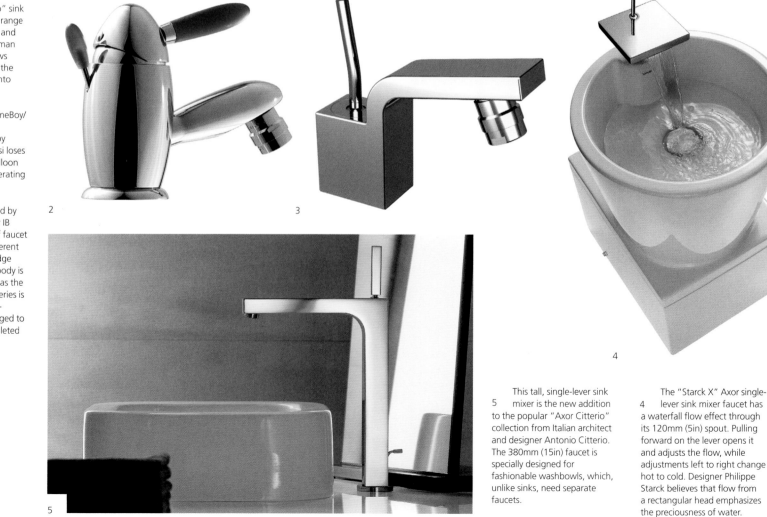

2

3

4

5

This tall, single-lever sink
5   mixer is the new addition to the popular "Axor Citterio" collection from Italian architect and designer Antonio Citterio. The 380mm (15in) faucet is specially designed for fashionable washbowls, which, unlike sinks, need separate faucets.

The "Starck X" Axor single-
4   lever sink mixer faucet has a waterfall flow effect through its 120mm (5in) spout. Pulling forward on the lever opens it and adjusts the flow, while adjustments left to right change hot to cold. Designer Philippe Starck believes that flow from a rectangular head emphasizes the preciousness of water.

The freestanding bathtub
6   faucet "Mem" by Sieger
Design for Dornbracht has a
wide, flat spout in chrome or
matt platinum. Panel controls
and the handheld shower, for
rinsing in the bath, are both
wall-mounted.

Hailed by its manufacturer,
7   Zucchetti, as a "modular
water management system,"
the "Isy*" system by Matteo
Thun revolutionized the
traditional faucet by making it
interchangeable. The single
plumbing mechanism is the
base for fitting on spouts and
handles of different sizes and
shapes. Names identify them
according to their function.
"Isystick" (top) is a sink mixer
faucet operated with a single

lever, while "Isyarc" (bottom)
is the floor-standing bathtub
faucet with wall-mounted disk
control. "Isyfresh" has an
elliptical section spout for
cascading water. All faucets
in the series are fitted with
Carbonplus treatment to prevent
the build-up of limescale.

"Vega," from the "Floor"
8   collection of floor-standing
mixers for sinks, bathtubs, and
showers by Rubinetterie Toscane
Ponsi, fills the Andrée Putman
bathtub for Hoesch, seen
without its brushed-steel
cladding to reveal its curvaceous
lines. Meticulous design applied
to the organization of space
distinguishes the "Floor"
collection, which comprises
four product ranges – "Vega,"

"Eco," "Saturno," and
"Mercurio." Mixers are made in
solid brass with chrome or nickel
finish, equipped with ceramic
disk cartridges, flexible water
induction tubes, and kits with
stainless-steel anchorings.
Ceramic cartridges hold the
temperature reliably and are a
neat installation replacement
for old-fashioned washers.

6

7

8

One of the Millennium Development Goals
agreed by all UN governments is to halve
the proportion of people who are without
access to safe water and sanitation.
According to the charity WaterAid, it
would cost an estimated extra £10 billion
($16 billion) each year to achieve this.
US and European households spend
more than this annually on pet food.

DESIGN INFLUENCE

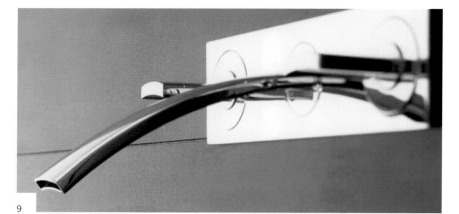

9

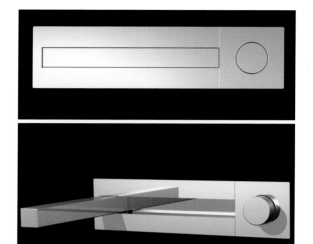

The amazing pack-flat
10   faucet from the Savil
Group in collaboration with
Giordan & Florian Design, who
patented the design and
launched it at the Milan
Furniture Fair in 2006, is so
discreet it is possible to mistake
it for a letterbox flap (top). Its
push-button controls make the
faucet swivel out and water
flow (below).

10

The elegant "Moon" rising
9   above the sink or bathtub
projects from its wall-mounted
metallic control panel. Designed
by Luca Ceri for Rubinetterie
Zazzeri, it features a convex
rectangular cross-section in
three different versions: the wall
mixer shown has three holes
and a single control mixer.

Antonio Citterio specified
11   his "Axor Citterio" sink
mixer faucets with cross fittings
by Hansgrohe in the Hotel
Bulgari in Milan. In this hotel,
created for the Italian jewelry
designer, every detail is like
a jewel, exquisitely set, even
the most prosaic objects such
as bathroom faucets.

11

The forerunner of all the
12   faucets that seek to
replicate a stream of water in
fluid styling. Danish designer
Arne Jacobsen created this
faucet, which is much loved by
architects around the world, in
the mid 20th century. The
stainless-steel circular sink and
wall-mounted faucet are both
made by Vola.

12

"Lulu" faucets by Sieger
13   Design for Dornbracht
are "a homage to Lulu de la
Falaise," the muse of Yves
Saint Laurent. She designed
accessories and jewelry for
30 years. The single-lever sink
mixer without pop-up waste
is operated by pulling
the lever forward to start then
left to right for hot and cold.   13

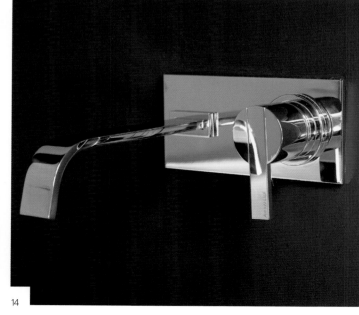

14

Slim, flat, and wide, the
14   "Blok Light" faucet by
Carlo Colombo for Antonio Lupi
is a refined version of the "Blok"
faucet with its spherical base.

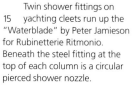

Twin shower fittings on
15 yachting cleets run up the
"Waterblade" by Peter Jamieson
for Rubinetterie Ritmonio.
Beneath the steel fitting at the
top of each column is a circular
pierced shower nozzle.

The wide, flat shape of the
16 spout means that the water
outlet is rectangular rather than
round, which creates a waterfall.
The "Aguablu" by Barbara
Sordina of Studio Marianelli for
Rubinetterie Zucchetti is boldly
geometric with a jet flow that
recalls water in its natural state.

15

"Love Me" unashamedly
17 seeks to be liked. IB
Rubinetterie cut away the
enclosure on the spout like a
quill pen so that water can be
seen and heard flowing down
the wide channel.

17

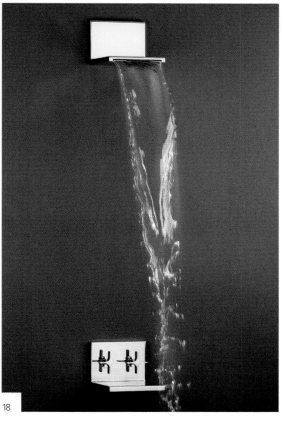

18

16

Cascading water from the
18 "Waterblade" by Peter
Jamieson for Rubinetterie
Ritmonio causes a free-fall of
water with all the pleasurable
sounds of flowing water
splashing into a vessel.

Water flowing gently from
19 the spout of the ceramic
"Vas" single-lever sink mixer,
part of Kohler's "Artist
Editions," is pleasing to the
ear and eye. Inspired by the
apothecary's pestle and mortar,
the "Bol" ceramic sink mixer
has a classical look, water filling
the entire body of the faucet.

The Grohe faucet "F1" by
20 FA Porsche Design is
controlled by dual levers at the
base, operated individually or in
combination to give the user full
control over water flow. Two
individually controlled water
channels are accommodated
within a single cartridge. The
faucet is finished in award-
winning ALU-XT to give a silky
aluminum look that is resistant to
damage, corrosion, and abrasion.

The curvaceous slimline
21 "Oceania" faucet by
Bathrooms International hides
a powerful below-sightline
jet system to create a forceful
flow of water.

ALSO SEE
kitchens pp.185, 201

19

20

21

bathrooms/furniture and furnishings

The idea of the bathroom as a separate, often small, cell in the house has changed – bathrooms have become much less self-conscious, more integrated, open spaces. Sleeping, working, showering, and bathing space may all be shared, and the areas where such activities take place are subject to gradual, but continual, change. The seamless transition from kitchen to living room found in many contemporary homes is now being replicated in the loosening of the boundary between the bathroom and the bedroom. Only the toilet now stands alone.

The bathroom is a place that now, more than ever, has to meet a range of different needs, a space that must adapt to suit the people who use it. Satisfying these changing requirements calls for a range of furniture. Contemporary designers see bathroom furniture no longer as simply a support for sinks or bathtubs or somewhere to stack the towels, but as a complete project. Cabinets and drawers fitted with mirrors on the doors and side lighting are more like living-room furniture than bathroom fixtures. Small, touch-free sensors take the place of a light switch. Inside drawers, sockets offer space for hairdryers.

New materials, such as waterproofed LG HI-MACS, which effortlessly glue sections together in long spans, have revolutionized bathroom furniture design. A slab stretching 3m begins at one end with a wall-height niche for a mirror and a sink below, then runs on as a dado-height shelf before plunging down into a hollowed-out bathtub in a new all-in-one bathroom fitting by Tretzo (*see* page 147).

1

The "Odue" bathtub
1 collection by Giorgio Gurioli and Marco Maggioni for Oasis. Here "Drops" are the wall-mounted mirrors and cupboards between ceiling and floor, and "Stylla" is the starfish-shaped, wall-mounted rack made of high-density polyurethane enameled in high gloss.

"Thais" is a modular
2 system by Altamarea of cupboard and shelf units sized between 350mm (14in) and 650mm (26in), with a variety of worktops and doors in Corian®, glass, marble, and wood. Purchasers can compose their own layout by adding modular units in different materials within the framework of the room.

Red roses are digitally
3 imaged onto a cabinet by Branchetti from Colorwash. Any digital image, picture, or pattern can be silkscreened onto bathroom cabinetry; roses do not have to be red, they can color-match tiles. The faucet, with a wide waterfall spout, is the wall-mounted "LoveMe" made by IB Rubinetterie.

With its modular "40"
4 system of multipurpose hanging units, Falper reinvented the bookcase as bathroom shelving. The "Wall System" shelves in dark or light wood, waterproof sealed, match suspended drawer and cupboard units with marble or glass tops, and can be accessorized with mobile units on castors, custom-made mirrors, and tilting wall and ceiling lights.

2

3

4

5

6

The "B:room" by Kei-en
5   Studio for Listone
Giordano avoids the word
bathroom because, say its
creators, it is designed as "a
haven, a place to relax, read and
regenerate." It "focuses on a
room that had been side-lined"
with raised levels and volumes
across horizontal and vertical
surfaces on a modular system
for walls, floors, and furniture,
including tables, shelves,
benches, and storage systems.

The "Organizer" shelves
6   that are open or concealed
behind sliding doors are by
young Spanish company Cosmic
and are part of the "Stock"
series that solves storage
problems in the bathroom. The
crimson wall-hung sink called
"Simplex" is in polypropylene.
Hidden within it are the water
inlet, outer pipes, and fixings.

7

8

Lacquer, wood, and steel
9   wall-hung shelves by Axia
with an enameled sink on a
slimline table. The look is
workmanlike, down to the filing
cabinet on wheels beneath the
work table, which doubles as
linen box.

▼ **ALSO SEE**

walls and ceilings p.36
flooring p.63

9

Designer Lino Codato for
7   Milledue positions his
"Kubik" system around the
basin, where most storage is
needed. Cupboards, drawers,
and back-lit shelves on a flexible
modular system allow many
different permutations across a
line-up of basic units in a variety
of finishes, from light, natural
oak or dark wenge wood to
colored oak and lacquer
finishes, as shown here.

An ingenious space-saving
8   piece by Merati. The
"Risma" wall-hung shelving
system, with rounded corners to
square recesses, is sometimes
hollowed out almost to the
façade to leave a towel rail,
sometimes left extended to
the wall as a framed shelf.

bathrooms/furniture and furnishings

Magicians used to perplex
11   their audiences by claiming
their illusions were all done with
smoke and mirrors. There is no
smoke here, but from a distance
the wall-mounted, mirrored
"Transimage" cabinet by Villeroy
& Boch allows a glimpse of
what is within. As the mirror
is approached, a concealed
detector switches off the interior
light that permits this view and
activates the mirror lighting.
As if by magic, the contents
of the cabinet vanish and the
previously transparent mirror
shows only an image of the
person gazing into it.

"Slim" is the name of
12   Agape's large, tall mirror –
1 x 2m (3ft 3in x 6ft 7in) – with a
slim profile framed in natural or
wenge-stained oak. It can be
wall-mounted horizontally or
vertically or, as here – where it
reflects Agape's "026" container
with mirrored door – propped
casually against the wall.

The singularly uncommon,
14   grand-scale "Common 01"
oak towel rail leans against the
wall like a ladder. It is part of the
"New Places" collection, a joint
venture by designer fittings and
accessories manufacturer
Dornbracht, the design studio
E15, and Alape, which makes
basins and washstands.

Fitted or freestanding
10   bathroom furniture from
Kohler tidies up the bathroom.
The "Purist" wall-mounted
cabinet houses, within natural
lavastone, the "Purist"
washbasin. The minimalist lines
are emphasized by the use of
black walnut.

"Aquavision" from CP Hart
13   is just what its name
promises, a waterproofed TV, in
recognition of the fact that
people may want to check share
prices, watch breakfast TV, or
read Teletext before leaving
home in the morning,
showered, shaved or made-up,
and ready to greet the day.

15

16

Inspired by the asymmetric
15 patterns formed by liquid
and the symmetrical shapes of
solid forms, "Espace" by Vitra
pools water in an elliptical
basin jutting out beyond the
rectangular drawer unit that
supports it. Sink units can
be fitted with a refrigerator –
the first of its kind for the
bathroom. The mirror unit
has integral touch-free lights
that turn on by simply passing
a hand over a sensor. Corner
and off-set basins help free
floorspace.

American architect Robert
16 Stern called his collection
of fluted bathroom accessories
for Valli & Valli "Doria" in
homage to the Greek Doric
orders, in which the use of
decoration emphasizes rather
than masks the structure, just
as the wreath-like lozenges on
his collection support the rails
and shelves.

17

Celebrated architects and
17 designers invited by Valli &
Valli to create a bathroom
accessory collection include
Andrée Putman, whose
"Punctuation" series is a
witty reference to the spatial
punctuation that small but
vital details contribute to
the scheme. Her design is
distinguished by the square
shape of the hook combined
with the rounded lines of the
accessories and by the union
between the chrome-plated
brass and the opaque satin
crystal glass.

Boffi 's modular glass cube
18 system for storage is seen
here stacked as long, thin, twin
glass towers. Two cubes side by
side, wall-mounted horizontally
above the washbasin, match
the dimensions of Boffi's mirror.

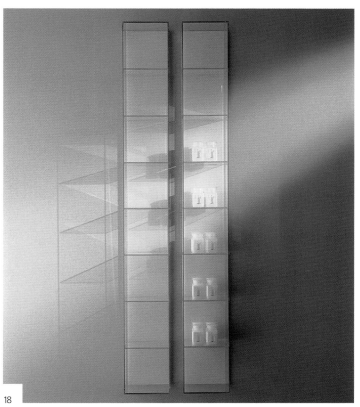

18

kitchens

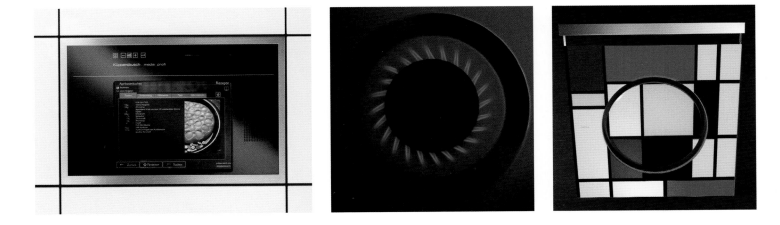

ABOVE LEFT There are more than 2,500 recipes on the "Media Profi" built-in screen by Küppersbusch which also reveals the contents of the fridge freezer and their best-before dates. The touch screen offers access to the internet, digital TV, CD, and DVD functions.

ABOVE CENTER Oblique gas flames on the Miele stove evenly and more efficiently distribute heat across pots and pans.

ABOVE RIGHT Silk-screen painted "Om" glass range hood has an almost vertical surface by Lorenzo Lispi, patented by Elica, who showcase it with a Mondrian.

LEFT Architectonic "Z" by Zaha Hadid, the international prize-winning architect, is made in DuPont Corian® by Ernestomeda. Appliances built into two elemental freestanding units which represent fire (cooking) and water (everything for food preparation including the kitchen sink). The workstation doubles as a multimedia center with a screen for TV and internet.

Everyone has their own idea of the perfect kitchen. It could be cluttered with trestle tables and everything but the sink hung from the rafters, with herbs growing indoors, like the busy, open cooks' kitchen designed for Dornbracht by Mike Meire (*see* page 184). Or maybe your style is more the American colonial kitchen by style guru Martha Stewart that the *Financial Times* described as "stylistically a blur of Norman Rockwell Americana refashioned for the *Desperate Housewives* generation" (*see* page 182).

The busy professional living alone in an inner-city apartment maybe wants a sushi bar, a microwave or gas-powered stove, coffee machine for Starbucks at home, and an under-counter wine cooler (*see* page 202). The family in the country house with a kitchen garden needs a fridge freezer, a deep double sink, and a contemporary cooking range that heats the flag-stoned floor. Keen cooks need Vario appliances by Gaggenau for global cuisine with a deep-fat fryer (for tempura, not chips), steamer, griddle, stove for a wok, and a tepanyaki grill. Call them kitchens with attitude, but there is one tailor-made for you at mass-produced prices. Custom-built kitchens are

1

2

First of four kitchens from the "LaCucina Alessi" collection by Alessandro Mendini, each with its own personality and materials. All four designs, "Agreste," "Sinuosa," "Geometrica," and "Trasparente" have column storage behind decorative doors and a work island with differently shaped and sized gas or ceramic cooking burners, sinks by Foster, faucets by Oras, and furniture by Valcucine. "Agreste" has a stainless-steel breakfast counter protected by a range hood of printed glass and steel with adjustable lighting. Leaf-shaped inlays decorate the ebonized wooden sliding doors on the four storage units.

2 The semi-transparent "Trasparente" kitchen has lilac countertops, and see-through doors and drawers with in-built lighting. The sink can be either "Ekotek" synthetic resin or stainless steel with steel or cast-iron grid gas stoves.

3 Graphs in two shades of green film create peaks and troughs across drawer fronts and glass doors on "Geometrica," which appears to float between cylindrical stainless steel drawer units. Along the wall, studded stainless-steel units conceal refrigerators and ovens.

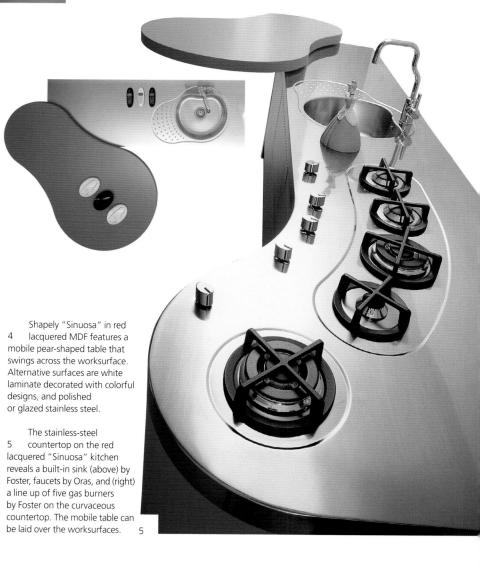

4 Shapely "Sinuosa" in red lacquered MDF features a mobile pear-shaped table that swings across the worksurface. Alternative surfaces are white laminate decorated with colorful designs, and polished or glazed stainless steel.

5 The stainless-steel countertop on the red lacquered "Sinuosa" kitchen reveals a built-in sink (above) by Foster, faucets by Oras, and (right) a line up of five gas burners by Foster on the curvaceous countertop. The mobile table can be laid over the worksurfaces.

5

so last century, whereas customizing your kitchen is a possibility in the 21st century.

Perhaps it is an architectonic piece designed like a mobile phone to hold many functions in a single shapely freestanding piece such as the "Z," made in a run of Corian®. The "Z" kitchen by Zaha Hadid lands very lightly upon its blades in any space big enough to take it.

When two Pritzker Prize-winning international architects, Zaha Hadid and Norman Foster, design kitchens for mass production, it shows the importance of the kitchen at the heart of the home.

"In the kitchen," Foster explains, "we not only prepare and consume food. We watch television, use computers, read, spend free time, enjoy the company of family and friends. Kitchens need to be capable of interpreting these new habits, also through the discreet use of technology, absolutely without special effects." His kitchen design for Dada, "Place," vertically moves the counter level by remote control, making it possible to respond to all those different needs. First installed at the Albion Riverside in London, the residential complex on the Thames designed by Foster and Partners for which Dada provided all the kitchens, "Place" is now in apartments designed by the architect all over the world.

This design response to individual and changing needs drives the design of the kitchen, the last room to break out of standardized components. Kitchen units and appliances stood still in a time warp, either anchored on plinths or tied by inflexible electricity flexes to the wall socket. Now they move out into the house with built-in appliances: freestanding fridges you can walk around, stoves and the sink in a bubble or a box, ovens with built-in elevators to transport food, and ventilation hoods that double as works of art or light shades take their place in the living room. Cooks in the Jamie Oliver generation entertain friends while cooking, so Gaggenau lined up its appliances on a counter with a backsplash that powers an unobtrusive ventilation system (see page 186) low enough to talk across. And they are talking points, all these innovative designs.

BELOW LEFT At last, a world first, the refrigerator that does not have to keep its back to the wall to hide unsightly ducting, grilles and wiring. Architect Renzo Piano's refrigerator for Smeg, the "FPD34," looks as good from behind as it does from the front. This freestanding refrigerator can take center stage in an open-plan kitchen.

BELOW RIGHT "coolMedia" stainless-steel and aluminum fridge freezer by Siemens integrates a flat-screen swivel TV with Nicam stereo sound, fasttext, a video games console, DVD, VCR, and camcorder. Inside, digital sensors control temperatures recorded on an LCD display. Independent cooling systems mean that the refrigerator can shut down, just leaving the freezer on when you are on holiday.

RIGHT Glass drawers support thick countertops that cantilever into tabletops in a balancing act for Poggenpohl by Spanish architect, Jorge Pensi. His "PlusModo" kitchen stretches the horizontal line for base units and wall-mounted cupboards. Large pull-out wooden sliding drawers without handles like trays are concealed beneath extra thick worksurfaces.

BELOW RIGHT Everything in this American classic colonial-style "Katonah" kitchen, down to the speckled eggs on the countertop that inspired the paint color, is from Martha Stewart, the best known brand in the USA for home furnishing. She designed new houses, inside and out, for a KB Homes development in North Carolina, with more to follow in Atlanta, Houston, and LA.

As appliances get smarter, kitchen furniture is simplified to bring back the table. Not to be confused with the workstation, Piero Lissoni's new kitchen for Boffi is almost just that: a single table with everything built into its clean, orderly lines, and all the wiring needed to power an international office while cooking global cuisine. Architect Andrea Branzi designed a room for the interior design show *Abitare Il Tempo* in Verona in 1997 that consisted of just one big table which was kitchen, office, and reading space. As he observed, "We move toward fluid functions, a space in which several shapes and possibilities exist. Making the most of rituals and the cultural value of food and diet are what matter most."

This branding of kitchens by designers with celebrity status has freed the kitchen from a line-up of expensively crafted cabinetry. Kitchens are morphing from the stolid line-up of cabinets and appliances. The first sign was when they were taken down off the walls and pulled away from them. Freestanding kitchens – or ones that projected slightly into the room like a breakfast bar – were described as islands and peninsula kitchens. Now the kitchen is more of an archipelago, with individual pieces clustered in the space available.

Architectural magazine *Domus* hypothesizes that "the more you can walk around it, the less kitchen-like it is." Even the refrigerator has a personality with retro-styling and assertive colors from Smeg, or the watch-me "Cool Media" of Siemens with a swiveling TV to track the cook's movements on its impressive front.

Cable management is becoming as important as it is in an office, which is one of the reasons that Bulthaup braces load-bearing walls for the "b3" kitchen with steel supports, and then panels them. Such tactics would be extreme were it not for its other function, to free floorspace by hanging everything in the kitchen on the wall, including a fully loaded, extra outsized stainless-steel American fridge freezer.

New materials have influenced expressive kitchens and their appliances. Honeycombed aluminum used for aircraft cabin floors makes its way into kitchens by

LEFT Close encounters with the "Sheer®" kitchen by Drag Design for Gatto Cucine puts a spin on workstations. At the touch of a button, the transparent meta-acrylic range hood rises to reveal a cooking and food preparation center in a carbon fiber bubble. Built into its girth of 1.5m (5ft) on the Corian® countertop are a double sink, stove, lava stone griddle, and wine cooler

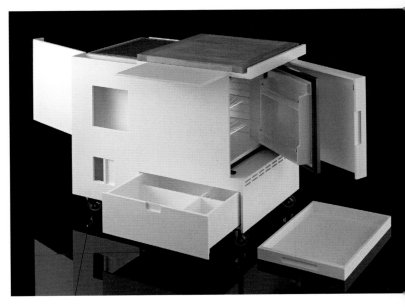

LEFT Forget simple, inflexible, closed kitchen modules. World renowned architect Norman Foster personalizes everyday space with his dynamic "Place" kitchen for Dada. Rounded table counters move up or down by remote control to adjust the height for the task in hand, whether you are eating, sitting down, or preparing food.

ABOVE Meals on wheels first rolled into kitchen design in 1963 when Joe Colombo launched "Machines for Living." In 2006 Boffi relaunched his innovative "Mini Kitchen" in a cart. Inside are a ceramic glass stove, mini refrigerator, drawers, sockets for electrical appliances, a solid teak cutting board, and pull-out countertop.

Snaidero that soar and plunge in shapely ways, more like aircraft wings than conventional units. Design duo Seymour Powell looked to the aeronautical industry to line their ovens for Mercury in a silicon from a meteorite that fell in Arizona 50,000 years ago, bonded at high temperatures to make Thermastone. Solid high-gloss acrylic Parapan® on vertical surfaces allows doors to contour around a kitchen. Corian® and LG HI-MACS are synthetics that can be pre-formed and molded to make almost any shape that a designer can dream up.

With changing shapes and an increasingly important role, the footprint of the kitchen is changing. Kitchens were traditionally planned around the sources of water and electricity, with the sink and dishwasher on the outer walls for drainage, and the two areas for food preparation and cooking in a triangle around it. Ikea describes this working triangle of activity as "pure ergonomics, really just a long word to explain a simple concept – don't make things more difficult than they need to be." But the designer of the "K12" for Boffi, architect Norbert Wangen, whose kitchen in a box only hints at your needs as it furnishes any space, dismisses such observations about ergonomics in today's world as: "Too static. Ergonomics assumes you don't move at all but spend 100 years in the same position… Chopping at the countertop, washing up, putting something in the oven. Ergonomic chairs are weird. Better by far to have a chair that ejects you. Better for your health, for your back. We are on the move all the time even when we're asleep. The sleeper turns on average 20 times a night. There is no optimum position. So let's build in change."

Change is certainly what kitchens are capable of doing. Nothing static: everything capable of dual function of movement. Now it is possible to cook in a bubble with the "Sheer®" by Gatto Cucine. Or in a cart like the one designed in 1963 by Joe Colombo. Boffi has brought this back into production, and updated it with a ceramic induction stove element that only heats up when a ferrous metal on the base of the cooking vessel touches the magnetic field.

Built-in electronic controls mean that smart kitchens can be set to open the garage doors for your arrival, having de-activated the burglar alarm and put the pre-set oven on to cook a meal left inside it. Refrigerators on the drawing board have a webcam inside so that you can sit at your desk in the office and check whether you need to buy milk or butter on the way home. Designers are creating big, powerful products with all kinds of options that recognize that people entertain at home and need more home help.

Tables that cook? Dishwashers without water? Stacking box refrigerators? Just some ideas from leading industrial design students around the world for the shape of things to come by 2015 if Electrolux patents them. Electrolux sponsors the DesignLab to prototype exciting new ideas for cooking, laundry, refrigeration, and dishwashing. Predictions are based upon space shrinking, especially in cities, and a universal theme among students was preserving the environment. Big

ABOVE As homespun as the Windsor chair and trestle table, with herbs in the sink, pots and utensils strung up overhead, this kitchen was installed in "The Farm Project" by Neo Noto studio artist Mike Meire. It was used to launch kitchen faucets by Dornbracht, the single-lever sink mixer "Tara Classic Profile," and the "Tara Classic" pillar faucet, by Sieger Design.

RIGHT A kitchen in a cupboard: you can put a kitchen in the smallest space of 1.4m (4ft 7in) in width, by using Ikea's "Värde." The mini kitchen is complete with two-ring ceramic stove, refrigerator, sink with mixer faucet, strainer and two fixed shelves, two adjustable shelves, spice rack, suspension rails with hooks, and a blackboard.

BELOW RIGHT Exuberant curves and ballooning shapes on faucets with ellipsoid handles in Michael Graves' mass-production line for Delta Faucet. Celebrated architect Michael Graves crowned Disney hotels with giant swans and dolphins, yet everyday household objects still get his attention.

BELOW LEFT Faucets by Stefano Giovannoni for the "La Cucina Alessi" collection made by Oras. Two ceramic disc handles in the standard version, a dishwasher valve in the special one, and an option to install an electronic faucet automatically dispensing hot water when a hand is placed near a photocell make it versatile.

consumers of power and emitting CFCs, appliances of the future have to be modular, adaptable, flexible, compact, and sustainable.

As children playing with a microscope in Africa know, it is possible to use the sun's ray angled through glass to start a fire. Now it becomes a cooking source: "CooKit" is a solar stove developed in many variations, initially in France, for which construction drawings can be downloaded from the internet. Cardboard, aluminum foil, a plastic bag, and a black pot are the only things needed for temperatures up to 82–121°C (180–250°F).

A refrigerator from Solatron Technologies in California runs on solar power compressor condensers that use less energy than a car headlight. Korean designer Hae-jin-Kim's "Hot Fridge" uses the hot air released by a refrigerator to recirculate it within. Energy-efficient American "Sub Zero" fridges use less energy than a 100W light bulb. Look for the A + or A++ rating when buying any appliance: it means it has passed the European energy efficiency test.

kitchens/into the living room

Before space became a luxury, kitchens occupied their own room, or rooms. When built-in cupboards and appliances replaced the pantry, scullery, laundry, and larder, the modern kitchen was born. In a 2006 Ikea survey of 14,000 people in 28 countries, 60 per cent said the kitchen is one of the two most important rooms in the home. None of them used the kitchen just to cook, and 69 per cent think their kitchen is too small. Laundry, cooking, homework, eating, washing up, watching TV, family discussions, charging mobile phones, surfing the net, socializing, feeding pets, playing board games: the list of activities they spelled out was endless.

Kitchens adapted to their demanding role in two ways: they grew longer and wider, and more like furniture. Units came down off the walls to take center stage. They grew curves and stood on poised feet instead of plinths. Countertops cantilevered off in all directions to bridge the gap between living, eating, and cooking space. Doors without handles open at fingertip touch, built-in lighting makes them appear to float.

As they advanced and changed shape, modular units stretched out to take over more living space. Measurements widened from 750 to 900mm (29 to 35in) with appliances keeping pace: Smeg's pizza stone and bread oven is only 480mm tall but it put on 50mm (2in) from 900 to 950mm wide (35 to 37in) to keep pace.

1

1 The Cinderella in every kitchen, the range hood, is transformed into a beautiful steel-cased pendant light. "Platinum" by Elica disguises the filters, motor, and electronics needed for silent, efficient air treatment within the Evolution system patented by Elica. Touch-sensitive rod controls different functions.

2 On the other side of the cherry veneer wall you could hang an XL American Amana refrigerator full of food and weighing a ton. Bulthaup's "b3" kitchen is designed so that 4m panels covering steel struts across load-bearing walls can carry up to 1 ton per meter, hooked into the grooves like these glass shelves.

2

3 Kitchen designers love the "Gaggenau AT 400 Ventilation Table" system because it lets cooks take center stage while whisking away the smell of cooking. Shown with a line-up of elements, griddles, and steamers in the "Gaggenau Vario" series, the range hood is where cooks want it – at countertop level.

4 A high-tech stainless-steel professional fridge freezer from Sub Zero, the "PRO 40" was given a new face in Milan 2006. A sepia drawing by Michelangelo digitally printed onto the Corian® cupboard fascia does not detract from its efficient dual refrigeration and triple evaporation which keeps food fresher for longer.

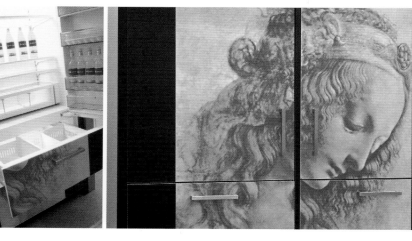

3

4

New sizes in the
5   multi-functional "Cube"
from Gatto Cucine increase the
depth of floor units from 600
to 650mm (23½ to 25½in) and
wall units to 350mm (13½in)
depth to hold more and sit
comfortably alongside modern
furniture in a single living and
dining space.

Low-level lighting and
6   deeply recessed mirrored
plinths create the illusion that
furniture floats above the floor
in this "Walnut and Silver"
collection by SmallBone of
Devizes. Its hub houses a
stove and an oven in a granite
countertop above dark walnut
open shelves, lined in faux
ostrich. Details like the beaten
silver handles and glass and
mirror insets decoratively link
the functional kitchen with
stylish living.

5

6

Rather than units, the
7   kitchen is furnished with
a series of benches and tables
with built in under-counter
lighting. A kitchen diner in the
spirit of our times, "Esprit" from
Leicht keeps food preparation
and dining zones on two tables
that face each other, divided by
a red lacquered panel. Those
three elements – tables and
panel – allow many different
spatial configurations.

7

⬇ **ALSO SEE**

introduction p.6
walls and ceilings p.40

kitchens/kitchens on the move

Telescopic, rotational, sliding, and gliding kitchens are on the move in their conquest of inner space. Electronic controls change both the function and appearance of kitchens as acrylic ventilation hoods zoom up and down over stoves. Workstations telescope at the push of a button to turn into tables. Faucets pop up when the lid of a seemingly static box, the "K11," lifts at the touch of a fingertip to reveal a sink and faucet. A fold-away stove cover doubles as a powerful air purification system. Its designer, architect Norbert Wangen, introduces a new idea for the person who does not want to live in a kitchen all the time yet likes to cook and entertain.

The advance of technology has put ventilation hoods, stolid cooking ranges, even wall-mounted ovens on the move. The "Liftmatic" oven on an elevator moves out of the hot zone when cooking time is up to place the finished dish at countertop level. Seymour Powell's red-hot cooking range for Mercury revs up temperatures with revolving handlebar controls on the front rail like a motorcycle. Its "Thermastone" oven is lined with materials found in the aerospace industry, never before cast in a domestic oven (*see also* page 184).

1

Beneath the hovering
3 semi-transparent meta acrylic hood of the "Sheer®" bubble kitchen by Gatto Cucine lies a carbon fiber workstation. Its circular diameter of 1.5m (5ft) is covered with a DuPont Corian® worksurface which contains (left to right) wine coolers, a double sink and drainers, and a ceramic induction cooking zone with pull-out wing tables. The

telescopic ventilation hood is driven by fingertip pressure on an electronic button, or by remote control. Beneath the tall canopy there is room for a swiveling upright faucet, and instead of being flush-mounted the semi-circular ceramic induction stove is upraised from the worksurface.

Flaps open at the touch of
1 a fingertip on the "K11" (left) to reveal a sink and pop-up faucet in one module, and stove with air-purification plant in its cover in the other. The "K2" monoblock top (below, center) glides open to double as a stainless-steel table, and reveals a sink and stove above the built-in refrigerator and dishwasher. Both kitchens are by Norbert Wangen for Boffi.

"Liftmatic" oven by
2 Siemens raises or lowers the oven floor on shafts to access dishes from three sides without doors or handles. Using less energy than a traditional oven, its vitreous china base cooks bread, pizza and croissants without a baking tray.

2

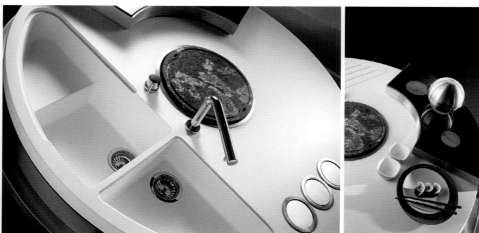

3

4

5

Designers Seymour Powell
4   power drive the Mercury
"Thermastone" oven with
two grips on the rail like
motorcycles to increase gas flow
and temperature. Inside, two of
the four ovens are cast in silicon
carbide (SiC) from a meteorite
in the Diablo canyon in Arizona.
Synthesized under extreme
temperature, its thermal and
mechanical properties are
second only to diamonds'.

↓ **ALSO SEE**

doors p.76

6

As kitchens move away
5   from the wall, powerful
ventilation above the stove
is important. Cumbersome
and traditionally static hoods
block sight lines. Miele's new
telescopic ventilation hood with
powerful air-suction telescopes
above cooking zones at the
touch of an electronic button.

This high-gloss aluminum
6   with white trim
Porcelanosa "G410" kitchen
has ceramic glass induction
stove, sink and faucet built into
aluminum worksurfaces. It can
be configured to fit almost any
space with just two pieces of
furniture. Work areas are
accessible from any direction.

Appliance manufacturer
7   Whirlpool looks for the
kitchen of the future. Designer
Dario Grasselli shows how
compactly furniture integrates
appliances. With an induction
stove, sink, combination
microwave, refrigeration, and
dishwasher, it packs all the
appliances into one piece.

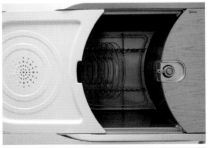

7

kitchens/kitchens in a box

In the 21st century, product innovation has been joined by visual innovation. When a shocking pink Smeg refrigerator with rounded edges and a 1950s-style door handle featured full page in *Vogue*, the trend for packaging what used to be known as "white goods" began. In today's crowded and competitive market for appliances, they must look good as well as deliver a technically superior performance. Smeg is a good example of a high-profile brand-building campaign.

Behind the many activities that take place in today's evolutionary kitchens, storage is still the main function. Stand-alone furniture without a range of wall-fixed cabinets makes a feature of packing a lot of function behind the packaging then highlighting it so that it does not look like a kitchen unit. Whirlpool's freestanding "Theater" kitchen turns banked storage boxes into a stage set. Even the static wall-mounted cupboard gets designer treatment from Ferruccio Laviani for Dada with floating glass rectangles set one above another, distanced from each other for maximum effect. For Boffi, Piero Lissoni mixes Corian®, colored ceramics, satin steel, and two kinds of ecological composite wood for the "Table System" and the "Zone" collection to integrate with existing kitchens.

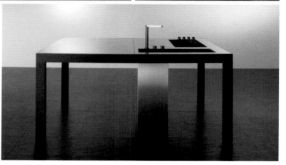

1

The "Zone" kitchen by
1 Piero Lissoni for Boffi plays with scale and volume with thin wood, glass, or aluminum countertops set on monumental oblong units on recessed stainless-steel plinths so they appear to hover. Inset on his "Table" system (bottom) is the stainless-steel sink (below) with "W1" fixed height and revolving spout on a faucet by Norbert Wangen for Boffi.

The iconic "Fab"
2 refrigerator by Smeg (far left) shows how white goods boldly colored can take the world by storm. Now Smeg prove that retro-styling can hide top technology with the 600mm (23½in) "Fab" dishwasher (below) with room for 14 place settings, 10 programs engineered to save off-peak electricity, and half-load cycles to save water.

Staging a domestic
3 experience at the "in:kitchen" show by Whirlpool Europe, the Ziba Europe design team built the "Theater" kitchen. While the chef cooks on a U-shaped table, the audience watches. Behind the theatrical backdrop of storage, a table, refrigerators, drawers, and ovens, are accessible in both directions.

2

3

↓ **ALSO SEE**
lighting p.139
bathrooms p.150

"Some parts of the home, especially the living room and kitchen, can become very versatile and virtually unique. Aesthetically speaking, the kitchen is the object of great attention – partly because today a kitchen costs more than a living room, and partly because it has become a community space. These days I think entering a house through the kitchen is an interesting route."

Alessandro Mendini, in.kitchen, Whirlpool Corporation

↑ **DESIGN INFLUENCE**

4

6

Back-lighting gives a
4   stack of glass-fronted boxes a drama that no Welsh dresser can hope to emulate. "Chroma" cabinet in the SieMatic "SL909" kitchens range bathes its contents in intense cobalt blue light. Either static or constantly changing on a computerized program, the spectrum of colors is mood-enhancing.

From Ikea, this beech
6   "Ärlig" kitchen features "Faktum" frames and a "Lagan" countertop, standing on "Capita" legs, with "Kosing" door handles. In the Ikea catalogue, a standard kitchen shown with different door front is priced to show how much
it would cost to get the same amount of kitchen in any given design, a useful exercise for the first-time home buyer.

5

Unusual floating glass-
5   sided and fronted boxes in the "Quadrante" kitchen designed by Ferruccio Laviani for Dada. Framed in wood covered with extruded aluminum, each glass box is attached independently with a space between so that it appears to float in its own space rather than stack.

Almost everything in the
7   Bulthaup "b3" kitchen – knife rack, towel rail, board, and utensil boxes – clips into the groove on the panelled walls shown on p.186. Freestanding units have hidden feet recessed beneath the units.

7

kitchens/opening up the box

When Electrolux asked industrial design students across the world for innovations in cooking, laundry, washing, and refrigeration products by the year 2015, they all anticipated space shrinking. Yet in an Ikea survey on kitchens, 60 per cent of participants admitted to having a "junk drawer" of bits and pieces they do not know what to do with. Either a clear-out or a storage plan is needed: pots and pans near the stove; plates and cutlery near to where you eat; cleaning products and waste disposal near the sink, and fiddly bits like cutlery trays, dividers for utensils, and condiment jars behind drawer fronts and cupboard doors. Inside the "K12" by Norbert Wangen for Boffi, deep drawers contain magnets shaped like "T"s and

"L"s to move about on magnetic surfaces to adapt to changing needs. Ikea's "Rationell" has dividers like pipe cleaners that clip together to make different shapes.

Alternatively, the junk drawer could be replaced with a smart one housing an appliance, like Neff's warming drawer which preheats dishes, keeps food warm and defrosts it. The busy professional who eats out a lot but needs somewhere to keep the sushi bento box can install a small fridge freezer under the counter. Packed-flat fast food chills out in a slimline drawer from Ariston. With Fisher & Paykel's genius dishwasher in a drawer, dirty plates and glasses can be stashed away in a drawer and washed when the guests have gone.

1

2

3

A 760mm (30in) triple
1   oven combines oven with microwave and warming drawer. Thermador's stainless-steel and glass three-in-one with "Personal Culinary Assistant™" changes to different cooking methods at a single-touch. The glass surface of the "Sens-A-Touch™" control panel is easily cleaned.

4

A built-in warming drawer
2   from Bosch keeps food warm, defrosts it, heats up plates, and even melts chocolate. The 290mm high (11½in) brushed-steel drawer fits 12 place settings inside, including serving dishes.

Deep drawers on telescopic
4   rails extend right out of Siemens capacious under-counter "EasyStore" stainless-steel refrigerator so that nothing is lost at the back. Eight two-liter bottles are held in grippers with moveable dividers to ensure stability. "AgION" coated walls prevent a build-up of bacteria, and on the door, Liquid Crystal Display panels record temperature rises and falls.

5

With adjustable
3   temperature and humidity levels, the stainless-steel Wolf 760mm (30 in) warming drawer with a 450W heating element will not let the steamed fish dry out while keeping the egg-fried noodles crisp. It is certified for use outside the kitchen, next to the barbecue. Five stainless-steel containers with lids are optional.

Neff warming drawer in
5   two sizes, small or large, to take six or twelve place settings, fits neatly under the Neff coffee center, microwave or (as shown) the Neff "B1664" oven. It warms plates and defrosts delicate dishes like ice cream while the oven's "ScrollControl" display electronically scrolls down menus with seventeen programs and retrieves stored recipes.

↓ **ALSO SEE**

bathrooms p.174

"Rationell" drawer dividers
6 clip together and slide to make adjustable partitions within shallow and deep drawers from Ikea. Interior fittings include cutlery trays, jars, plate holders, and dividers. The "Rationell" range works with "Faktum" kitchen frames to make a fully extendable drawer so that its contents can be viewed at a glance.

The planked oak veneer
7 of the Leicht "Espirit" is light, but the storage capacity of these long and deep, 500–1200mm (1ft 7in–4ft), drawers is heavy duty. The emphasis is on horizontal space within the drawers that glide smoothly open with barely visible ergonomic aluminum-edged handles.

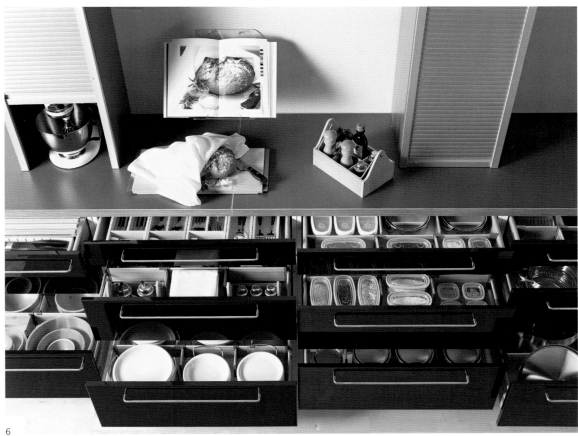

6

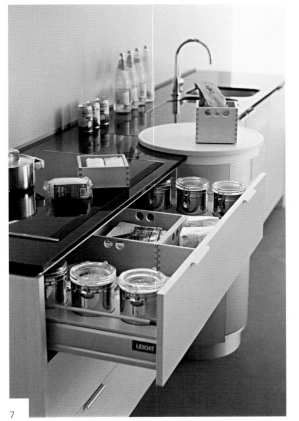

7

8

9

10

Need even more space?
8 Nolte's "Gullwing" drawer, fronted with "Solar Yellow" gloss finish, creates extra room for storing smaller items inside a standard 600, 800, or 900mm deep (23½, 31½, or 35in) pan drawer. Wing-shaped side panels slide over the main body of the drawer, depending on whether it is open or closed.

A dishwasher in a drawer,
9 the "DishDrawer®" gave a little-known New Zealand company Fisher & Paykel its foothold on the global marketplace. The EZKleen resin coating applied to the brushed stainless-steel finish can be cleaned with a soapy sponge. Behind its flat door panel, with recessed controls, is space for 24 place settings. There are 4 eco-friendly washing cycles.

Santos has many dividers
10 for storage in the 650mm deep (25½in) drawers of the base units in its "Minos" kitchen. Trays, drawers, dividers, cutting boards – the objective is to achieve neat interior spaces where everything is easily seen, and close at hand for the cook. Like a wooden cribbage board, pegs in the perforated base can be moved to change the space.

11

12

13

An organized kitchen with a place for everything is what every cook needs. Here, this cutlery drawer made of beechwood from Leicht reveals an interior arrangement of utter simplicity on a curved bow front. Leicht kitchens also feature drawers that close silently.

11

Fully extendable self-closing drawers in Ikea's "Rationell" range include hidden extras like this cutting board with a tray for crumbs. This fits beneath the countertop over the silver-colored powder-coated steel tray.

12

Extra storage in the pull-out slide and glide "Faktum" cupboard at Ikea. With sturdy, fully extending drawers and a depth of 570mm (22⅓in), the cupboard is ideal for keeping supplies that the cook does not need every day, like dried and canned goods, and bottles.

13

14

Blum makes drawer sides and backs, bases, and runners for other kitchen manufacturers to build into units. The Blum corner allows access to the far corners of the drawers. Stable and self-closing, the drawers integrate the Blumotion soft-close system.

14

A carousel with double shelves large enough to store pots and pans is another way to transform overlooked corner space. Leicht's "Avance" carousel is handle free and flexible, allowing classic "L" or "U" shapes to be planned.

15

15

kitchens/breaking out of the box

Shapely kitchens on the curve rival monumental mono-block kitchens much loved by minimalists. Solid natural materials – wood, marble, and stone – demand those vast unbroken cubed shapes. New materials are making it possible to break out of the box. There is not a set square on site in these kitchens that sweep around space, encompassing sinks and appliances within curved fronts, anticipating eating around a table rather than perching on a line-up of bar stools like a cafeteria. Highly technical materials like LG HI-MACS® and Corian®, joined on large spans, make it easier to achieve these rounded forms than timber technology, where five separate molds can be required to make different door curves in a tight space. High-gloss acrylic Parapan® can be thermo-molded into curved door fronts that break out of the rigorous line-up of kitchen units as vividly as the 20 intense colors it comes in. Hour-glass curves can be manipulated to follow any curve. Aluminum honeycomb, more commonly used in the airplane industry for cabin floors than in the kitchen industry, bridge gaps between banks of appliances with plunging heights and audacious curves. Lightweight and strong, these new materials make resilient countertops, which is why designers like them so much.

1

2

The "Skyline" (above and right) swoops around corners like a Scaletrix™ track to make full use of small spaces. Designed by Lucci and Orlandini for the smaller home sharing kitchen space with the living room, wraparound countertops can be customized by Snaidero, making them especially suitable for elderly and disabled people. The "Skylab" center island for food preparation (right) supports a glass-topped table.

"Venus" corners tightly on the curves as you would expect from the Ferrari design studio, Pininfarina for Snaidero. Aluminum honeycomb panel doors beneath ice-white tops are finished with Microtouch leather-effect material. In association with Fiat's research center, Snaidero fitted LED lights into aluminum shelves, evenly distributing light inside cupboards to save 83 per cent of energy compared to halogen.

3

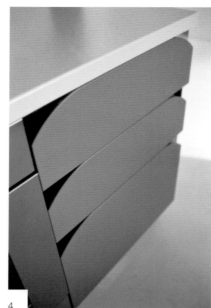

4

Changes of height from
3　countertop to dining table
are achieved seamlessly in
DuPont Corian®, which has
come a long way since its arrival
as a material for worksurfaces
and backsplashes in the 1970s.
As solid wood becomes a luxury
– and teak a no-no – Corian®
adapts heavily grained wood
hues as well as many plain
colors. Non-porous, it bonds
with scarcely visible joins.

Drawer fronts on the Gatto
4　Cucine "Tiare" range are
contoured at the edges to pull
away from the straight front
and make handles obsolete.
Drawer edges, rounded and
smoothed for easy access,
disguise the fact that behind
them, the drawers are straight
sided and strengthened with
anodized aluminum.

6

5

It is unusual for a sink to
5　break out into a curve but
the "Henley" by Stoneham is
gently cambered for easy access
to all the compost and waste
bins, as well as all the cleaning
stuff stored below the sink in
Blum drawers.

A built-in, ceramic glass
6　stove, the "EW 957," with
a central wok cooking zone
from Küppersbusch. To cook
directly on the ceramic glass
surface or in a wok pan in the
center, five separate cooking
zones adapt to different pan
dimensions. With sensor touch
electronic controls and stove
graphics, cooking takes on a
whole new dimension.

The oval design of the
7　"TR 90DX" ceramic stove
made by Spanish company
Teka is replicated in the lines of
the co-ordinating wall-mounted
"DX90" hood freestanding
above an island unit. The fluid
lines and glass lighten up the
wall-mounted hood.

7

8

9

The semi-circular kitchen
8 in an apartment designed
by Ian Alcorn relies on high-gloss
solid acrylic Parapan® for
the curves on door fronts that
are concave. Thermo-formed
to create curves in 20 colors,
Parapan® reinvents itself
below (picture 11) in great
convex shapes.

Lined up along the wall,
9 natural cherry cabinet
fronts from Arrital balloon
into a bow-fronted melamine
unit finished in aluminum.
This arrangement of curved
shapes and straight lines
balances the varying heights
of the taller storage units with
drawers, and lower countertops.

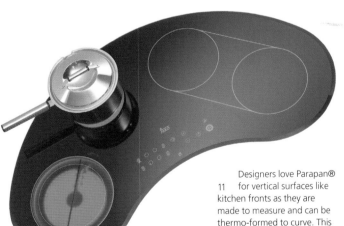

10

Designers love Parapan®
11 for vertical surfaces like
kitchen fronts as they are
made to measure and can be
thermo-formed to curve. This
vivid red kitchen has Parapan®
doors and a Pianoforte
countertop and backsplash.

Kidney-bean shaped Teka
10 ceramic stove, the "VRTC
90," has a bevelled edge which
lies flush with the worksurface.
Four cooking zones are mapped
out in lines across its black glass
surface, and the shape means
that cooks no longer risk burns
leaning across heated pans to
reach pots at the back.

11

kitchens/countertops, backsplashes, and unit fronts

Backsplashes don't have the same importance in kitchens now that appliance manufacturers have worked to make them obsolete. Deeper sinks, more accurate faucets with rotating spouts aimed at saving water, not splashing it about, and stoves with curvaceous easy-clean tops are designed to make that rather awkward transition between countertop and wall, the backsplash, less relevant.

Countertops are the real hard workers of the kitchen, the hands-on surface absorbing the daily ritual of food preparation and covering the most visible mileage. In today's kitchen, countertops have to stand in as a desk for homework, a bar for entertaining, even a tabletop for computers. Natural materials such as slate or stone are counterbalanced by some of the new synthetics. When it comes to units, door fronts can be wood, steel, bamboo, laminate, opaque glass, or in the case of Spagnol's "Ice," a plasma screen TV. Parapan® is a popular synthetic material that is 100 per cent recyclable.

1

2

3

1　Not for the faint of heart, this transparent kitchen is made entirely of custom-cut Saint-Gobain glass. The kitchen, called "Simplicity," was created by Italian designer Ennio Arosio for Carlo Santambrogio, exclusively for Smirk in the UK, and every aspect of it – the sink, faucet, and base for the heating element – is made of crystal clear glass.

3　Thirty years ago Italian industrial design guru Marco Zanuso designed the "Elam E5" kitchen, and its multi-functional units are still prized today. The bespoke cabinet system, co-ordinated by Tisettanta Design Lab, is versatile, easily integrating contemporary appliances.

2　The entire wall behind the stove and range becomes one gigantic backsplash. Black speckled Corian® makes a dramatic backdrop in this kitchen. Its smooth tactile surface has a definite man-made feel to it that does not try to imitate other materials, which is why designers like it. Also, it is warm to the touch and cuts easily so that the ceramic induction stove fits smoothly into its speckled black surface.

5　Super slim low profile "Laser" sink with an extra large bowl from Franke sits flush without clamps, rails, or screws. The Slimfix® system simply drops into a cut out, where gripping anchored beneath the rim holds it firm.

6　The Astracast "Geo" composite sink looks and feels like granite, but does not need a fork-lift truck nor a reinforced steel joist beneath it to support it. The bold square shape and linear design shown here in Volcano Black is made of a composite mixed with metallic particles to reflect light and includes anti-bacterial protection.

4

4　"Solitaire" freestanding table and island unit made from stainless steel in the "SteelArt" kitchen by Blanco. Widths change from a substantial panel at the top end to a reversal of the volume at the far end.

5

6

7 Lacquered surfaces are a classic for door fronts and have a luster that can never be dulled. Gray, anthracite, and cream silk matt lacquered surfaces come alive against the vivid background of orange in the Leicht "Espirit" kitchen.

8 Composed of more than 90 per cent natural quartz aggregates, along with pigment and polyester resins, CaesarStone quartz surfaces are harder than granite and just as resistant to chipping and cracking. The engineered stone is easy to incorporate into kitchen design as it can be shaped and bent, and is heat resistant, impervious to stains, and low maintenance.

9 "Le Pietre" by Cerim is made of 13 ceramic stones in different designs and colors. Porcelain is used for floors, and white body ceramic for walls like this one, realistically mimicking stone, down to the perfectly squared edges of each rectangular slab.

9

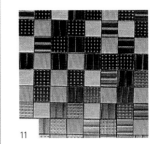

11

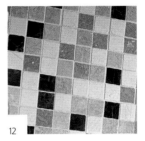

12

7

8

10 The Rolls Royce of one-off kitchens made in Italy, Strato Cucine has always combined the best of old and new materials – Carrerra marble and metal in the "Non Plus Ultra" collection designed by Marco Gorini, combines the sculptor's favorite material with industrial steel.

11 Vitrum "High Tech" glass tiles by CeramGres are mounted on mesh for easy installation. The textured collage of the "Hoshi" studded tiles, with ridged "Shimo" tiles and shimmering "Yuki" inset with waffle indentations on "Harashi" make an interesting collage.

12 Mosaics are an ancient art form, made easier to install with Mandarin Stone's range of polished limestone and marble chips already set into tiles in the mosaic pattern. "Chara" comes in a range of dramatic colors.

13 Gradations of gray and white colors of this "Mosaic Design" countertop on the Siematic high-gloss lacquered "SL 909" kitchen. Made from 10 x 10mm (⅜ x ⅜in) marble pieces combined with Venetian glass tesserae, no two kitchen worksurfaces are alike since each piece of work is handcrafted for the owner. Siematic "Mosaic Design" countertop comes in 100 x 100mm (3⅞ x 3⅞in) ceramic tiles in a single tone or two-tone chessboard.

14 Wall tile mosaics in the "Muro" range from Cosentino for backsplashes to complement the Silestone quartz composites of the work surfaces. The quartz tiles are on a preformed backing sheet for easier installation and contain Microban anti-bacterial agent.

15 Light plays on the pearly acrylic sheet with translucent Perspex® from Lucite® in this kitchen designed by two Polish interior designers, Agnieszka Stefañska and Bibianna Szyszko-Stein. They say it is designed for their ideal client: "the modern woman who is more than a domestic goddess." Divided by an illuminated back-lit wall of Perspex®, the cooking and eating areas match the pink of the shelves. The refrigerator and appliances are hidden in co-ordinated cabinets made from Perspex® colored Frost Blush Pink and Pearlescent Candy.

13

14

10

15

All good kitchens are designed for cooks, of course, but this selection of appliances illustrates the well-known fact that global cuisine impacts upon our tastes not just when eating out but cooking at home. Appliance manufacturers respond with machines that can healthily steam organic vegetables bought at the Farmers' Market, toast Parma ham and mozzarella mixes for a quick lunchtime snack, crisp the egg white batter on prawns for Japanese tempura (which is a healthier reason to buy a deep-fat fryer), and hold the wok firm at a high heat in a hollowed out ceramic stove for dim sum.

Following the Western rituals of wine and coffee, there are appliances designed to deliver both to perfection. Making good-quality coffee at home used to be a hassle, requiring industrial-sized machines, pressure, and steam. Now sleeker models that can be built into kitchen units are available, and they will transform coffee beans into piping hot espresso, mochatto, latte, or cappuccino at the push of a button.

And wine buyers can choose between the top-of-the-range American Sub Zero wine cooler which holds 138 bottles, or smaller ones that slip under the countertop. It is a matter of individual taste and budget.

1 Induction cooking on ceramic glass means that a magnetic field on the stove is triggered when a ferrous-based cooking pot is placed on it. It heats instantly while the glass all around remains ice cold. With the "Bosch Touch Control Oven" you could put your hand on the front surface while a pan cooks at the back of the stove.

2 Steaming is the healthy way to cook, but as anyone who has tried the traditional way of steaming over a pan of water knows, if you are not careful, you can end up with soggy, tasteless fish or veg. Cooking in the Neff "Mega System" steam oven occurs at 100°C, for a gentle way of preparing food that keeps in nutrients and the delicious taste without any unwanted fats.

3 The "ZoneSmart™" on this ceramic electric stove by Thermador sizes up the pan, which triggers the sensor to activate exactly the number of zones needed to heat the pot. It recognizes when the pan has been removed and then turns off the element. When the pan is returned, the element automatically heats up again.

4 For every Italianate who enjoys a bruschetta or panini or just a plain cheese toastie, the "AMC957" from the Whirlpool "6th Sense" range is ideal. It sits directly on top of the stove, but safety comes first. The non-conductive, heat-proof handles make flipping them swift, while the double-sized toasting holds two sandwiches. With a non-stick Teflon interior, it doubles to sear roasted vegetables, Mediterranean style.

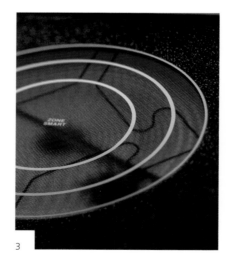

1

3

4

5 Designed to be wall mounted at eye-level, the "EB 388" extra-wide professional oven from Gaggenau has a brushed stainless-steel drop-down contoured door. Big enough for 2 Thanksgiving turkeys, the oven has 11 heating methods, pyrolytic self-cleaning and a temperature sensor.

2

5

6

↓ **ALSO SEE**

bathrooms p.166

7

There are many schools for Japanese food – sushi, sashimi, teriyaki and tepanyaki – all with their own rituals, placements, and stoves. This tepanyaki styled "Misura" L-shaped kitchen from Effeti sears meat, fish and vegetables at high heat with flavorings to be served directly into bowls on the bar below.
6

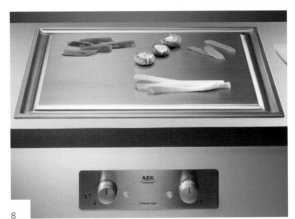

8

Miele point out that "tepan" means "grilled on a hot table." Tepan lets food cook in its own juices with little or no fat. Miele's three models, "TepanYaki," "Tepan," and "Tepan Mobile," all in stainless-steel plate. The "Tepan" dips slightly in the center to keep in the juices. Like a wok, intense heat is produced in the center. The edges are ideal for simmering or keeping food warm.
7

Such is the popularity worldwide of Japanese food that mass-market appliance manufacturer AEG makes the "Teppan Yaki" stainless-steel stove that no longer limits the cook to the size of a saucepan. Two temperature zones mean that foods requiring different temperatures can be cooked at the same time. The stainless-steel surface heats up fast, with even distribution, and it is easy to clean too.
8

The Zip "HydroTap" unique innovation is that at the push of a button it delivers freshly filtered boiling water for tea, coffee, or soup, as well as chilled water, from the same unit. The faucet does not have to be installed on a sink, although it does require plumbing. The "Hydrotap" range includes four versions – boiling only, chilled only, boiling and chilling, and a mixer unit.
9

The "Instant-Hot™ Water Dispenser" from KitchenAid boasts it can quickly and safely produce up to 60 cups of near-boiling water an hour straight out of the faucet. Hand-finished and made of solid brass, the faucet can handle hard, soft, city, or well water. It could signal the end of the flex for the kettle.
10

A home kitchen that's as flexible as one in a restaurant is every cook's dream. Gaggenau's "Vario 400" series lines up various special duty appliances in identical modular sizes from a griddle to a wok and teppanyaki grill (below right) and (left to right) steamer for healthy eating which drains straight into the sink; electric deep fat fryer for tempura; and electric barbecue grill.
11

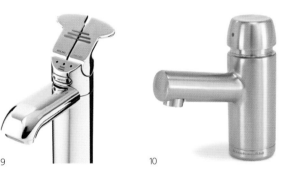

9

10

11

kitchens/cooks' kitchens

12

12 Not the first to design a coffee maker Neff's "Coffee Center" model C7660 won the "iF" award for outstanding international design. It holds 400g (14oz) of fresh beans and a large 1.8lt (3pt) water tank on fully programmable temperature and timer functions, with ClearText™ display in a choice of languages. A special frothing nozzle makes great cappuccino.

13 Miele coffee's new "CVA 4080" coffee maker features a conical bean grinder to ensure the very best cup of freshly ground coffee. Easy to refill, different brands of coffee can be exchanged simply.

14 The secret to the frothy top on every cup of cappuccino or latte from Gaggenau's CM200 is the "Aroma Whirl." After brewing, the internal piping is thoroughly rinsed to ensure full flavor. A flexible option is to set the amount of coffee and water. Espresso is efficiently dispensed.

17 LG's new "Titanium TV Side by Side" refrigerator freezer combines technology with entertainment on the LCD touch screen for TV, DVD, VHS, radio, and cable. LG's BioShield™ and BioSilver™ work against bacteria to keep food fresher for longer. It has a digital temperature control and an alarm that sounds if the door is left ajar.

13

14

15 Oenophiles with good wines but no cellar can chill the bubbly, cool the whites and keep the reds at sommelier standards with the Siemens "KF 18WA40" wine cooler. It holds up to 32 bottles of wine on 4 vibration-free contoured shelves, and has 2 other shelves for party food storage. Electronic LED display allows the selection of the correct temperature, and it has a swift chill function.

16 Full-size wine storage from Sub-Zero in the "430." It holds 147 750ml bottles with a specially lit shelf for prize bottles between the two separate wine compartments, each individually controlled for humidity and temperature. Sturdy rust-proof roller-guide shelves faced with cherrywood have an extension for easy access.

15

16

17

18

19

20

21

22

23

Electrolux sponsors the Design Lab for product design students around the world. Some ideas to be realized by the year 2015:

18 Futuristic refrigerators designed by students from the University of Notre Dame in the USA. The "Soho" adapts to many living environments, as it is lightweight and designed for multi-configuration stacking, while using water and resources efficiently.

19 "N-refrigerator" is a refrigerator with reduced dimensions composed of independent modules designed by students at the Escola Superior de Artes e Design (ESAD) in Portugal. Ideal for the city singleton frequently buying food in small quantities.

20 Electronic grids inset within a wooden table top allow the use of induction tables like hotplates, food mixers and laptops without cords or plugs. The "2015," as students at Central Saint Martins in London call their invention, is designed to be put into production by Electrolux in that year.

21 "Hot-Pot Party," designed by Chinese students at the Design School of Southern Yangtze University, is a mobile cooking unit with many cooking zones functioning at the same time to stack on pull-out tables.

22 Breaking out of the big white box, a washer/dryer that doubles all week as a laundry basket. At the touch of a button the "Washman" washes the load then empties it into the dryer unit below. This clever machine was designed by students from the Czech Academy of Arts with a team from the Academy of Fine Arts and Design in Slovakia.

23 A waterless dishwasher that runs on carbon dioxide, cleaning dishes in a closed loop programme. No chemicals are used. Curvaceously formed and environmentally sustainable, the eco-chic "Rockpool" dishwasher is designed by Australian students at the University of New South Wales.

directory

walls and ceilings

2 Jane
Tel: 813 832 5263
sales@2jane.com
www.2jane.com

3Form (Futimis Systems)
2300 South 2300 West
Suite B
Salt Lake City, Utah 84119, USA
Tel: 801 977 0400
Fax: 801 977 0491
info@3-form.com
www.3-form.com

Abet Laminati
Viale Industria 21
12042 Bra (CN), Italy
Tel: +39 0172 419111
Fax: + 39 0172 431571
abet@abet-laminati.it
www.abet-laminati.it

60 West Sheffied Ave.
Englewood, NJ 07631, USA
Tel: 801 201 541 0700
801 800 228 2238
Fax: 801 201 541 0701
abetusa@aol.com
www.abetlaminati.com

Alias
Via dei Videtti 2
24064 Bergamo
Grumello Del Monte, Italy
Tel: +39 035 44 22 511
Fax: +39 035 44 22 590
info@aliasdesign.it
www.aliasdesign.it

Alivar
Via B.Cellini 190
50028 Tavarnelle (FI), Italy
Tel: +39 055 80 70 115
Fax: +39 055 80 70 127
alivar@alivar.com
www.alivar.com

Alusion (Cymat Corporation)
6320-2 Danville Road
Mississauga
Ontario L5T 2L7, Canada
Tel: 905 696 2419
Fax: 905 696 9300

info@alusion.com
www.alusion.com

Amanda J Simmons
ACME Studio 52
165 Childers Street
Deptford SE9, UK
Tel: +44 (0) 7868 780090
amanda.simmons@btinternet.com
www.amandajsimmons.co.uk

Arma Architectural Materials
Via Monelli
2 Pedemontana Angolo Ghiarola
Vecchia
41042 Fiorano Modenese (MO)
Italy
Tel: +39 0536 911 489
Fax: +39 0536 911 490
info@armaitalia.it
www.armaitalia.it

Armstrong
2500 Columbia Avenue (17603)
P.O. Box 3001
Lancaster, PA 17604, USA
Tel: 717 397 0611
www.armstrong.com

Arpa Ceramiche
Scandiano RE, Italy
Tel: 00 39 0522 341311
Fax: 00 39 0522 520115
info@arpaceramiche.it
www.arpaceramiche.it

Artcoustic
Distributor USA, Canada, Mexico:
St John Group
4396 Saddlestone Drive
Bellingham, WA 98226, USA
Tel: 360 756 2205
Fax: 360 647 1087
artcoustic@artcoustic.com
www.artcoustic.com

UK & Ireland sales office:
Tel: +44 (0) 1245 400 904
Fax: +44 (0) 1245 400 910
salesuk@artcoustic.com

Bang & Olufsen
Peter Bangs Vej 15
P.O. Box 40
DK-7600 Struer
Denmark

Tel: +45 96 84 11 22
Fax: +45 96 84 50 33
www.bang-olufsen.com

Stockists:
UK: +44 (0) 1189 692 288
USA: 847 590 4900

Bark Cloth
Talhauser Strasse 18
D – 79285 Ebringen, Germany
Tel and fax: +49 (0)700 22 75
25 68
barkcloth@barkcloth.de
www.barktex.com

Barrisol
Stretch Ceilings (UK) Ltd
Doman Road
Yorktown Industrial Estate
Camberley, Surrey GU15 3DF, UK
Tel: +44 (0) 1276 681000
Fax: +44 (0) 1276 406900
info@barrisol.co.uk
www.barrisol.co.uk

Bisazza
36041 Alte Vincenza, Italy
Tel: +39 0444 707 511
Fax: +39 0444 492
088info@bisazza.com
www.bisazza.com

3540 NW 72nd Ave.
Miami, FL 33122, USA
Tel: 800 Bisazza
info@bisazzausa.com

Bowers & Wilkins
Dale Road
Worthing
West Sussex BN11 2BH, UK
info@bwspeakers.com
www.bwflatspeakers.com

Stockists:
UK: +44 (0) 1903 221800
USA: 978 664 2870

Cabot
Industrie Park Hoescht
Building D660
Frankfurt am Main
Germany
Tel: +49 69 305 29331
www.cabot-corp.com

Cafe Interiors
The Mill
Greenside Lane
Droylsden, Manchester M43 7AJ
UK
Tel: +44 (0) 161 371 5550
Fax: +44 (0) 161 371 5552
info@cafeinteriors.co.uk
www.cafeinteriors.co.uk

CanvasRus
Ladds House
Old Otford Road
Sevenoaks
Kent TN14 5EZ, UK
Tel: +44 (0) 1732 454 092
sales@canvasRus.co.uk
www.canvasrus.co.uk

Casa Dolce Casa
Via Viazza Il Tronco, 45
41042 Fiorano Modenese (MO)
Italy
Tel: +39 0536 84 1011
Fax: +30 0536 84 1001
info@casadolcecasa.com
www.casadolcecasa.com

942 Curie Drive
Alpharetta, GA 30005, USA
Tel: 678 393 8050
Fax: 678 393 8930

Citterio
Via Don Giuseppe Brambilla 16/18
23844 Sirone (Lecco), Italy
Tel: +39 031 853545
Fax: +39 031 853529
vendite@citteriospa.com
www.citteriospa.com

Color Kinetics
10 Milk Street, Suite 1100
Boston, MA 02108, USA
Tel: 617 423 9999
Fax: 617 423 9998
info@colorkinetics.com
www.colorkinetics.com

CuoioArredo
Divisione di Cuoificio Bisonte
Via Masini, 36
56029 S. Croce sull'Arno(Pisa)
Italy
Tel: +39 0571 30036
Fax: +39 0571 33894

info@cuoioarredo.it
www.cuoioarredo.it

Dalsouple
P.O. Box 140
Bridgwater, Somerset, TA5 1HT
UK
Tel: +44 (0) 1278 727777
Fax: +44 (0)1278 727788
info@dalsouple.com
www.dalsouple.com

Digetex
Birtle Bleach Works
Elbut Lane
Bury
Lancashire BL9 6UX
UK
Tel: +44 (0) 161 762 0482
Fax: +44 (0) 161 797 4505
enquiries@digetex.com
www.digetex.com

Dool Design
19 Rue Paul Bert
75011 Paris
France
Tel: +33 (0) 1 4348 6144
dooldesign@hotmail.com

Driade
Via Padana inferiore 12
29012 Fossadello di Caorso (PC)
Italy
Tel: +39 0523822628
com.it@driade.com
www.driade.com

Droog Design
Staalstraat 7a
1011 JJ Amsterdam
The Netherlands
Tel: +31 (0) 20 523 5050
Fax: +31 (0) 20 320 1710
info@droogdesign.nl
www.droogdesign.nl

DuPont Corian
Wedgwood Way
Stevenage
Herts SG1 4QN
UK
Tel: +44 (0) 1438 734000
Fax: +44 (0) 1483 734836
eu-info@dupont.com
www.dupont.com

US contact:
1007 Market Street
Wilmington, DE 19898, USA
Tel: 302 774 1000

Elumin8 Systems
1 Nimrod Way
Ferndown BH21 7SH, UK
Tel: +44 (0) 1202 865 138
Fax: +44 (0) 1202 865 101
enquiries@elumin8.com
www.elumin8.com

Emdelight
Friedberger Landstr. 645
60389 Frankfurt a. M.
Germany
Tel: +49 (0) 69 47 88 15 0
Fax: +49 (0) 69 47 88 15 77
info@emdelight.com
.

FEG
Superstrada Valassina
20034 Giussano (MI)
Italy
Tel: +39 0362 8691
Fax: +39 0362 869280
info@gruppofeg.it
www.gruppofeg.it

Formica Limited
Coast Road
North Shields
Tyne & Wear NE29 8RE
UK
Tel: +44 (0) 191 259 3000
Fax: +44 (0) 191 258 2719
formica.limited@formica.co.uk
www.formica.co.uk

Forms + Surfaces
6395 Cindy Lane
Carpinteria, CA 93013
USA
Tel: 805 684 8626
Fax: 805 684 8620
marketing@forms-surfaces.com
www.forms-surfaces.com

Front
Tegelviksgatan 20
11641 Stockholm
Sweden
Tel: +46 (0) 8710 0170
everyone@frontdesign.se
www.frontdesign.se

Fusion Glass Designs
365 Clapham Road
London SW9 9BT
UK
Tel: +44 (0) 20 7738 5888
Fax: +44 (0) 20 7738 4888
info@fusionglass.co.uk
www.fusionglass.co.uk

Futimis Systems – see 3Form

GKD
Metallweberstrasse 46
D-52353 Düren
Germany
Tel: +49 (0) 2421 803 0
Fax: +49 (0) 2421 803 211
info@gkd.de
www.creativeweave.de

GKD-USA Inc.
825 Chesapeake Drive
Cambridge, MD 21613, USA
Tel: 800 453 8616
sales@gkdusa.com
www.gkdmetalfabrics.com

Glas Platz
Auf den Pühlen 5
D-51674 Wiehl-Bomig
Germany
Tel: +49 (0) 2261 78 90 0
Fax: +49 (0) 2261 78 90 10
info@glas-platz.de
www.glas-platz.de/index.htm

Groupe Foin
Immeuble Edison
Z.I. Paris Nord II
33 Rue des Vanesses
BP 55288 Villepinte
95958 Roissy CDG Cedex
France
Tel: +33 1 499 03906
Fax: +33 1 499 03916
foin@bacou-dalloz.com
www.groupe-foin.com

Gooding Aluminium
1 British Wharf
London SE14 5RS
UK
Tel: +44 (0) 20 8692 2255
Fax: +44 (0) 20 8469 0031
sales@goodingalum.com
www.goodingalum.com

Heideveld Polyester
Europaweg 24
NL – 8181 BH Heerde
The Netherlands
Tel: +31 (0) 57 869 2058
Fax: +31 (0) 57 869 4651
info@heideveld-polyester.nl
www.heideveld-polyester.nl

Home Cinema
Gecko Inc Ltd
Tel: +44 (0) 20 8603 0480
info@gecko.uk.com
www.homecinema.uk.com

H&R Johnson Tiles
Harewood Street
Stoke-on-Trent ST6 5JZ, UK
Tel: +44 (0)1782 575575
Fax: +44 (0)1782 577377
sales@johnson-tiles.com
www.johnson-tiles.com

H&R Johnson USA
122 Tices Lanes
East Brunswick, NJ 08816, USA
Tel: 732 698 0900
Fax: 732 698 9589
Usa1@johnson-tiles.com

Hyperion Tiles
67 High Street
Ascot
Berkshire SL5 7HP, UK
Tel: +44 (0) 1344 620211
Fax: +44 (0) 1344 620100
ascot@hyperiontiles.com
www.hyperiontiles.com

INAX
5-1 Koie-Honmachi
Tokoname
Aichi Pref
479-8585
Japan
www.inax.co.jp

Ineos
P.O. Box 13
The Heath
Runcorn
Cheshire WA7 4QF
Tel: +44 (0) 1928 515525
Fax: +44 (0) 1928 513890
info@ineosfluor.com
www.ineosfluor.com

Jenny Wilkinson Design
The Studio
8 Woodfield
Harefield UB9 6DJ, UK
Tel: +44 (0) 1895 822856
jenny@paint-by-numbers.co.uk
www.paint-by-numbers.co.uk

Kreon Architectural Lighting
Lakeside House
1 Furzeground Way
Stockley Park East
Uxbridge
Middlesex UB11 1BD, UK
Tel: +44 (0) 208 622 3036
Fax: +44 (0) 208 622 3241
salesuk@kreon.com
www.kreon.com

Lea Ceramiche
Via Cameazzo 21
41042 Fiorano Modenese (MO)
Italy
Tel: +39 0536 837 811
Fax: +39 0536 830 326
www.ceramichelea.com

Lewis Tsurumaki Lewis
147 Essex Street
New York, NY 10002, USA
Tel: 212 505 5955
Fax: 212 505 1648
office@ltlarchitects.com
www.ltlarchitects.com

Lightfader (manufactured
by TAL)
Joos de ter Beetstlaan 33
8740 Pittem
Belgium
Tel: +32 (0) 51 464341
Fax: +32 (0) 51 464342
info@lightfader.be
www.lightfader.be

Linn Products
Glasgow Road
Waterfoot
Eaglesham
Glasgow G76 0EQ
UK
Tel: +44 (0) 141 307 7777
Fax: +44 (0) 141 644 4262
helpline@linn.co.uk
www.linn.co.uk

Litracon
Litracon Bt
Tanya 832
6640 Csongrád
Hungary
Tel: +36 30 255 1648
info@litracon.hu
www.litracon.hu

Lucite International
Queens Gate
Queens Terrace
Southampton SO14 3BP, UK
Tel: +44 (0) 870 240 4620
Fax: +44 (0) 870 240 4626
contactus@lucite.com
www.luciteinternational.com

Lutron
7200 Suter Rd
Coopersburg, PA 18036-1299
USA
Tel: 610 282 3800
intsales@lutron.com
www.lutron.com/smarthouse

UK contact:
Lutron House
6 Sovereign Close
Wapping, London E1W 3JF, UK
Tel: +44 (0) 207 702 0657
Fax: +44 (0) 207 480 6899
lutronlondon@lutron.com

Louverlite
Ashton Road
Hyde
Cheshire SK14 4BG, UK
Tel: +44 (0) 1618 825 000
Fax: +44 (0) 1618 825 009
jamie.marsden@louvolite.com
www.louvolite.com

Magscapes (UK)
5 Albemarle Way
Clerkenwell
London EC1V 4JB, UK
Tel: +44 (0) 20 7336 8674
info@magscapes.com
www.magscapes.com

Marotte
47 rue Eugène Berthoud – BP 87
93402 Saint-Ouen Cedex
Paris
France

directory

Tel: +33 (0) 1 49 48 13 60
Fax: +33 (0) 1 40 12 28 87
contact@marotte.fr
www.marotte.fr

Metall-FX
Unit 18, Manningford Bohune
Estate
Pewsey
Wiltshire SN9 6NL, UK
Tel: +44 (0) 1980 630020
Fax: +44 (0) 1980 630080
info@metall-fx.com
www.metall-fx.com

Mission International
Audio Group, IAG House
Sovereign Court
Ermine Business Park
Huntingdon
Cambridge PE29 6XU, UK
Tel: +44 (0) 1480 447700
Fax: +44 (0) 1480 423701
info@mission.co.uk
www.mission.co.uk

Muraspec
74–78 Wood Lane End
Hemel Hempstead
Herts HP2 4RF, UK
Tel: +44 (0) 8705 117 118
Fax: +44 (0) 8705 329 020
customerservices@muraspec.com
www.muraspec.com

My Foto Wall
90 New North Road
Huddersfield
West Yorkshire HD1 5NE, UK
Tel: +44 (0) 1484 344096
customer-services@myfotowall.
com
www.myfotowall.com

Niall McLaughlin
168 Portobello Road
London W11 2EB, UK
Tel: +44 (0) 20 7792 0973

Nathan Allan Glass
110-12011 Riverside Way
Richmond, BC
Canada V6W 1K6
Tel: 604 277 8533
Fax: 604 277 1515
www.nathanallan.com

Omni Decor
Via del Lavoro, 1
22036 Erba (CO)
Italy
Tel: +39 031 633701
Fax: +39 031 610331
info@omnidecor.net
www.omnidecor.net

Oxeon AB
Fältspatsgatan 2
SE-421 30 Västra Frölunda
Sweden
Tel: +46 (0) 31 709 33 80
Fax: +46 (0) 31 709 33 89
contact@oxeon.se
www.oxeon.se

Panasonic UK
Panasonic House
Willoughby Road
Bracknell
Berkshire RG12 8FP
UK
Tel: +44 (0) 8705 357357
www.panasonic.co.uk

Panelite
3341 S. La Cienega Place
Los Angeles, CA 90016
USA
Tel: 310 202 1115
Fax: 310 202 1151
info@panelite.us
www.e-panelite.com

Pastoe
Rotsoord 3
Postbus 2152
NL-3500 GD Utrecht
The Netherlands
Tel: +31 (0) 30 258 55 55
Fax: +31 (0) 30 252 23 40
ums@pastoe.nl
www.pastoe.nl

Perspex – see Lucite p. 205

Philips Electronics UK Ltd.
The Philips Centre
Guildford Business Park
Guildford
Surrey GU2 8XH
UK
Tel: +44 (0) 1293 776675
www.philips.com/cineos

Pilkington
Prescot Road
St Helens
Merseyside WA10 3TT, UK
Tel: +44 (0) 1744 28882
Fax: +44 (0) 1744 692660
www.pilkington.com

Pilkington North Ameirca
P.O. Box 799
811 Madison Avenue
Toledo, OH 43695, USA
Tel: 419 247 3731
Fax: 419 247 3821

Planolux
Piazza Giustinian Recanati, 7
31100 Treviso
Italy
Tel: +39 0422 419133
Fax: +39 0422 580347
info@planolux.it
www.planolux.it

Polaron
26 Greenhill Crescent
Watford Business Park
Watford
Herts WD18 8XG, UK
Tel: +44 (0) 1923 495495
Fax: +44 (0) 1923 228796
www.polaron.co.uk

Rex Ceramiche
Via Canaletto 24
41042 Fiorano (MO)
Italy
Tel: +39 0536 840 111
Fax: +39 0536 840 750
www.rex-cerart.it

Rogier Sterk
St Peterlaan 115
6821 HG Arnhem
The Netherlands
Tel: +31 (0) 6 2748 3351
Fax: +31 (0) 26 445 1600
info@rogiersterk.nl
www.rogiersterk.nl

Ron Arad Associates
62 Chalk Farm Road
London NW1 8AN, UK
Tel: +44 (0) 20 7284 4963
Fax: +44 (0) 20 7379 0499
www.ronarad.com

Ross Lovegrove
Studio X
21 Powis Mews
London W11 1JN, UK
Tel: +44 (0) 20 7229 7104
Fax: +44 (0) 20 7229 7032

Royal Tichelaar Makkum
Postbus 11
8754 ZN Makkum
The Netherlands
Tel: +31 (0) 515 231 341
Fax: +31 (0) 515 232 555
info@tichelaar.nl
www.tichelaar.nl

Schott Desag (Germany)
Hattenbergstrasse 10
D-55122 Mainz
Germany
Tel: +49 (0) 6131 66 3662
Fax: +49 (0) 6131 664 011
info@schott.com
www.schott.com

Schott
Drummond Road
Astonfields Industrial Estate
Stafford ST16 3EL, UK
Tel: +44 (0) 1785 223166
Fax: +44 (0) 1785 223522
Info.uk@schott.com
www.schott.com

555 Taxter Road
Elmsford, NY 10523, USA
Tel: 914 831 2200
Fax: 914 831 2201
info@us.schott.com
www.us.schott.com

Sharp Electronics UK
4 Furzeground Way
Stockley Park
Uxbridge UB11 1EZ, UK
Tel: +44 (0) 20 8734 2000
www.sharp.co.uk

Shoji Designs
PO Box 1122
Olalla, WA 98359
USA
Tel: 253 857 4712
Fax: 253 857 4015
info@shojidesigns.com
www.shojidesigns.com

Sim2 Multimedia
SIM2 UK Ltd
Steinway House
Worth Farm
Little Horsted
East Sussex TN22 5TT
UK
Tel: +44 (0) 1825 750850
Fax: +44 (0) 1825 750851
info@sim2.co.uk
www.sim2.com

SIM2 USA
10108 USA Today Way
Miramar, FL 33025
Tel: 954 442 2999
Fax: 954 442 2998
vperez@sim2usa.com

Sky Design
1240 North Horman Avenue
Chicago, IL 60651
USA
Tel: 888 2784660
Fax: 773 2783548
www.skydesign.com

SmartComm Group
45 Cressex Enterprise Centre
Lincoln Road
High Wycombe HP12 3RL
UK
Tel: +44 (0) 1494 471 912
Fax: +44 (0) 1494 472 464
info@smartcomm.co.uk
www.smartcomm.co.uk

Solutia
575 Maryville Centre Drive
St Louis, MO 63141
USA
Tel: 314 674 1000

European contact:
Rue Laid Burniat, 3
Parc Scientifique – Fleming
B-1348 Louvain-la-Neuve (Sud)
Belgium
Tel: +32 10 48 12 11
Fax: +32 10 48 12 12
www.solutia.com

Sommers Plastic Products
P.O. Box 4356
31 Styertowne Road
Clifton, NJ 07012

USA
Tel: 973 777 7888
Fax: 973 777 7890
sales@sommers.com
www.sommers.com

Sonance
212 Avenida Fabricante
San Clemente, CA 92672-7531
USA
Tel: 800 582 7777
customerservice@sonance.com
www.sonance.com

Stone & Ceramic Warehouse
51–55 Stirling Road
London W3 8DJ
UK
Tel: +44 (0) 20 8993 5545
Fax: +44 (0) 20 8752 0281
gen@stoneandceramicwarehouse.
co.uk
www.stoneandceramicwarehouse.
co.uk

Swarovski
Perrywood Business Park
Honeycrock Lane
Salfords
Surrey RH1 5JQ
UK
Tel: +44 (0) 1 737 856 805
Fax: +44 (0) 1 737 856 880
customer.relations.gb@swarovski.
com
www.swarovski.com

The Light Lab
20–22 Vestry Street
London N1 7RE
UK
Tel: +44 (0) 20 7278 2678
Fax: +44 (0) 20 7427 2363
info@thelightlab.com
www.thelightlab.com

Total Panel System
Caspe, 97–101
08013 Barcelona
Spain
Tel: +34 (0) 93 247 88 70
Fax: +34 (0) 93 265 45 54
info@totalstone.com
www.totalstone.com

Vanceva (a Solutia brand)
Solutia Inc
575 Maryville Centre Drive
St. Louis, Missouri 63141
USA
Tel: 314 674 1000
Fax: 314 674 7021
glazin@solutia.com
www.vanceva.com/design

Vetroarredo
Via Reginaldo Giuliani, 360
c.a.p. 50141 Firenze
Italy
Tel: +39 055 44951
Fax: +39 055 455295
www.vetroarredo.com

Visiomatic
Weissacher Strasse 1
D-70499 Stuttgart
Germany
Tel: +49 711 83948 830
Fax: +49 711 83948 8388
contact@visiomatic.com
www.visiomatic.com

Yamigiwa
Konoike Building 1F
3-6-1 Kita kuhoji-cho
Chuo-ku
Osaka
501-0058 Japan
Tel: +81 6 2258 6561
Fax: +81 6 2258 6563
press@yamagiwa.co.jp
www.yamagiwa.co.jp

flooring

Aganippe Pavimenti
Zona Industriale 13
Val di SAngo
Lanciano
Italy
Tel: +39 0872 50611
Fax: +39 0872 50628
info@aganippe.com
www.aganippe.com

Alloc
Fiboveien 26
NO-4580 Lyngdal
Norway
Tel: +47 38 34 22 00

Fax: +47 38 34 37 44
alloc@alloc.no
www.alloc.com

Almatec
Viale Virgilio 48
41100 Modena
Italy
Tel: +39 059 888411
Fax: +39 059 848808
info@improntaitalgraniti.com
www.impronta.it

I7200 Fullerton Road
Springfield VA 22150, USA
Tel: 703 455 9200
Fax: 703 455 4619
us@improntaitalgraniti.com
www.improntaitalgraniti-usa.com

Alternative Flooring Company
3b Stephenson Close
East Portway
Andover SP10 3RU
Hampshire
UK
Tel: +44 (0) 1264 335111
Fax: +44 (0) 1264 336445
sales@alternativeflooring.com
www.alternativeflooring.com

Antron (Invista)
4123 East 37th Street North
Wichita, KS 67220
USA
Tel: 877 446 8478 (toll-free
in the US and Canada)
or 001 770 792 4221
(international)
antroncarpetfibres@btconnect.com
www.antron.invista.com
www.invista.com

Bill Amberg
21–22 Chepstow Corner
London W2 4XE
UK
Tel: +44 (0) 20 7727 3560
Fax: +44 (0) 20 7727 3541
www.billamberg.com

American Hardwood Export Council
1111 19th Street, NW
Suite 800

Washington, DC 20036, USA
Tel: 202 463 2720
Fax: 202 463 2787
www.ahec.org/

3 St Michael's Alley
London EC3V 9DS
UK
Tel: +44 (0) 20 7626 4111
Fax: +44 (0) 20 7626 4222
info@ahec-europe.org
www.ahec-europe.org

Amtico
UK Sales Division
Kingfield Road
Coventry
West Midlands CV6 5AA
www.amtico.com

Amtico International Inc.
The Amtico Studio
6480 Roswell Road
Atlanta, GA 30328
Tel: 404 267 1900
Fax: 404 267 1901

Apavisa Porcelanico
Ctra. Castellón
San Juan de Moró, Hm. 7,5
12130 San Juan De Moro
Castellón
Spain
Tel: +34 964 701 120
Fax: +34 964 701 195
info@apavisa.com
www.apavisa.com

Appiani
Via Pordenone, 13
31046 Oderzo (TV)
Italy
Tel: +39 0422 815 308
Fax: +39 0422 814 026
info@appiani.it
www.appiani.it

Ariostea
Via Cimabue, 20
42014 Castellarano (RE)
Italy
Tel: +39 0536 816 811
Fax: +39 0536 816 838
info@ariostea.it
www.ariostea.it

Armstrong – see p. 204

ASN Natural Stone
2415 17th Street
San Francisco, CA 94110
USA
Tel: 415 626 2616
Fax: 415 626 3578
infowest@asnstone.com
www.asnstone.com

Azteca Ceramica
Ctra CastellÓn
Alcoralum 19, 7
12110 Alcora
Spain
Tel: +34 964 367 500
Fax: +34 964 367 444
comercial@aztecaceramica.com
www.aztecaceramica.com

Azuvi
Av Italia 58
12540 Villareal
Castellón
Spain
Tel: +34 964 509 100
Fax: +34 964 509 115
azuvi@azuvi.com
www.azuvi.com

Beige Design
1025 Carleton Street, No. 14
Berkeley, California 94710, USA
Tel: 510 666 0892
thom@beigedesign.com
www.beigedesign.com

Bisazza – see p. 204

Boen Bruk
N-4658 Tveit
Norway
Tel: +47 38 06 66 00
Fax: +47 38 06 66 01
boenbruk@boen.no
www.boen.com

Bolon
Box 73
SE–523 22 Ulricehamn
Sweden
Tel: +46 (0) 321 53 04 00
Fax: +46 (0) 321 53 04 50
info@bolon.se
www.bolon.se

directory

Boral Timber
Six Campbell Court
Novato, CA 94947
USA
Tel: 800 267 2560
Fax: 415 893 0253
info@boraltimber.com
www.boraltimber.com

Café Interiors – see p. 204

CeraCasa
PO Box 33
12110 Alcora, Castellón
Spain
Tel: +34 964 361 611
Fax: +34 964 360 967
ceracasa@ceracasa.com
www.ceracasa.com

Cerámicas Diago
Partida Benadresa s/n
12006 Castellón
Spain
Tel: +34 964 340 717
Fax: +34 964 218 444
ceramicas@diago.com
www.diago.com

Cerim
Via Canaletto, 24
41042 Fiorano
Italy
Tel: +39 0536 840111
Fax: +39 0536 844750
www.cerim.it

Christine van der Hurd
260 Fifth Avenue
Suite 11
New York, NY 10001
USA
Tel: 212 213 6541
Fax: 212 213 6836
info@vanderhurdstudio.com
www.vanderhurdstudio.com

Continental Cut Stone
P.O. Box 37
Florence, TX 76527
USA
Tel: 254 793 2329
Fax: 254 793 2358
info@continentalcutstone.com
www.continentalcutstone.com

Craigie Stockwell Carpets
81 York Street
London
W1H 1QH
UK
Tel: +44 (0) 20 7224 8380
Fax: +44 (0) 20 7224 8381
www.craigiestockwellcarpets.com

CuoioArredo – see p. 204

Dalsouple – see p. 204

Droog Design – see p. 204

Eco Timber
1611 Fourth Street
San Rafael, CA 94901
USA
Tel: 415 258 8454
Fax: 415 258 8455
www.ecotimber.com

Effepimarmi
69, Via Del Commercio Nord
56034 Casciana Terme (PI)
Italy
Tel: +39 0458 002 200
Fax: +39 0498 077 130
info@effepimarmi.it
www.effepimarmi.it

Floor Gres
Via Canaletto 24
41042 Fiorano
Modenese (MO)
Italy
Tel: +39 0536 840 111
Fax: +39 0536 844 750
info@floorgres.it
www.floorgres.it

Forest Stewardship Council
FSC International Center
Charles-de-Gaulle 5
53113 Bonn
Germany
Tel: + 49 (228) 367 66 0
Fax: + 49 (228) 367 66 30
www.fsc.org
fsc@fsc.org

Forbo International SA
Lindenstrasse 8
Postfach 1041
CH - 6341 Baar

Tel. +41 58 787 25 25
Fax +41 58 787 20 25
info@forbo.com www.forbo.com

Front – see p. 205

Fusion Glass Designs –
see p. 205

GKD – see p. 205

Gobbetto
Via Carroccio, 16
20123 Milan
Italy
Tel: +39 02 83 222 69
Fax: +39 02 89 404 269
gobbetto@gobbetto.com
www.gobbetto.com

Goodwin Heart
Pine Company
106 SW 109th Place
Micanopy, FL 32667-9442
USA
Tel: 800 336 3118
or 352 466 0339
Fax: 352 466 0608
goodwin@heartpine.com
www.heartpine.com

Grespania Ceramica
CV·16 (Ctra. Castellón-Alcora),
Km 2,200 P.O. Box 157
12080 Castellón
Spain
Tel: +34 964 344 411
Fax: +34 964 344 401
www.grespania.com
mail@grespania.com

Heuga
Tel: +1 800 4384 2266
www.heuga.com

Hyperion Tiles – see p. 205

Ibero Alcorense
Ctra Castellón Teruel Km 19
Camino Foyes Ferraes s/n
12110 Alcora Castellón
Spain
Tel: +34 964367536
Fax: +34 9644361088
ibero@iberoalcorense.com
www.iberoalcorense.com

Ikea
www.ikea.com

Iris Ceramica
Via Ghiarola Nuova, 119
41042 Fiorano Modenese (MO)
Italy
Tel: +39 0536 862 111
Fax: +39 0536 862 452
www.irisceramica.com
mkng@irisfmg.com

Iris Fabbrica Marmi e Graniti
Via Ghiarola Nuova, 119
41042 Fiorano Modenese
Modena (MO)
Italy
Tel: +39 0536 862 340
www.irisfmg.com

Junckers UK
Wheaton Road
Witham
Essex CM8 3UJ
UK
Tel: +44 (0) 1376 534 700
Fax: +44 (0) 1376 514 401
brochures@junckers.co.uk
www.junckers.co.uk

Karastan
508 East Morris Street
Dalton, GA 30721
USA
Tel: 800 234 1120
www.karastan.com
karastan@rsvpcomm.com

Kasthall
Box 254
511 23 Kinna
Fritslavägen 42
Sweden
Tel: +46 320 20 59 00
Fax: +46 320 20 59 01
info@kasthall.se
www.kasthall.se

Lea Ceramiche – see p. 205

Le Qr
Via Soresi, 23/a
12084 Mondovi' (CN)
Italy
Tel: +39 0174 551020
Fax: +39 0174 481937

info@leqr.it
www.leqr.it

Listone Giordano
www.listonegiordano.com

Linie Design
Granlyet 7
3540 Lynge
Denmark
Tel: +45 48189066
Fax: +45 48189275
info@liniedesign.dk
www.liniedesign.dk

Malibu Stone
3730 Cross Creek Road
Malibu, CA 90265, USA
Tel: 310 456 9444
Fax: 310 456 8569
malibu.stone@verizon.net
www.malibustonemasonry.com

Mirage Floors
1255–98th Street
Saint-Georges
Quebec
Canada G5Y 8J5
Tel: 418 227 1181
Fax: 418 227 1188
www.miragefloors.com

Missoni Home
T & J Vestor Spa
Via Roma, 71/b
21010 Golasecca (VA)
Italy
Tel: +39 0331 950 311
Fax: +39 0331 959 011
sales@tjvestor.it
www.missonihome.it

Mohawk Carpet
Tel: 800 266 4295
www.mohawkcarpet.com

Mountain Lumber
6812 Spring Hill Road
Ruckersville, VA 22968, USA
Tel: 434 985 3646
Fax: 434 985 4105
sales@mountainlumber.com
www.mountainlumber.com

Mykon
5 Stukeley Business Centre
Blackstone Road
Huntingdon PE29 6EF
Cambridgeshire
UK
Tel: +44 (0) 1480 415070
Fax: +44 (0) 1480 450181
sales@mykon-systems.com
www.mykon-systems.com

Nani Marquina
Església 10, 3er D
08024 Barcelona
Spain
Tel: +34 932 376 465
Fax: +34 932 175 774
info@nanimarquina.com
www.nanimarquina.com

Navarti
Ctra Onda-Villareal km 3.5
12200 Onda (Castellón)
Spain
Tel: +34 964 776 262
Fax: +34 964 770 000
global@navarti.com
www.navarti.com

Onix Mosaico
Ronda Circunvalación Este, P25
U.I.6
12200 Onda (Castellón)
Spain
Tel: +34 964 776 287
Fax: +34 964 776 284
onix@onixmosaico.com
www.onixmosaico.com

John Pawson
Unit B, 70-78 Yorkway
London N1 9AG
UK
Tel: +44 (0) 20 7837 2929
Fax: +44 (0) 20 7837 4929
email@johnpawson.com
www.johnpawson.com

Parentesi Quadra
Via Arcoveggio 11
51039 Quarrata (PT)
Italy
Tel: +39 0573 730 98
Fax: +39 0573 731 44
info@parentesiquadra.it
www.parentesiquadra.com

Pergo
Head office
Strandridaregatan 8
PO Box 1010
231 25 Trelleborg
Sweden
Phone: +46 410 363100
Fax: +46 410 155 60
cc.uk@pergo.com
www.pergo.com

PO Box 13113
Kingsbury Link
Piccadilly
Tamworth B77 9DJ
UK
Tel: +44 (0) 1827 871 840
Fax: +44 (0) 1827 871 850

Peronda
Avda Manuel Escobedo 26
12200 Onda
Spain
Tel: +34 964 602 012
Fax: +34 964 600 361
webmaster@peronda.es
www.peronda.es

Porcelanosa
Marshall House
468–472 Purley Way
Croydon CR0 4RG
UK
Tel: +44 (0) 870 8110 550
Fax: +44 (0) 870 8110 584
www.porcelanosa.co.uk

Quick-Step Flooring
Ooigemstraat 3
8710 Wielsbeke
Belgium
Tel: +32 (0) 56 675211
Fax: +32 (0) 56 675212
info@quick-step.com
www.quick-step.com

Reed Harris
Riverside House
27 Carnwath Road
London SW6 6JE
UK
Tel: +44 (0) 207 736 7511
Fax: +44 (0) 207 736 2988
www.reedharris.co.uk

Rex Ceramiche – see p. 206

Rhodes Architectural Stone
2011 East Olive Street
Seattle, WA 98122
USA
Tel: 206 709 3000
Fax: 206 709 3003
www.rhodes.org

Rogier Sterk – see p. 206

Royal Mosa Meessenerweg
3586224 AL Maastricht
P.O. Box 1026
6201 BA Maastricht
The Netherlands
Tel + 31 (0)43 368 94 44
Fax +31 (0)43 368 93 35
www.mosa.nl

Royal Tichelaar Makkum –
see p. 206

Rubber Flooring Company
Units 12 & 13
Smallshaw Industrial Estate
Burnley
Lancashire BB11 5SX
UK
Tel: +44 (0) 1282 411 014
Fax: +44 (0) 1282 411 015
www.therubberflooringcompany.
co.uk

Saar Oosterhof
vormgever@saar.nl
www.saar.nl

Shaw Floors
P.O. Drawer 2128
616 E. Walnut Avenue
Dalton, GA 30722-2128
USA
Tel: 800 4417429
www.shawfloors.com

Smile Plastics
Mansion House
Ford
Shrewsbury SY5 9LZ
UK
Tel: +44 (0) 1743 850 267
Fax: +44 (0) 1743 851 067
smileplas@aol.com
www.smile-plastics.co.uk

Smith & Fong
Company USA
375 Oyster Point Boulevard #3
South San Francisco, CA 94080
USA
Tel: 650 872 1184
Fax: 650 872 1185
info@durapalm.com
www.durapalm.com

Stile
Via dei Laghi 18
Bivio Lugnano
06018 Trestina Citta di
Castello (PG)
Italy
Tel: +39 075 864 7616
Fax: +39 075 864 7630
stile@stile.com
www.stile.com

Stepevi UK
274 King's Road
London SW3 5AW, UK
Tel: +44 (0) 20 7376 7574
Fax: +44 (0) 20 7376 7577
info@stepevi.com
www.stepevi.com

Swisstex
P.O. Box 9258
Greenville
SC 29604-9258
USA
Tel: 864 845 7541
Fax: 864 845 5699
swisstex@foampartner.com
www.swisstex.com

Tabu
Via Rencati 110
22063 Cantù (CO)
Italy
Tel: +39 031 714 493
Fax: +39 031 711 988
info@tabu.it
www.tabu.it

Tiles of Spain (ASCER)?
Camino Caminás s/n?12003
Castellón
Spain
Tel: +34 964 727 200?
Fax: +34 964 727 212
global@ascer.es
www.spaintiles.info

The Rug Company
124 Holland Park Avenue
London W11 4UE
UK
T: +44 (0) 20 7229 5148
F: +44 (0) 20 7792 3384
sales@therugcompany.co.uk
www.therugcompany.co.uk

Tufenkian Carpets
919 3rd Avenue
Ground Level
New York, NY 10022
USA
Tel: 212 475 2475
info@tufenkiancarpets.com
www.tufenkiancarpets.com

Tutto Parquet – see Listone
Giordano

Woodnotes
Tallberginkatu 1B
00180 Helsinki
Finland
Tel: +358 9 6942200
Fax: +358 9 6942221
woodnotes@woodnotes.fi
www.woodnotes.fi

Zimmerman, Jonathan
Tel: 415 923 9278
z@zdomes.com
www.zdomes.com

doors

G&S Allgood
297 Euston Road
London NW1 3AQ
UK
Tel: +44 (0) 20 7387 9951
Fax: +44 (0) 20 7383 7950
email@allgood.co.uk
www.allgood.co.uk

Bisca
Sawmill Lane
Helmsley
North Yorkshire YO62 5DQ
UK
Tel: +44 (0) 1439 771 702
Fax: +44 (0) 1439 771 002
info@bisca.co.uk
www.bisca.co.uk

directory

Cocif
Via Ponte Ospedaletto, 1560
47020 Longiano (FC)
Italy
Tel: +39 0547 56144
Fax: +39 0547 54094
info@cocif.com
www.cocif.com

Colombo Design
Via Baccaniello, 22
24030 Terno D'Isola (BG)
Italy
Tel: +39 035 49 49 001
Fax: +39 035 90 50 44
info@columbodesign.it
www.colombodesign.it

Coop Legno
Via Saint-Eusebio 4/G
41014 Castelvetro di Modena
(MO)
Italy
Tel: +39 05970 2712
Fax: +39 05970 2254
www.cooplegno.com

Dorma UK
Wilbury Way
Hitchin
Herts SG4 0AB
UK
Tel +44 (0) 1462 477600
Fax +44 (0) 1462 477601
autos@dorma-uk.co.uk
www.dorma-uk.co.uk

Fioravazzi
Via Zanina 18
Loc. Birbesi di Guidizzolo
Mantova
Italy
Tel: +39 0376 84953 12
Fax: +39 0376 849533
www.fioravazzi.com

FSB (Franz Schneider Brakel)
Nieheimer Strasse 38
33034 Brakel
Germany
Tel: +49 5272 608 0
Fax: +49 5272 608 300
info@fsb.de
www.fsb.de

Fusital (see Valli & Valli UK)

Via Concordia, 16
20055 Renate (MI)
Italy
Tel: +39 0362 982 1
vendite.italia@vallievalli.com
www.vallievalli.com

Garofoli
Via Recanatese 37
Castelfidardo (AN)
Italy
Tel: +39 0717 27 171
Fax: +39 0717 80 380
www.garofoli.com

GD Dorigo
Via G. Pascoli, 23
31053 Pieve di Soligo (TV)
Italy
Tel: +39 0438 840153
Fax: +39 0438 82268
info@gd-dorigo.com
www.gd-dorigo.com

Ghidini
Via Chiesa 42/44
25060 Brozzo di Marcheno (BS)
Italy
Tel: +39 030 89691
Fax: +39 030 8960333
info@ghidini.com
www.ghidini.com

Hafele UK
Swift Valley Industrial Estate
Rugby
Warwickshire CV21 1RD; UK
Tel: +44 (0) 1788 542020
Fax: +44 (0) 1788 544440
www.hafele.co.uk
www.hafeleamericas.com

3901 Cheyenne Drive
Archdale, NC 27263
Tel: 336 434 2322
Fax: 336 431 3831

Henry Glass
Via Boarie 35 (zona industriale)
31046 Oderzo (TV)
Italy
Tel: +39 0422 209411
Fax: +39 0422 209490
info@henryglass.it
www.henryglass.it

HEWI Heinrich Wilke
Prof.-Bier-Strasse 1–5
34454 Bad Arolsen
Germany
Tel: +49 5691 82 0
Fax: +49 5691 82 319
www.hewi.com

Inner Door
Royds Enterprise Park
Future Fields
Bradford
West Yorkshire
BD6 3EWUK
Tel: +44 (0) 845 128 3958
Fax: +44 (0) 845 128 3959
www.innerdoor.co.uk

Jeld-Wen Doors USA
P.O. Box 1329
Klamath Falls, OR 97601
USA
Tel: 800 535 3936
www.jeld-wen.com/jwlb

Laura Meroni
Via Nuova Valassina
22060 Arosio (CO)
Italy
Tel: +39 031 761 450
Fax: +39 031 763 311
info@laurameroni.com
www.laurameroni.com

Louverlite – see p. 205

Lualdiporte
Via Piemonte 13
20010 Mesero (MI)
Italy
Tel: +39 02 9789248
Fax: +39 02 97289463
info@lualdiporte.com
www.lualdiporte.com

Mandelli
Via Rivabella, 90
20045 Besana in Brianza (MI)
Italy
Tel: +39 0362 96 99 1
Fax: +39 0362 96 99 20
www.mandelli.it

Export office:
Tel: +39 0362 96 99 1
Fax: +39 0362 96 99 30

McDowell and Benedetti
68 Rosebery Avenue
London EC1R 4RR
UK
Tel: +44 (0) 20 72788810
Fax: +44 (0) 20 72788844
email@mcdowellbenedetti.com
www.mcdowellbenedetti.com

Movi
Via Don Guanella 2
22060 Arosio (CO)
Italy
Tel: +39 031 761 414
Fax: +39 031 762 181
info@movi.it
www.movi.it

Nathan Allan Glass Studios –
see p. 206

Olivari
Via Matteotti 140
28021 Borgomanero (NO)
Italy
Tel: +39 0322 835080
Fax: +39 0322 846484
olivari@olivari.it
www.olivari.it

Portarredo (Invisibile)
Via C. Besana SNC
44011 Argenta (FE)
Italy
Tel: +39 0532 800 960
Fax: +39 0532 318 703
info@portarredo.com
www.linvisible.it

Porte Zanini
37021 Corbiolo di Bosco Chiesa
Nuova (VR)
Italy
Tel: +39 045 70 50 988
Fax: +39 045 6780 108
info@zaniniporte.com
www.zaniniporte.com

Randi
Mirabellevej 3
DK-8900 Randers
Denmark
Tel: +45 86 42 75 22
Fax: +45 86 43 93 14
randi@randi.dk
www.randi.dk

Rimadesio
Via Furlanelli, 96
20034 Giussano (MI), Italy
Tel: +39 0362 3171
www.rimadesio.it

Schott – see p. 206

Scrigno
Via Casale, 975
47828 S. Ermete di Santarcangelo
di Romagna (RN), Italy
Tel: +39 0541 757711
Fax: +39 0541 758744
or +39 0541 757780
scrigno@scrigno.it
www.scrigno.net

Tecnoline
Lötzener Str.2-4D-28084 Bremen
Germany
Tel: +49 421 43735 0
Fax: +49 421 43735 25
info@tecnoline.de
www.tecnoline.de

Tre-P
Via dell'Industria, 2
20034 Birone di Giussano (MI), Italy
Tel: +39 0362 861120
Fax: +39 0362 310292
trep@trep-trepiu.com
www.trep-trepiu.com

Valli & Valli UK
Unit 8 Hedging Lane Industrial
Estate, Hedging Lane
Dosthill, Tamworth
Staffordshire B77 5HH, UK
Tel: +44 (0) 1827 283 655
Fax: +44 (0) 1827 280 553
sales@valliandvalli.co.uk
vallivalli-uk@valli.force9.nex
www.vallievalli.com

windows

AG Plastics
Spinnerijstraat 100
B-8530 Stasegem Harelbeke
Belgium
Tel: +32 (0) 56 20 00 00
Fax: +32 (0) 56 21 95 99
info@agp.be
www.agplastics.com

Andersen
100 Fourth Avenue North
Bayport, MN 55003-1096
USA
Tel: 651 264 5150
www.andersenwindows.com

Balcony Ltd
Unit 1b Ivydene Industrial Estate
Ivydene Lane
Ashurstwood
West Sussex RH19 3TN
UK
Tel: +44 (0) 1342 410 411
Fax: +44 (0) 1342 410 412
effi@balcony-ltd.com
www.balcony-ltd.com

Colt Group
New Lane
Havant
Hampshire PO9 2LY
UK
Tel: +44 (0) 2392 451 111
Fax: +44 (0) 2392 454 220
info@coltgroup.com
www.coltgroup.com

Green Building Store
11 Huddersfield Road
Meltham
West Yorkshire HD9 4NJ
UK
Tel: +44 (0) 1484 854 898
Fax: +44 (0) 1484 854 899
info@greenbuildinstore.co.uk
www.greenbuildingstore.co.uk

Greenpeace
Canonbury Villas
London N1 2PN, UK
Tel: +44 (0) 20 7865 8100
Fax: +44 (0) 20 7865 8200
info@uk.greenpeace.org
www.greenpeace.org.uk

Groupe Foin – see p. 205

Hunter Douglas Europe
Piekstraat 2
3071 El Rotterdam
The Netherlands
Tel: +31 10 486 9911
Fax: +31 10 484 7910
info@hde.nl
www.hunterdouglas.nl

Jeld-Wen Doors– see left

Louverlite – see p. 205

Madico USA
45 Industrial Parkway
Woburn, MA 01888
USA
Tel: 800 225 1926
Fax: 781 935 6841
info@madico.com
www.madico.com

Marvin Windows & Doors
P.O. Box 100
Warroad, MN 56763
USA
Tel: 800 537 7828
www.marvin.com

UK address:
Canal House
Catherine Wheel Road
Brentford
Middlesex TW8 8BD
UK
Tel: +44 (0) 208 5698 222
Fax: +44 (0) 208 5606 374
sales@marvinUK.com
www.marvin-architectural.com

Omni Decor – see p. 206

Pella Windows
Pella Corporation
Customer Service Department
102 Main Street
Pella, Iowa 50219
USA
www.pella.com

Pilkington – see p. 206
www.keepupworld.com

Saint-Gobain
81 Aldwych House
London WC2B 4HQ
UK
Tel: +44 (0) 20 7400 8800
Fax: +44 (0) 20 7400 8899
info@saint-gobain.co.uk
www.saint-gobain.co.uk

Sanei Hopkins
300 Aberdeen House
22–24 Highbury Grove

London N5 2EA
UK
Tel: +44 (0) 207 704 1901
Fax: +44 (0) 207 704 9048
info@saneihopkins.co.uk
www.saneihopkins.co.uk

Schott – see p. 206

Scrigno – see left

Seufert-Niklaus
Lindenweg 2
97654 Bastheim
Germany
Tel: +49 (0) 97 73 91 81 0
Fax: +49 (0) 97 73 91 81 30
info@seufert-niklaus.de
www.seufert-niklaus.de

Silent Gliss
Star Lane
Margate
Kent CT9 4EF
UK
Tel: +44 (0) 1843 863 571
Fax: +44 (0) 1843 864 503
info@silentgliss.co.uk
www.silentgliss.co.uk

Sivoia QED – see Lutron p. 205

Solatube International, Inc.
2210 Oak Ridge Way
Vista, CA 92081
USA
Tel: 760 597 4400
Fax: 760 599 5181
www.solatube.com

Soltag
Rued Langgaards Vej
Copenhagen
Denmark
www.soltag.net

Targetti
Via Pratese 164
50145 Florence
Italy
Tel: +39 055 37 911
Fax: +39 055 37 91 26 6
targetti@targetti.it
www.targetti.com

Vanceva – see p. 207

Velux
Aadalsvej 99
2970 Horsholm
Denmark
Tel: +45 45164000
Fax: +45 45164002
www.velux.com

Weather Shield USA
531 N Eighth Street
PO Box 309
Medford, WI 54451
USA
Tel: 800 477 6808
www.weathershield.com

WoodTrade F. Hecht
Dillberg 16
D-97828 Marktheidenfeld
Germany
Tel: +49 93 91 / 91 62 76
Tel: +49 93 91 / 91 62 77
office@woodtrade-svl.com

staircases

Albini & Fontanot
Via P. Paolo Pasolini, 6
47852 Cerasolo Ausa (RN)
Italy
Tel: +39 0541 906 111
Fax: +39 0541 906 124
www.albiniefontanot.com

Arcways
1076 Ehlers Road
Neenah, WI 54956
USA
Tel: 800 558 5096
Fax: 920 725 2053
info@arcways.com
www.arcways.com

Andrew Moor Associates
14 Chamberlain Street
London NW1 8XB
UK
Tel: +44 (0) 20 7586 8181
Fax: +44 (0) 20 7586 8484
andrew@andrewmoor.co.uk
www.andrewmoor.com

Balcony Ltd – see left

Barrett Lloyd Davis Associates
535 Kings Road
London SW10 0SZ
UK
Tel: +44 (0) 20 7838 5555
Fax: +44 (0) 20 7838 5556
mail@blda.co.uk
www.blda.co.uk

Bisca – see p. 209

Boundary Metal Ltd.
The Steel Works
Colthrop Business Park
Colthrop Lane
Thatcham
Berkshire RG19 4LP
UK
Tel: +44 (0) 1635 879818
Fax: +44 (0) 1635 879810
enquiries@boundary-metal.co.uk
www.boundary-metal.co.uk

Tsao & McKown
20 Vandam Street
Tenth Floor
New York, NY 10013
USA
Tel: 212 337 3800
Fax: 212 337 0013
info@tsao-mckown.com
www.tsao-mckown.com

Canal Engineering
Lenton Lane
Nottingham NG7 2PQ
UK
Tel: +44 (0) 115 986 6321
Fax: +44 (0) 115 986 0211
enquiries@canalengineering.co.uk
www.canalengineering.co.uk

Corrigan, Soundy & Kilaiditi
93A High Street
Eton
Windsor SL4 6AF
UK
Tel: +44 (0) 1753 840 519
Fax: +44 (0) 1753 868 227
info@cskarchitects.co.uk
www.cskarchitects.co.uk

Edilco
Via Verona 12
37060 Sona (VR)
Italy

Tel: +39 04560 82222
Fax: +39 04560 80100
info@edilco.it
www.edilco.it

Eva Jiricna Architects
38 Warren Street
London W1T 6AE
UK
Tel: +44 (0) 20 7554 2400
Fax: +44 (0) 20 7388 8022
mail@ejal.com
www.ejal.com

Gooding Aluminium – see
p. 205
www.goodingalum.com

HEWI Germany – see p. 210

Joel Berman Glass
1–1244 Cartwright Street
Vancouver BC V6H 3R8
Canada
Tel: 604 684 8332
Fax: 604 684 8373
info@jbermanglass.com
www.jbermanglass.com

Ladders Online
T.B. Davies (Cardiff)
Penarth Road
Cardiff CF11 8TD
UK
Tel: 08450 647647
Fax: 029 2070 2386
info@tbdavies.co.uk
www.ladders-online.com

LightGraphix
20 Bourne Road
Industrial Park
Crayford
Kent DA1 4BZ
UK
Tel: +44 (0) 1322 527629
Fax: +44 (0) 1322 524902
light@lightgraphix.co.uk
www.lightgraphix.co.uk

Light & Motion
(Lichttechnik, Austria)
Paulusgasse 13
A 1030 Vienna
Austria
Tel: +43 1 714 23 260

Fax: +43 1 713 06 76
info@lightandmotion.at
www.lightandmotion.at

Limestone Gallery
Arch 47 South Lambeth Road
London SW8 1SS
UK
Tel: +44 (0) 20 7735 8555
Fax: +44 (0) 20 7793 8880
info@limestonegallery.com
www.limestonegallery.com

Luigi Rosselli Architects
15 Randle Street
Surry Hills 2010
New South Wales
Australia
Tel: +61 292 811 498
Fax: +61 292 810 196
www.luigirosselli.com
luigiroselli@netspace.net.au

Muvis (Lights)
Via Turati, 32
20121 Milano
Italy
Tel: +39 02 62694718
Fax: +39 02 29062781
info@muvis.com
www.muvis.com

Mykon – see p. 209

Nathan Allan Glass – see
p. 206

Rick Mather Architects
123 Camden High Street
London NW1 7JR
UK
Tel: +44 (0) 20 72841727
Fax: +44 (0) 20 72677826
info@rickmather.com
www.rickmather.com

Ross Lovegrove – see p. 206

Simon Conder Associates
Nile Street Studios
8 Nile Street
London N1 7RF, UK
Tel: +44 (0) 20 7251 2144
Fax: +44 (0) 20 7251 2145
sca@simonconder.co.uk
www.simonconder.co.uk

Tacchini
Via Domodossola 19
20030 Baruccana di Seveso (MI)
Italy
Tel: +39 0362 504 182
Fax: +39 0362 552 402
info@tacchini.it
www.tacchini.it

heating and cooling

Actis
infos@actis-isolation.com
www.actis-isolation.com

Aestus
Unit 5
Strawberry Lane Industrial Estate
Strawberry Lane
Willenhall
West Midlands WV13 3RS
UK
Tel: +44 (0) 870 403 0115 for UK
distributor
Tel: +44 (0) 1902 632 256
Fax: +44 (0) 1902 635 800
sales@aestus-radiators.com
www.aestus-radiators.com

Antrax
Via Boscalto 40
31023 Resana (TV)
Italy
Tel: +39 0423 7174
Fax: +39 0423 717474
antrax@antrax.it
www.antrax.it

BedZed
homes@peabody.org.uk
www.bedzed.org.uk

**Bill Dunster Architects Zed
Factory Ltd**
24 Helios Road
Wallington
Surrey SM6 7BZ
UK
Tel: +44 (0) 20 8404 1380
Fax: +44 (0) 20 8404 2255
www.zedfactory.com

Bisque
23 Queen Square
Bath BA1 2HX
UK
Tel: +44 (0) 122 547 8500
Fax: +44 (0) 122 547 8586
mail@bisque.co.uk
www.bisque.co.uk

Brandoni
Via O. Pigni 2
60022 Castelfidardo (AN)
Italy
Tel: +39 071 7822 026
Fax: +39 071 7821 772
info@brandoni.com
www.brandoni.com

Brilliant
Thwaites Close
Blackburn BB1 2QQ, UK
Tel: +44 (0) 1254 682384
Fax: +44 (0) 1254 672647
info@brilliantfires.co.uk
www.brilliantfires.co.uk

**Building Research
Establishment UK**
Garston, Watford
WD25 9XX, UK
enquiries@bre.com.uk
Tes: +44 (0)1923 664000
www.bre.co.uk

Casa Vieja
Lamps Plus
20250 Plummer Street
Chatsworth, CA 91311
USA
Tel: 800 7821967
www.lampsplus.com

**Centre for Alternative
Technology** (CAT)
Machynlleth
Powys
SY20 9AZ
Wales, UK
Tel: +44 (0) 1654 702 400
Fax: +44 (0) 1654 702 782
www.cat.org.uk

Celcius Italia
Corso Emanuele Filiberto 8
23900 Lecco
Italy

Tel: +39 0341 220376
Fax: +39 0341 220187
info@celsiusitalia.it
www.celsiusitalia.it

Clivet
Via Camp Lonc, 25
32030 Villapaiera - Feltre (BL)
Italy
Tel: +39 0439 3131
Fax: +39 0439 313382
info@clivet.it
www.clivet.itCordivari

Zona Industriale Pagliare
64020 Morro D'Oro (TE)
Italy
Tel: +39 085 80401
Fax: +39 085 80414 18
info@cordivari.it
www.cordivari.it

CVO Firevault
UK Showroom:
36 Great Titchfield Street
London W1W 8BQ
UK
Tel: +44 (0) 207 580 5333
Fax: +44 (0) 207 255 2234
enquiries@cvofirevault.co.uk
www.cvo.co.uk

Head office:
Unit 4 Beaumont Square
Durham Way South
Aycliffe Industrial Park, Newton
Aycliffe, County Durham DL5 6SW
UK

Diligence (Focus Fires)
22 Dart Mills
Old Totnes Road
Buckfastleigh TQ11 0NF
UK
Tel: +44 (0) 1364 644 790
Fax: +44 (0) 1364 644 791
www.diligenceinternational.com

Dimplex
Millbrook House
Grange Drive
Hedge End
Southampton SO30 2DF, UK
Tel: +44 (0) 870 077 7117
Fax: +44 (0) 870727 0109
www.dimplex.co.uk

Dru Heating
Drugasar
Deans Road
Manchester M27 0JH
UK
Tel: +44 (0) 161 793 8700
Fax: +44 (0) 161 727 8057
info@drufire.co.uk
www.drufire.co.uk

Ecolec
Sharrocks Street
Wolverhampton WV1 3RP
UK
Tel: +44 (0) 1902 457 575
Fax: +44 (0) 1902 457 797
enquiries@ecolec.co.uk
www.ecolec.co.uk

Elgin & Hall
Adelphi House
Hunton
Nr. Bedale
North Yorkshire DL8 1LY
UK
Tel: +44 (0) 1677 450 712
Fax: +44 (0) 1677 450 713
info@elgin.co.uk
www.elgin.co.uk

Feilden Clegg Architects
21 Great Tichfield Street
London W1W 8BA
UK
Tel: +44 (0) 20 7323 5737
Fax: +44 (0) 20 7323 5720
london@feildenclegg.com
www.feildenclegg.com

Fondis
18 rue Guy de Place
BP 60010 Vieux Thann
68801 Thann Cedex
France
Tel: +33 (0) 389 377 500
Fax: +33 (0) 389 377 589
www.fondis.com

Friends of the Earth
26-28 Underwood Street
London N1 7JQ
UK
Tel: +44 (0) 20 7490 1555
Fax: +44 (0) 20 7490 0881
www.foe.co.uk
www.foe.org

Gruppo Piazzetta
Via Montello 22
31010 Casella D'Asolo (TV)
Italy
Tel: +39 04235271
Fax: +39 0423 55178
infopiazzetta@piazzetta.it
www.gruppopiazzetta.com

Heat & Glo
Hearth & Homes Technologies
20802 Kensington Boulevard
Lakeville, MN 55044
USA
Tel: 952 985 6000
Fax: 952 985 6001
info@heatnglo.com
www.heatnglo.com

Home Depot
Tel: 800 4300 3376
www.homedepot.com

Hunter Fan Company
11660 Central Parkway
Jacksonville, FL 32224
USA
Tel: 901 743 1360
Fax: 901 248 2435
global@hunterfan.com
www.hunterfan.com

Irsap / Officina Delle Idee
Via Delle Industrie 211
45031 Arquà Polesine (RO)
Italy
Tel: +39 042 546 6611
Fax: +39 042 546 5044
officinadelleidee@irsap.it
www.officina-delle-idee.com/

JIS
Warehouse 2
Nash Lane, Off Church Road
Haywards Heath
West Sussex RH17 7NJ
UK
Tel: +44 (0) 1444 831 200
Fax: +44 (0) 1444 831 900
info@jiseurope.co.uk
www.jiseurope.co.uk

King & Miranda Design Srl
Via Savona, 97
Milano 20144
Italy

Tel: +39 0248953851
Fax: +39 0247711872info@kingmiranda.com
www.kingmiranda.com

Lamps Plus
www.lampsplus.com

LG
1000 Sylvan Avenue
Englewood Cliffs
New Jersey 07632
USA
Tel: 800 243 0000
customerservice@lge.com
us.lge.com (US website)
uk.lge.com (UK website)

Limestone Gallery – see left

Mark Gajewski
G Squared Art
PO Box 2480
Avila Beach, CA 93424
USA
Tel: 877 8585333
info@g2art.com
www.g2art.com

MHS
35 Nobel Square
Burnt Mills Industrial Estate
Basildon
Essex SS13 1LT
UK
Tel: +44 (0) 1268 591010
Fax: +44 (0) 1268 728202
www.mhsradiators.com
sales@modular-heating-group.co.uk

Minka Aire
1151 W. Bradford Ct.
Corona, CA 92882
USA
Tel: 951 735 9220
Fax: 951 735 9758
sales@minkagroup.net
www.minkagroup.net

The Modern Fan Company
709 Washington St
Ashland, OR 97520
USA
Tel: 541 4828545

Fax: 541 4828418
info@modernfan.com
www.modernfan.com

The Platonic Fireplace Company
Phoenix Wharf
Eel Pie Island
Twickenham TW1 3DY
UK
Tel: +44 (0) 208 891 5904
Fax: +44 (0) 208 892 2590
info@platonicfireplaces.co.uk
www.platonicfireplaces.co.uk

The Radiator Company
TRC House,
Units 13-14, Charlwoods Road
East Grinstead
West Sussex RH19 2HG
UK
Tel: +44 (0) 8707 302 250
Fax: +44 (0) 1342 302 260
sales@theradiatorcompany.co.uk
www.theradiatorcompany.co.uk

Radiating Style
Unit 15 Thompson Road
Hounslow
Middlesex TW13 3UH
UK
Tel: +44 (0) 870 072 3428
Fax: +44 (0) 208 577 9222
sales@radiatingstyle.com
www.radiatingstyle.com

Rudloe Stoneworks
Leafield Stoneyard
Potley Lane
Corsham
Wiltshire SN13 9RS
UK
Tel: +44 (0) 122 581 6400
Fax: +44 (0) 1225 811 343
sales@rudloe-stone.com
www.rudloe-stone.com

Runtal Italia
Via Provinciale 15/D
24040 Lallio (BG)
Italy
Tel: +39 035 455 1511
Fax: +39 035 455 1512
info@runtalitalia.it
www.runtalitalia.it

Satyendra Pakhalé
R.J.H Fortuynplein 70
1019 WL Amsterdam
The Netherlands
Tel: +31 20 419 72 30
Fax: +31 20 419 72 31
info@satyendra-pakhale.com
www.satyendra-pakhale.com

Sonnenkraft
Sonnenkraft SolarSystems GmbH
Industriepark
A-9300 St. Veit/Glan
Germany
Tel: +43 (0) 4212 45010 400
Fax: +43 (0) 4212 45010 477
england@sonnenkraft.com
www.sonnenkraft.co.uk

Sunovation
Vital-Daelen-Strasse
D-63911 Klingenberg-Trennfurt
Germany
Tel: +49 (0) 9372 949109
Fax: +39 (0) 9372 949110
info@sunovation.de
www.sunovation.de

Terry Pawson Architects
206 Merton High Street
London SW19 1AX
UK
Tel: +44 20 854 325 77
Fax: +44 20 854 386 77
tpa@terrypawson.com
www.terrypawson.com

Tubes Radiatori
Via Boscalto 32
31023 Resana (TV)
Italy
Tel: +39 0423 7161
Fax: +39 0423 7150 50
tubes@tubesradiatori.com
www.tubesradiatori.com

Unico System International
Unit 3 Ynyshir Industrial Estate
Llanwonno Road
Porth CF39 0HU
UK
Tel: +44 (0) 1443 684828
Fax: +44 (0) 1443 684 838
scott@unicosystem.com
www.unicosystem.com

directory

Unico
7401 Alabama Ave.
Saint Louis, MO 63111-9906
Tel: 800 5527 0896
Fax: 314 457 9000

Viessmann
Hortonwood 30
Telford
Shropshire TF1 7YP
UK
Tel: +44 (0) 1952 675 000
Fax: +44 (0) 1952 675 040
info@viessmann.co.uk
www.viessmann.co.uk

Vogue UK
Units 6–10, Strawberry Lane
Industrial Park
Strawberry Lane
Willenhall
West Midlands WV13 3RS
UK
Tel: +44 (0) 870 403 0111
Fax: +44 (0) 870 403 0112
sales@vogue-uk.com
www.vogue-uk.com

Zehnder
B15 Armstrong Mall
Southwood Business Park
Farnborough
Hampshire GU14 0NR
UK
Tel: +44 (0) 1252 515151
Fax: +44 (0) 1252 522 528
sales@zehnder.co.uk
www.zehnder.co.uk

lighting

3M
3M Center
St. Paul, MN 55144-1000
USA
Tel: 888 364 3577
www.3m.com

Alivar – see p. 204
Anglepoise
6 Stratfield Park
Elettra Avenue
Waterlooville PO7 7XN
UK
Tel: +44 (0) 2392 250 934

Fax: +44 (0) 2392 250 696
sales@anglespoise.co.uk
www.anglepoise.co.uk

Artek oy ab
Lemuntie 3-5 B
FI-00510 Helsinki
Finland
Tel: +358 10 617 3460
Fax: +358 10 617 3491
info@artek.fi
www.artek.fi

US distributor:
Herman Miller Inc.
855 East Main Avenue
Zeeland, MI 49464-0302
USA
Tel: 616 654 8321
Fax: 616 654 5817

UK agent:
twentytwentyone
18C River Street
London EC1R 1XN
UK
Tel: +44 (0) 20 7837 1900
Fax: +44 (0) 20 7837 1908
artek@twentytwentyone.com
www.twentytwentyone.com

Artemide
Via Bergamo, 18
20010 Pregnana Milanese (MI)
Italy
Tel: +39 02935 181
Fax: +39 02935 90254
info@artemide.com
www.artemide.com

Atelier Mendini
24 Via Sanno
20135 Milano (MI)
Italy
Tel: +39 02 59900974
www.ateliermendini.it

**Baldinger Architectural
Lighting**
19-02 Steinway Street
Astoria, NY 11105
USA
Tel: 718 204 5700
Fax: 718 721 4986
info@baldinger.com
www.baldinger.com

Barovier & Toso
Palazzo Contarini
Fondamenta Vetrai, 28
30141 Murano (VE)
Italy
Tel: +39 041739 049
Fax: +39 041527 4385
showroom.murano@barovier.com
www.barovier.com

Belux
Klünenfeldstrasse 20
CH-4127 Birsfelden
Switzerland
Tel: +41 61 316 74 01
Fax: +41 61 316 75 99
belux@belux.com
www.belux.com

Blauet
C/ Palencia 34–44 Bjos
08027 Barcelona
Spain
Tel: +34 93 579 40 02
Fax: +34 93 579 71 00
info@blauet.com
www.blauet.com

B.Lux
Poligono Eitua, 70
48240 Berriz-Bizkaia
Spain
Tel: +34 946 827 272
Fax: +34 946 824 902
info@grupoblux.com
www.grupoblux.com

Byblos Art Hotel
Via Cedrare 78
37029 Corrubbio di Negarine
Verona
Italy
Tel: +39 045 6855555
Fax: +39 045 6855500

Concord Lighting
174 High Holborn
London WC1V 7AA
UK
Tel: +44 (0) 171 497 1400
Fax: +44 (0) 171 497 1404

Droog Design – see p. 204

Emdelight – see p. 205

Equipoise Lighting UK
Kable House
Amber Drive
Langley Mill
Nottingham NG16 4BE
UK
Tel: +44 (0) 7770 412163
Fax: +44 (0) 1332 781060
www.equipoiselighting.co.uk

Erco Leuchten GmbH
Postfach 24 60
58505 Lüdenscheid
Germany
Tel: +49 23 515510
Fax: +49 23 51551300
info@erco.com
www.erco.com

UK contact:
38 Dover Street
London W1S 4NL
Tel: +44 (0) 20 74080320
Fax: +44 (0) 20 74091530
info.uk@erco.com

US contact:
160 Raritan Center Parkway
Suite 10
Edison, NJ 08837
USA
Tel: 732 2258856
Fax: 732 2258857
info.us@erco.com

Flos
Via Angelo Faini, 2
25073 Bovezzo
Italy
Tel: +39 030 24381
Fax: +39 030 2438250
info@flos.it
www.flos.com

FontanaArte
Alzaia Trieste 49
20094 Corsico
Italy
Tel: +39 02 45121
Fax: +39 02 2512660
info@fontanaarte.it
www.fontanaarte.it

Foscarini
Via delle Industrie, 27
30020 Marcon

Venice
Italy
Tel: +39 041595 3811
Fax: +39 041595 3820
foscarini@foscarini.com
www.foscarini.com

iGuzzini Illuminazione
Via Mariano Guzzini, 37
62019 Recanate (MC)
Italy
Tel: +39 07175 881
Fax: +39 07175 88295
iguzzini@iguzzini.it
www.iguzzini.com

Ingo Maurer
Kaiserstrasse, 47
80801 Munich
Germany
Tel: +49 89381 6060
Fax: +49 89381 60620
info@ingo-maurer.com
www.ingo-maurer.com

Isamu Noguchi Museum
32–37 Vernon Boulevard
Long Island City, NY 11106
USA
Tel: 001 718 204 7088
Fax: 001 718 278 2348
info@noguchi.org

Kreon – see p. 205

Leucos
Via Moglianese, 29/31
30037 Scoze (VE)
Italy
Tel: +39 041 5859111
Fax: +39 041 447598
info@leucos.it
www.leucos.it

Leucos USA, Inc.
11 Mayfield Ave.
Edison, NJ 08837
Tel: 732 225 0010
Fax: 732 225 0250

Louis Poulsen
Nyhavn 11
Postboks 7
1001 København K
Denmark
Tel: +45 70 33 14 14

Fax: +45 33 29 86 69
info@lpmail.com
www.louis-poulsen.dk

Luceplan
Via E.T. Moneta, 44/46
20161 (MI)
Italy
Tel: +39 026 62421
Fax: +39 026 6203400
info@luceplan.com
www.luceplan.com

Lucitalia
Via Pellizza da Volpedo, 50
20092 Cinisello Balsamo (MI)
Italy
Tel: +39 02612 6651
Fax: +39 02660 0707
lucitalia@luceitalia.it
www.lucitalia.it

Lutron – see p. 205
Matsushita Electric Industrial
1006, Oaza Kadoma
Kadoma City
Osaka
Japan
Tel: +81 6908 1121
Fax: +81 6908 2351
www.mei.co.jp

O Luce
Via Brescia, 2
20097 San Donato Milanese (MI)
Italy
Tel: +39 029849 1435
Fax: +39 029849 0779
info@oluce.com
www.oluce.com

Pandul
Søllingsvej 4
DK 2920 Charlottenlund
Denmark
Tel: +45 36458 303
Fax: +45 36458 203
info@pandul.dk
www.pandul.dk

Reggiani SpA Illuminazione
Viale Monza 16
20050 Sovico (MI)
Italy
Tel: +39 039 2071 1
Fax: +39 039 2071 999

point@reggiani.net
www.reggiani.net

Santa & Cole
Santisima Trinidad del Monte, 10
08017 Barcelona
Spain
Tel: +34 934 183 396
Fax: +34 934 183 812
info@santacole.com
www.santacole.com

Speirs and Major Associates
Lighting Architects
Well Court Hall
Dean Village
Edinburgh EH4 3BE
UK
Tel: +44 (0) 1312 264474
Fax: +44 (0) 1312 205331
info@samassociates.com
www.samassociates.com

**Swarovski Crystal Palace
Collection**
2nd Floor
14-15 Conduit Street
London W1S 2XJ
UK
Tel: +44 (0) 20 7016 6780
Fax: +44 (0) 20 7016 6770
www.swarovskisparkles.com

29 West, 57th Street, 8th Floor,
New York, NY 10019
Tel: 212 935 4200 x 191
Fax: 212 935 8800

Tecnolumen
Lötzener Strasse, 2–4
D-28207 Bremen
Germany
Tel: +49 421 430 417 0
Fax: +49 421 498 668 5
info@tecnolumen.de
www.tecnolumen.de

Vos Pad
100 Watermans Quay
Regent on the River
William Morris Way
London SW6 2UW
UK
Tel: +44 (0) 207736 4117
info@vossolutions.com
www.thevospad.com

Woka Lamps Vienna
Palais Breuner
Singerstrasse, 16
A-1010 Vienna
Austria
Tel: +43 1513 2912
Fax: +43 1513 88505
info@woka.com
www.wokalamps.com

Zumtobel AG
Höchster Strasse 8
A-6850 Dornbirn
Austria
Tel: +43 (0)5572 509-0
Fax: +43 (0)5572 509-601
enquiries@zumtobel.com
www.zumtobelgroup.com

bathrooms

Agape
Via Po Barna 69
46031 Correggio Micheli di Bagnolo
San Vito (MN), Italy
Tel: +39 0376 250311
Fax: +39 0376 250 330
info@agapedesign.it
www.agapedesign.it

Alape
Am Gräbicht 1-9
D-38644 Goslar
Post Box 1240
D-38602 Goslar
Germany
Tel: +49 5321 5580
Fax: +49 5321 5584 00
info@alape.com
www.alape.com

Il Bagno Alessi
Via Faentina 213
L QUADRIFOGLIO
Via Guercino, 2
20154 Milano, Italy
Tel: +39 02 33606808-11
Fax: +39 02 33606807
ufficiostampa@quadrifogliocomuni
cazione.it
www.ilbagnoalessi.com

Altamarea
by Tecnolac srl
Via Istria 1/3 z.i.

31046 Oderzo (TV)
Italy
Tel: +39 0422 71 3212
Fax: +39 0422 816 818
altamarea@tecnolac.it
www.altamareabath.it

Alternative Plans
4 Hester Road
London SW11 4AN
Tel: 020 7228 6460
sales@alternative-plans.co.uk
www.alternative-plans.co.uk

Antonio Lupi
73/75 Via Mazzini
50050 Stabbia
Cerreto Guidi
Florence
Italy
Tel: +39 057 1586881
Fax: +39 057 1586885
lupi@antoniolupi.it
www.antoniolupi.it

Axia
18 Via del Credito Castelfranco
31093 Veneto (TV)
Italy
Tel: +39 0423496222
Fax: +39 0423743733
axia@axiabath.it
www.axiabath.it

Axor – see Hansgrohe

Bathrooms International
4 Pont Street,
London SW1X 9EL
UK
Tel: +44 (0) 20 7838 7788
Fax: +44 (0) 20 7838 7789
sales@bathroomsint.com
www.bathroomsint.com

Bisazza – see p.204

Boffi
Via Oberdan 70
20030 Lentate Sul Seveso (MI)
Milan
Italy
Tel: +39 0362 5341
Fax: +39 0362 565077
info@boffi.com
www.boffi.com

Box Art
Via Maragliano 5R
50144 Firenze
Italy
Tel: +39 055 333 081
Fax: +39 055 331 033
info@boxart.org
www.boxart.org

Ceramica Catalano
10134 Fabrica di Roma (VT)
Italy
Tel: +39 0761 5661
Fax: +39 0761 574304
info@catalano.it
www.catalano.it

Ceramica Flaminia
SS Flaminia km 54630
01033 Civita Castellana (VT)
Italy
Tel: +39 076 154 2030
Fax: +39 076 154 0069
ceramicaflaminia@ceramicaflaminia
.it
www.ceramicaflaminia.it

Cesana
Via Dalmazia 3
20059 Vimercate (MI)
Italy
Tel: +39 039635 38 1
Fax: +39 039685 1166
cesana@cesana.it
www.cesana.it

Cesana UK
Chipnall House,
Chipnall
Shropshire TF9 2RB
Tel: +44 (0) 1630 661 666
www.cesana.it

Colourwash Bathrooms
18 Weir Road
London SW19 8UG
UK
Tel: +44 020 8944 2695
Fax: +44 020 8947 3559
sales@colourwash.co.uk
www.colourwash.co.uk

Industrias Cosmic
C/Cerdanya 2
Pol. Ind. La Borda
Aptdo. Correos P.O. Box 184

08140 Caldes de Montbui
Barcelona
Spain
Tel +34 902 155 500
Fax +34 902 155 505
Info@icosmic.com
www.icosmic.com

C.P. Hart
Newnham Terrace
Hercules Road
London SE1 7DR
UK
Tel: +44 (0) 20 7902 5250
Fax: +44 (0) 20 7902 1030
adrians@cphart.co.uk
www.cphart.co.uk

Dornbracht
Kobbingser Muhte 6
Postbox 1454
D5858 Iserlohn
Germany
Tel: +44 (0) 1889 271930
Tel: +49 2371 4330
Fax: +49 2371 33232
info@dornbracht.de
www.dornbracht.com

Dornbracht
Unit 8
Bow Court
Fletchworth Gate
Coventry CV5 6SP
UK
Tel: +44 (0) 2476717129
Fax: +44(0) 247618907
sales@dornbracht.co.uk
www.dornbracht.co.uk

DuPont Corian– see p. 204

Durat®
Tonester Ltd.
Huhdantie 4,
21140 Rymättylä
Finland
Tel: +358 (0)22 52 1000
Fax: +358 (0)22 52 1022
contact@durat.com
www.durat.com

Duravit UK
Unit 7 Brudenell Drive
Brinklow
Milton Keynes

Buckinhamshire MK10 0DE
UK
Tel: +44 (0) 870 7307 787
www.duravit.com

Effegibi
Via Gallo 769
47022 Borello di Cesena (FC)
Italy
Tel: +39 054 737 2881
Fax: +39 054 737 2924
info@effegibi.it
www.effegibi.it

Even
54 Via dell'Artigianato
35012 Camposampiero
(PD)
Italy
Tel: +39 0499303577
Fax: +39 0499303587
info@evendesign.it
www.evendesign.it

Falper
Via Veneto 7-9
40064 Ozzano Emilia
Bologna
Italy
Tel: +39 051799319
Fax: +39 051796495
info@falper.it
www.falper.it

Fantini Fratelli
Via M Bucharroti 4
28010 Pella No
Italy
Tel: +39 0322 969 127
Fax: +39 0322 969 530
fantini@fantini.it
www.fantini.it

Flair International
Bailieborough
Co. Cavan
Ireland
Tel: +353 429 665294
info@flairshowers.com
www.flairshowers.com

Grohe
Blays House
Wick Road
Englefield Green
Egham, Surrey TW20 0HJ

UK
Phone +44 (0)871 200 3414
Fax +44 (0)871 200 3415
info@grohe.co.uk
www.grohe.com

Hansgrohe
Auestrasse 5–9
D-77761 Schiltach
Germany
Tel: +49 (0) 7836510
Fax: +49 (0) 7836511300
info@hansgrohe.com
www.hansgrohe.com

UK contact:
Units D1 and D2
Sandown Park Industrial Estate
Royal Mills
Esher
Surrey KT10 8BL
Tel: +44 (0) 870 7701972
Fax: +44 (0) 870 7701973
info@hansgrohe.co.uk
www.hansgrohe.co.uk

Hansa
Hansa Metallwerke AG
Sigmaringer Str. 107
D-70567 Stuttgart
Germany
Tel: +49 711 16 14 0
Fax: +49 711 16 14 3 68
info@hansa.de
www.hansa.de

Hoesch
D52 372 Kreuzau,
Post bag 10 04 24
Germany
Tel: +49 2422 54180
Fax: +49 2422 54184
www.hoesch.de

Hotel Bulgari, Milano
Via Privata Fratelli Gabba, 7/b
20121 Milano
Italy
Tel: +39 028058051
Fax: +39 02080 5805 222
www.bulgarihotels.com

Hotel Silken Puerta
America, Madrid
Avenida de América, 41
28002 Madrid

Spain
Tel: +34 917 445 400
Fax: +34 917 445 401
hotel.puertamerica@hotels-silken.com
www.hotelpuertamerica.com

IB Rubinetterie
Via dei Pianotti 3/5
25069 Sarezzo (BS)
Italy
Tel: +39 0308 02101
Fax: +39 0308 03097
info@ibrubinetterie.it
www.ibrubinetterie.it

Ideal Standard
The Bathroom Works,
National Avenue,
Kingston upon Hull HU5 4HS
UK
Tel: +44 (0) 1482 346461
Fax: +44 (0) 1482 445886
www.ideal-standard.co.uk

Jacuzzi Brands
777 S. Flagler Drive
Suite 1100–West
West Palm Beach, FL 33401
USA
Tel: 561 514 3838
www.jacuzzibrands.com

Kaldewei
Beckumer Strasse 33-35
D-59229 Ahlen
Germany
Tel: +49 23 82 78 50
Fax: +49 23 82 78 52 00
info@kaldewei.de
www.kaldewei.com

UK contact:
Unit 7, Sundial Court
Tolworth Rise South
Surbiton
Surrey KT5 9RN
Tel: +44 208 337 1441
Fax: +44 208 337 1998
info@kaldewei-uk.com
www.kaldewei.com

Kohler UK
Cromwell Road
Cheltenham
Gloucestershire GL52 5EP

UK
Tel: +44 (0) 870 850 5561
www.kohleruk.com

Kos
Viale de la Comina 17
33170 Pordenone
Italy
Tel: +39 0434 363405
Fax: +39 0434 551292
info@kositalia.it
www.kositalia.it

Langham Hotel
1C Portland Place
London W1B 1JA
UK
Tel: +44 (0) 7636 1000
Fax: +44 (0) 20 7323 2340

Laufen
Laufen House
Crab Apple Way
Vale Business Park
Evesham
Worcestershire WR11 1GP, UK
Tel: +44 1386 422768
Fax: +44 1386 765502
laura.soer@uk.laufen.com
www.laufen.co.uk

LG Hi-Macs UK
1 Draper Street
Southborough
Tunbridge Wells
Kent TN4 0PG, UK
Tel: +44 (0) 1892 543008
Fax: +44 (0) 1892 549147
www.naturalacrylicstone.com

Limestone Gallery – see p.212

Listone Giordano – see p.208

Lute Suite, Amsterdam
Amsteldijk Zuid 54–58
1184 VD Ouderkerk aan de Amstel
The Netherlands
Tel: +44 700 598 0735
Fax: +44 870 134 3055
www.arc-corporate-housing.com

Matki Showering
Churchward Road
Yate
Bristol BS37 5PL, UK

Tel: +44 (0) 1454 322888
Fax: +44 (0) 1454 315284
helpline@matki.co.uk
www.matki.co.uk

Merati
Via Carlo Porta, 67
20038Seregno (MI)
Italy
Tel: +39 03623 20472
Fax: +39 03623 20473
info@merati.com
www.merati.com

Milldue Arredi
7 Via Balegante,
31039 Riese Pio X
Treviso
Italy
Tel: +39 04237 55233
Fax: +39 04234 56319
milldue@milldue.it
www.milldue.com

Oasis
Via 1 Maggio 8
33070 Buddia
Italy
Tel: +39 0434 654752
Fax: +39 0434 654850
www.oasisbagni.com

Ondine
Interbath Inc
655 North Baldwin Park
Blvd
City of Industry,
CA 91746-1502, USA
Tel: 800 423 9485
www.ondineshowers.com

Original Bathrooms
143-145 Kew Road
Richmond-upon-Thames
Surrey TW9 2PN, UK
Tel: +44 (0) 20 8940 7554
Fax: +44 (0) 20 8948 8200
sales@original-bathrooms.
co.uk
www.original-bathrooms.
co.uk

Pharo (part of Hansgrohe)
Auestr. 5-9
77761 SchiltachGermany
Tel: +49 (0) 7836/51-0

Fax: +49 (0) 7836/51-2512
info@hansgrohe.com
www.pharobodytime.com

Porcelanosa – see p. 209

Rapsel
13 Via Volta
20019 Settimo Milanese
(MI), Italy
Tel: +39 023355 981
Fax: +39 023350 1306
rapsel@rapsel.it
www.rapsel.it

Regia
Via Vigevano
Zona Industriale
20053 Taccona Di Muggiò
(MI), Italy
Tel: +39 0392782510
Fax: +39 0392782571
info@regia.it
www.regia.it

UK distributor:
Tel: +44 (0) 20 8367 4314

Respect
2 Brestkaya ulitsa d. 6
125047 Moscow
Russia
Tel. +7 (95) 2000928
Fax +7 (95) 2503582
respect@respect-design.com
www.respect-design.com

Rubinetterie Ritmonio
Zona Industriale Roccapietra
4 Via Indren
13019 Varallo (VC)
Italy
Tel: +39 01635 60000
Fax: +39 01635 60100
info@ritmonio.it
www.ritmonio.com

Rubinetterie Toscane
Ponsi
Via A. Volta 2
55049 Viareggio
Italy
Tel: +39 0584 427 611
Fax: +39 0584 46 117
info@ponsi.com
www.ponsi.com

Rubinetterie Zazzeri
Via del Roseto 56/64
50012 Bagno a Ripoli
Florence
Italy
Tel: +39 05569 6051
Fax: +39 05569 6309
info@zazzeri.it
www.zazzeri.it

Savil
Via Monte Guglielmo 71
I-25060 Cogozzo
Villa Carcina
Brescia
Italy
Tel: +39 0308900437
Fax: +39 0398901056
www.savil.it

Teuco UK
Suites 312-314
Business Design Centre
52 Upper Street
London N1 0QH
UK
Tel: +44 20 7704 2190
Fax: +44 20 7704 9756
info@teuco.co.uk
www.teuco.co.uk

Titan
Strada Ascrittizi, 7
47891 Falciano
Republic of San Morino
Tel: +378 877 111
Fax: +378 908 154
titan@titan.sm
www.titan.it

Tretzo
Tel: +44 199 445 199
geoff@tretzo.com
www.tretzo.com

Valli & Valli UK – see
p. 210

Villeroy & Boch
Suite 8
Wilmslow House
Grove Way
Wilmslow
Cheshire SK9 5AG
UK
Tel: +44 (0) 1625 5252 02

Fax: +44 (0) 1625 5845 35
wellness-uk@villeroy-boch.
com
www.villeroy-boch.com

VitrA
Park 34
Collett Way
DidcotOxon OX11 7WB
UK
Tel: +44 (0) 1235 750990
Fax: +44 (0) 1235 750980
info@vitrauk.com
www.vitrauk.com

Vola
Lunavej 2
DK-8700 Horsens
Denmark
Tel: +45 7023 5500
Fax: +45 7023 5511
sales@vola.dk
www.vola.dk

Wet
Via G. Colombo 81/2
20133 Milano
Italy
Tel: +39 (0) 22668 3109
Fax: +39 (0) 25412 5735
wet@wet.co.it
www.wet.co.it

West One Bathrooms
45-46 South Audley Street
London W1K 2PY
UK
Tel: +44 (0) 207499 1845
Fax: +44 (0) 207629 9311
sales@westonebathrooms.
com
www.westonebathrooms.
com

Zucchetti Rubinetteria
29 Via Molini di Resiga
28024 Gozzano(NO)
Italy
Tel: +39 0322954700
Fax: +39 0322954823
marketing@zucchettirub.it
www.zucchettionline.com

kitchens

AEG / Electrolux
55-57 High Street
Slough SL1 1DZ
UK
Tel: +44 (0)8705 950 950
www.aeg.co.uk

Arrital
Via Casut 103
33074 Fontanafredda (PN)
Italy
Tel: +39 0434567411
Fax: +39 0434999728
info@arritalcucine.com
www.arritalcucine.com

Astracast
Holden Ing Way
Birstall
West Yorkshire WF17 9AE
Tel: + 44 (0) 1924 477466
Fax: +44 (0) 1924351297
marketing@astracast.co.uk
www.astracast.co.uk

Blanco
Oxgate Lane
London NW2 7JN
UK
Tel: +44 (0) 20 8450 9100
Fax: +44 (0) 20 8208 0095
info@blanco.co.uk
www.blanco.co.uk

Blum UK
Mandeville Drive
Kingston
Milton Keynes
Buckinghamshire MK10
0AW
UK
Tel: +44 (0) 1908 285700
Fax: +44 (0) 1908 285 701
info.uk@blum.com
www.blum.co.uk
www.dynamicspace.com

Boffi
Via Oberdan 70
20030 Lentate Sul Seveso
(MI)
Italy
Tel: +39 0362 5341

Fax: +39 0362 565077
info@boffi.com
www.boffi.com

Bosch
Old Wolverton Road
Wolverton
Milton Keynes
Bucks MK12 5PT
UK
Tel: +44 08706 000535
www.boschappliances.co.uk

Bulthaup
37 Wigmore Street
London W1U 1PP
UK
Tel: +44 (0) 20 7495 3663
Fax : +44 (0) 20 7495 0139
info@bulthaup.co.uk
www.london.bulthaup.com

Caesar Stone
Kibbutz Sdot Yam
MP Menashe 38805
Israel
Tel: +972 4 6364555
Fax: +972 4 6261268
export@caesarstone.com
www.caesarstone.com

UK contact:
Trans-Pennine Trading Estate
Gorrels Way,Rochdale
Lancashire OL11 2PX
Tel: +44 1706 869 691
Fax: +44 1706 869 860
general.enquiries@ebor.co.
uk

Ceramgres
Vicolo Spercenigo 21
31030 Mignagola di
Carbonera
Treviso
Italy
Tel: +39 0422 396366
Fax: +39 0422 396478
info@ceramgres.com
www.ceramgres.com

Cerim Ceramiche
Florim S.P.A
Via Canaletto 24
41042 Fiorano (MO)
Italy

directory

Tel: +39 0536 840911
Fax: +39 0536 8444750
info@cerim.it
www.cerim.it

Cosentino
Avda. Gumersindo Lorente s/n
Colonia Fin de Semena
28022 Madrid
Spain
Tel: +34 (0) 91 3291521
Fax: +34 (0) 91 3293420
madrid@cosentino.es
www.silestone.com

Dada
Strada Provinciale 31
20010 Mesero
Milano
Italy
Tel: +39 0297 20791
Fax: + 39 0297 289561
dada@dadaweb.it
www.dadaweb.it

UK contact:
Mark Nicholas Design
48 Penton Street
London
UK
Tel: +44 (0) 20 7278 7573
Fax: +44 (0) 20 7833 2273

Delta Faucet
55 E. 111 Street
PO Box 40980
Indianapolis, IN 46280
USA
Tel: 317 848 1812
www.deltafaucet.com

Dornbracht – see p. 216

Dupont Corian – see p. 204

Effeti
174 Via B Cellini
50028 Tavarnelle Valdi Pese (FI)
Italy
Tel: +39 055807091
Fax: +39 0558070085
effeti@effeti.com
www.effeti.com

Elam srl/Tissetanta Brand
Via Tofane 37
20034 Guissano (MI)
Italy
Tel: +39 03623191
Fax: +30 0362319300
www.tisettanta.com

Elica
Via Dante 288
60044 Fabriano An
Italy
Tel: +39 07326 101
Fax: +39 0732 610 249
info@elica.it
www.elica.it

Ernestomeda
2/8 Via dell'Economia
61025 Montelabbate (PU)
Italy
Tel: +39 0721 48991
Fax: +39 0721 4899 780
info@ernestomeda.it
www.ernestomeda.com

Fisher & Paykel UK
209 Purley Way
Croydon CR9 4RY
UK
Tel: +44 (0) 845 6001934
www.fisherpaykel.co.uk

Pleasant Oak Farm
Hob Lane
Balsall Common CV7 7GX
UK

Foster
Via M.S Ottone 18-20
42041 Brescello (RE)
Italy
Tel: +39 0522687425
Fax: +39 0522687639
info@fosterspa.com
www.fosterspa.com

Franke UK
West Park, Manchester
International Office Centre
Styal Road
Manchester M22 5WB
Tel: +44 (0) 161 436 6280
Fax: +44 (0) 161 436 2180
info.uk@franke.com
www.franke.co.uk

Gaggenau UK
Grand Union House
Old Wolverton Road
Milton Keynes
Wolverton MK 12 5PT
Buckinghamshire
UK
Tel: +44 8708 402003
mks-gaggenau-showroom@
bshg.com
www.gaggenau.com

Gatto
Via Direttisimo del Conero 51
60021 Camerano Ancona
Italy
Tel: +39 071730121
Fax: +39 0717301298
gatto@gattocucine.com
www.gattocucine.com

Hae-jin Kim
Tel: +82 2557 0326
hae-jin.kim@alumni.rca.ac.uk

IKEA – see p. 208

Kitchen Aid USA
www.kitchenaid.com

KB Homes
10990 Wilshire Blvd, 7th Floor
Los Angeles, CA 90024, USA
Tel: 310 2314000
Fax: 310 2314222
customerrelations@kbhome.com
www.kbhome.com

Küppersbusch
Postfach 10 01 32
D-45801 Gelsenkirchen
Germany
Tel: +49 (0) 2094010
Fax: +49 (0) 209401303
info@kueppersbusch.de
www.kueppersbusch.de

La Cucina Alessi (see Foster,
Oras, and ValCucine)
Alessi spa
28882 Crusinallo
Italy
Tel: +39 0323 868611
Fax: +39 0323 641605
info@alessi.com
www.alessi.com

Leicht
106 Culverden Down,
Tunbridge Wells,
Kent TN4 9SW
UK
Tel: +44 (0) 1892 519 383
www.leicht.com

LG Electronics UK
LG House
250 Bath Road
Slough
Berkshire SL1 4DX
UK
Tel: +44 (0) 1753 491500
uk.lge.com

Lucite
Queens Gate
Queens Terrace
Southampton SO14 3BP
UK
Tel: +44 (0) 870 2404620
Fax: +44 (0) 870 240 4626
contactus@lucite.com
www.lucite.com

Mandarin Stone
Unit 1 Wonastow Industrial Estate
Monmouth NP25 5JB
UK
Tel: +44 (0) 1600 715444
Fax: +44 (0) 1600 715494
info@mandarinstone.com
www.mandarinstone.com

Maytag UK
2 St Annes Boulevard
Foxboro Business Park
Redhill
Surrey RH1 1AX
UK
Tel: +44 (0) 1737 231132
Fax: +44 (0) 1737 778822
www.maytag.co.uk

Mercury Appliances
Whisby Road
Lincoln LN 3QZ
UK
Tel: +44 (0) 1522 881 717
Fax: +44 (0) 1522 880 220
sales@mercury-appliances.co.uk
www.mercury-appliances.co.uk

Miele UK
Fairacres
Marcham Road
Abingdon
Oxfordshire OX14 1TW
UK
Tel: +44 (0) 1235 554455
Fax: +44 (0) 1235 554477
info@miele.co.uk
www.miele.co.uk

Neff
Grand Union House
Old Wolverton Road
Wolverton
Bucks MK12 5PT
UK
Tel: +44 (0) 870 513.3090
www.neff.co.uk

Nolte Kuchen
32584 Löhne
Germany
Tel: +49 57238990
Fax: +49 5732899265
info@nolte-kuechen.de
www.nolte-kuechen.de

Oras
Isometsäntie 2
P.O. Box 40
26101 Rauma
Finland
Tel: +358 (0) 2 83 161
Fax: +358 (0) 2 831 6200
info.finland@oras.com
www.oras.com

Parapan
Thistle House
Thistle Way
Gildersom Spur, Wakefield Road
Morley
Leeds LS27 7JZ
UK
Tel: +44 (0) 1132 012240
Fax: 44 (0) 1132530 717
info@parapan.co.uk
www.parapan.co.uk

Poggenpohl Group UK
447–481 Finchley Road
London NW3 6HS
UK
Tel: +44 (0) 20 7794 7801
Fax: +44 (0) 20 7794 1379

info@normanglennkitchens.co.uk
kitchens@poggenpohl-group.co.uk
www.poggenpohl.co.uk

Porcelanosa – see p. 209

Santos
15882 Boqueixón
Santiago de Compostela
A Coruña
Spain
Tel: +34 981566448
Fax: +34 981 573737
santos@santos.es
www.santos.es

Schiffini spa Mobil Cucine
19020 Ceparana di BNolano (La
Spezia)
Via Genova 206
Italy
Tel: +39 01879501
Fax: +39 01879 32399
info@schiffini.it
www.schiffini.it

Sharp UK – see p. 206

SieMatic
Osprey House
Rookery Court
Primett Road
Stevenage
Hertfordshire SG1 3EE
UK
Tel: +44 (0) 1438 369327
Fax: +44 (0) 1438 36892
info@siematic.co.uk
www.siematic.com

Siemens UK
Siemens House
Oldbury
Bracknell
Berkshire RG12 8FZ
UK Tel: Tel: +44 (0)1344 396000
www.siemens.co.uk

Smallbone of Devizes
220 Brompton Road
London SW3 2BB
UK
Tel: +44 (0) 20 7581 9989 (UK)
www.smallbone.co.uk

Smeg UK
3 Milton Park
Abingdon
Oxon OX14 4RN
UK
Tel: +44 (0) 870 990 9907
Fax: +44 (0) 870 990 9337
customer.service@smeguk.com
www.smeguk.com

Smirk
364 Old York Road
London SW18 1SP
UK
Tel: +44 (0) 20 8870 5557
info@smirk.co.uk
www.smirk.co.uk

Snaidero Group
Viale Rino Snaidero Cavaliere del
Lavoro 15
33030 Majano (UD)
Italy
Tel: +39 0432 9521
Fax: +39 0432 952 235
linaverdi@snaidero.it

UK agent:
Asselle
14-18 Old Street
London EC1V 9BH
UK
Tel: +44 (0) 20 7253 2806
Fax: +44 (0) 20 7250 3910
snaidero@asselle.co.uk
www.snaiderogroup.com

Spaziostrato
Via Francesco Burlamacchi 5
20135 Milano
Italy
Tel: +39 02540 50 321
Fax: +39 0254126821
info@spaziostrato.com
www.spaziostrato.com

Solatron Technologies
www.partsonsale.com

Stoneham
Powerscroft Road
Footscray
Sidcup, Kent DA14 5DZ
UK
Tel: +44 (0) 208300 8181

Fax: + 44 (0) 208300 8183
kitchens@stoneham.plc.uk
www.stoneham-kitchens.co.uk

Sub Zero
6B Imprimo Park
Lenthall Road
Debden, Loughton
Essex IG10 3UF, UK
Tel: +44 (0) 20 8418 3800
Fax: +44 (0) 20 8418 3899
info@sub-zero.eu.com
www.westye.eu.com

Teka
177 Milton Park
Abingdon OX14 4SE, UK
Tel: +44 (0) 1235 861916
Fax: +44 (0) 1235 832137
info@teka.co.uk
www.teka.com

Thermador USA
5551 McFadden Avenue
Huntingdon Beach, CA 92649
USA
Tel: 800 656 9226
www.thermador.com

bibliography

Numbers in brackets refer to references within this edition of *Contemporary Details*

Bellati, Nally, *New Italian Design*, Rizzoli International Publications, 1990 (p.81)

Cohen, Jean-Louis, *Scenes of the World to Come: European Architecture and the American Challenge*, 1893–1960, Flammarion, 1995 (p.106)

Cooper, Ed Mae, *Starck*, Taschen, 2004 (p.117)

Day, Lucienne; BBC broadcast, *Looking at Things*, 1950 (p.69)

Forest Stewardship Council, www.fsc-uk.org (p.61); www.fscus.org

Foster, Norman, *On Foster... Foster On*, Prestel Publishing Ltd, 2000 (pp.73, 81)

Fuad-Luke, Alastair, *The Eco Design Handbook: a Complete Sourcebook for the Home and Office*, Thames & Hudson, 2005

Gates, Bill, *The Road Ahead: Living and Prospering in the Information Age*, Viking/Penguin Group (USA) Inc, 1996 (p.35)

in.kitchen, Whirlpool Corporation (p.191)

Kneipp, Sebastian, *My Water Cure*, Pilgrims Publishing, 2002 (p.165)

Le Corbusier, *Essential Le Corbusier: "L'Esprit Nouveau" Articles*, Architectural Press, 1998

Lloyd Morgan, Conway, *Philippe Starck*, Universe Publishing, 1999 (p.145)

Loos, Adolf; Newman, J.O. (translator), Smith, J.H. (translator), *Spoken into the Void: Collected Essays*, 1897–1900, The MIT Press, 1987 (p.156)

McCarthy, Donnachadh, *Saving the Planet Without Costing the Earth: 500 Simple Steps to a Greener Lifestyle*, Fusion Press, 2004

Moore, Charles W.; Lidz, Jane (photographer), *Water and Architecture*, Harry N. Abrams, Inc, 1994 (p.154)

Patton, Phil, *Michael Graves Designs: The Art of the Everyday Object*, Melcher Media, 2004 (pp.28, 81)

Pawson, John, *Minimum*, Phaidon, 1998 (Text on pp.45, 47 and 81 reproduced from *Minimum* by John Pawson © 1996 Phaidon Press Limited)

Peter, John, *The Oral History of Modern Architecture: Interviews with the Greatest Architects of the Twentieth Century*, Harry N. Abrams Inc, 1994 (pp.53, 95)

Sottsass, Ettore, *The Curious Mr Sottsass* (text on pp.71, 74 and 81 from *The Curious Mr Sottsass: Photographing Design and Desire* by Ettore Sottsass. Copyright © 1996 Ettore Sottsass. Reproduced by kind permission of Thames & Hudson London, Ltd)

van Hinte, Ed, *Material World* with *Frame* magazine, Birkhauser, 2003

Tanizaki, Jun'ichiro, *In Praise of Shadows*, Leete's Island Books Inc, 1991 (pp.18, 19, 134)

Tischhauser, Anthony; Major, Mark; Speirs, Jonathan, *Made of Light: The Art of Light and Architecture*, Birkhauser Verlag AG, 2005 (p.138)

Water Aid, www.wateraid.org

index

index

acknowledgments

Trolling the world – and the web – to keep up to date with new technology that affects the way we live in the 21st century has been an absorbing task for a year. I would like to thank Mitchell Beazley and in particular Giulia Hetherington, the head of picture research, for never swerving from the goal of making this a comprehensive sourcebook for homemakers, interior designers, and architects. Rebecca Douglas Home was invaluable in drawing up picture lists and compiling the directory.

Shaping the book for publication was a team effort with Anna Sanderson, Fiona Kellagher, Catherine Emslie, Jenny Faithfull, and Casey Farley pooling their talents to make the book both international and topical – and to bring it out on time. In particular, I would like to thank the senior editor, Suzanne Arnold, who pulled it all together. For endlessly seeking the wow factor in style and content, I would like to thank in particular Tim Foster, Sarah Rock, and Victoria Burley.

To all those manufacturers, architects, and designers who shared their innovative ideas and products, a very big thank you.

Nonie Niesewand

photographic acknowledgments

Mitchell Beazley would like to thank all the designers, manufacturers, distributors, and their public relations agents who have kindly supplied images for publication in this book, and who are credited in the captions alongside the images. Additional sources and credits are as follows.

Key: page numbers are followed by figure numbers or directionals: a above, b below, c centre, l left, r right.

7l manufactured by TAL, Belgium, www.tal.be; 8ar Rick Mather Architects; 9c View/Raf Makda; 12 Lewis Tsurumaki Lewis Architects; 14a & b Tensta Konsthall/Anna Lönnerstam; 18/2 Nicholas Kane; 20/7 architect: Rojkind Arquitectos; 20/8 see 7l; 20/12 architect: Solutia/Studio UDA/photo Alberto Ferrero; 22/3 Solutia/façade manufacturer: Euroalmuminios Barbosa SA, window manufacturer: Arino-Duglass/photo Serge Brison; 24/2 photo Wolfgang Schwager; 30/2 View/Richard Glover; 35/13 photo Philip Bier; 41/14 Alamy/Arcaid/Richard Bryant; 45 photo Thom Faulders; 46bl Tensta Konsthall/Anna Lönnerstam; 54/2 & 3, 55/6, 56/9, 10, 11, & 12, 57/1, 2, 3, & 4 Tile of Spain; 56/13 Reed Harris; 82/16 G & S Allgood; 84 Sanei Hopkins/Amir Sanei; 88 photo Laurie Black; 92/12 photo Oliver Schuster; 89l photo courtesy of Weather Shield Windows & Doors, USA; 96 Arcaid.co.uk/Richard Bryant; 99 View/Chris Gascoigne; 100/2 Ladders Online (T B Davies Ltd); 100/4 View/Richard Gover; 102/1 Arcaid.co.uk/John Edward Linden; 103/6 Arcaid.co.uk/Richard Bryant; 104/1, 105/3, 106/7 Ladders Online (T B Davies Ltd); 108 View/Dennis Gilbert; 113l & r The Radiator Company; 114/1, 2, & 3 Arcaid.co.uk/Richard Bryant; 18/20 & 21 The Radiator Company; 128 Byblos Art Hotel Villa Amista, Verona; 131b The Isamu Noguchi Foundation and Garden Museum; 133ar Lutron; 140/2 Michael Graves & Associates; 141/8 architect: Hilde Cornelissen/photo Serge Brison; 146l & r Lute Suites; 203 all Electrolux.